Scott-land

Scott-land

The Man Who Invented A Nation

Stuart Kelly

1006190573

First published in Great Britain in 2010 by Polygon, an imprint of Birlinn Ltd
West Newington House
10 Newington Road
Edinburgh
EH9 1QS

www.polygonbooks.co.uk

ISBN 978 1 84697 107 5

British Library Cataloguing-in-Publication Data
A catalogue record for this book is available on request from the British Library.

The publishers acknowledge subsidy from the Scottish Arts Council towards
publication of this volume

Typeset by IDSUK (DataConnection) Ltd
Printed by MPG Books, Bodmin

To my nephews Danny, Frazer and Finlay, wishing them all 'the will to do, the soul to dare', as Scott says in *The Lady of the Lake*, and, as always to Sam, who like the young Lochinvar has ever been 'so faithful in love and so dauntless in war'.

Contents

CONTENTS

Introduction

As a teenager, I was once offered, as part payment for helping carry out the terms of a will, my pick of the remnants of a library. I took the collected works of Shelley, Byron, Tennyson, Longfellow, Browning and Masefield. When I was asked if I wanted a complete set of the Waverley Novels as well, I declined. My dad – a Kirk Session Clerk and six-foot rugby player – asked me why I hadn't taken them. With all the worst tones of a supercilious, weedy sixteen-year-old, I told him that Scott was, to my mind, just a second-rate Dickens, a pale shadow of Dumas, and anyway I read real novels, like D M Thomas's *The White Hotel* and Lawrence Durrell's *Alexandria Quartet* and Robert Nye's *Falstaff*. Or something like that. I hadn't actually read a word of Scott. Scott was old-fashioned – I had seen *Ivanhoe* on TV and preferred *The Vikings*. He was all about things I wanted to escape from: the Scottish Borders, chivalry, macho culture, second-rate art. I was going home to write a poem a bit like *The Waste Land* and thought I was the first person in the world to be mildly depressed and too clever for my own good.

Scott was prehistorical, and I was gasping for the future. Scott was where I was from, not where I was going. Scott haunted my childhood. He was there in statues, monuments, busts and plaques; street-names, road signs and business hoarding; he was our little-known region's most famous son, the omnipresent Great Unknown. I eventually picked up one of the Waverley Novels. It wasn't even a novel. A real novel, as I knew, involved sexual dysfunction, random violence, typographical experimentation and lots of references to books I should have read, and then did. This *Waverley* thing was some kind of literary trilobite, edging its feeble antennae and malformed claws out of the soup of the dumb old Borders towards the eventual apotheosis of meta-reflexive deconstructions of contemporaneous marginality. I didn't throw books in those days, so I carefully replaced it on the shelf and went back to reading *The Magus*.

It took me a long time to like Scott. First, I had to learn that my liking of something was a pretty paltry measure of its aesthetic and cultural worth, and studying English at Oxford knocked some of that arrogance out of me. For this relief, much thanks. The Oxford Version of English was very Oxford and very English. It stirred in me a tiny, insistent, unexpected pang of *Heimweh*. Not nationalism, not local pride, not even the usual English translation of that German word, homesickness. It was real *Heimweh*: home-sore. I was sore for not being in the home I had left, and I was sore for that rejected home not being recognised in all the away-places.

Liking Scott started with liking writers who liked Scott. If Byron, Goethe and Hugo had found Scott immensely admirable, who was I to gainsay their enthusiasm? There were contemporary writers and critics, of vastly different political persuasions – people such as Allan Massie, A N Wilson, Angus Calder and James Robertson – who found in Scott a sensibility, an irony, a spirit of innovation and a sophistication to which I was blind. Until I read Scott, all my opinions about him would be lazy plagiarisms. When I did, I found a novelist who was not a 'second-rate Dickens' but the successor to the most daring writers of the eighteenth century: Henry Fielding, Jonathan Swift, Laurence Sterne. The opening pages of *Waverley* had the very self-awareness I had thrilled to in its more strident and jejune form in the pages of the fading avant-garde. The plot mechanics creaked in places, the descriptions maundered on to no discernible purpose and the characters were sometimes cardboard cut-outs: all these criticisms stand. But they do not annihilate Scott's qualities of wit, slyness, grandeur, empathy and originality.

When I came back to Scotland, it was not to the country I had left. I managed to be in England throughout one of the most exciting periods for Scottish literature and Scottish politics. There was a sense of confidence tethered to an air of just grievance, a feeling of new possibilities and a willingness to reassess some tightly held and self-serving myths. I had heard a fair few old jokes in

Oxford about Scotland ('Do you know how copper wire was invented? Two Scotsman saw a penny lying in the street at the same time'). They seemed as if they came from another age, about another country.

A degree of distance is sometimes the best way to clear the mind of stereotypes. As I reacquainted myself with the country of my birth, Scott, more than William Wallace, John Knox, Adam Smith, James Maxton or Margaret Thatcher, seemed to be the pivotal figure. He was the Unionist who preserved the idea of a Nation; the self-made Laird who left no line; the literary celebrity who craved anonymity; the disillusioned Romantic; the successful failure and failed success. He was Scotland's most problematic identity entrepreneur. In all the debates about whither Caledonia and whence Alba and stands Scotland where it did, between the Tartan Army and Silicon Glen, Scott was like Banquo, the invisible presence at the feast whose mere memory created shudders.

Loving Scott, rather than merely liking him, came later, and came directly from a sense of his neglect. Kevin Williamson, the editor of the radical Scottish literary magazine *Rebel Inc.*, which was quick to publish writers such as Irvine Welsh, wrote on his blog, *The Scottish Patient*, that 'It should be noted that Sir Walter Scott was not a great Scottish patriot nor even a particularly good writer – his prose is stodge – but he was an arse-licking royalist, a falsifier of Scottish history and a Tory cunt of the worst order'. To labour the point, Williamson also posts photographs of himself dancing on Sir Walter Scott's grave. Robert Burns was a tax collector; James Hogg, the 'Ettrick Shepherd' was a Tory; and Hugh MacDiarmid once expressed the hope that the Luftwaffe would flatten London; none of them is treated as a pariah.

This book is *not* an attempt to make Scott popular again. We do not read nowadays as we did in the early nineteenth century, and expecting everyone to suddenly scrape away 200 years of programming from their brains is as idle and foolhardy as putting on Scarlatti in a nightclub and expecting the dancers to fall into waltzes. Times, tastes, things change: Scott knew this. He is not just still readable, he is enjoyable and even breath-catching, but you will need to learn to love a certain slowness. If you play a 78 rpm record at the 33⅓ setting, then you miss the music. Literature can't be put on shuffle.

Instead, this is a plea, a journey, an argument and an analysis. Parts are biography, parts are critique, parts are polemic, parts are travelogue. Parts are satire and parts are psychology, parts are outrage and parts, I hope, are insight. It is also a thanatography, the underused genre of the life after life, a map of decay, where laurels and worms contend over a reputation. Scott's reputation is a story which begins with being compared to Shakespeare and ends with being called a cunt: or worse. At least Williamson detests Scott. In John Aberdein's novel, *Amande's Bed*, the American time and motion man is surprised that the citizens of Edinburgh erected a monument to Scott of the Antarctic. Scott has sunk to a pristine blank, about whom few care and fewer even know.

Scott was a complex man, and he left a contradictory legacy. *Scott-land* is a Baedeker to an imaginary country; the physical space we call Scotland overlaid with the psychic, iconic space he contrived. At this crossroads of cliché and estrangement, radicalism and conservatism, progress and nostalgia, the ghost of Scott waits to be exorcised or appeased. I choose to appease him. I think it's time to alight.

Arrival

Imagine travelling from London to Edinburgh by train. Somewhere between the ruined cottages on red sandstone cliffs and the austere white cube of a nuclear power station, England changes into Scotland. There are no signs, no special announcements, not even a perceptible change in the quantity of heather or pine trees. It is unlikely you will suddenly see people wearing kilts, or hear bagpipes in the air, or that the breakfast baguettes on the refreshment trolley will abruptly come with square sausage. Borders on maps are definitive. On the ground they are hazy and permeable. You might realise that Berwick is technically English while Dunbar is technically Scottish. You might even know that Berwick, although English, has a Scottish postcode. But the cross hatches of county and country, region and nation are invisible.

Whenever I'm returning to Edinburgh, I always get that involuntary jolt, not of recognition or dislocation, but of sad sameness. It's worse at night, or if I've dozed off, when there's no landscape. The streaks of sodium-lit lock-ups, the spires that could be churches but are probably arts centres or social work offices, the same neon glimpses – Hertz, Shell, Ford, Tesco, McDonalds – make everywhere anywhere. Behind my own reflection, the same rosebay willowherb, ragwort and Japanese knotweed, the same plastic bags and discarded bottles pass for nature. The linguist Ferdinand de Saussure used trains to discuss identity. Regardless of which physical train you're in, what's important is its departure time. The 18:30 is the 18:30 whether it's the *Flying Scotsman*, the *Waverley* or the *Northern Lights* actually pulling the coaches. Whichever line or train you're on, what you'll see outside is the desolate margin of railway sidings.

Certainly, when you step out onto the platform at Edinburgh Waverley there is no indication that this is Scotland. There's not

even a Welcome to Scotland sign. The bing-bong tannoy announcements have that ubiquitous, synthetic, halting timbre. A large screen
seeps *Sky News* next to the Departures Board. The miniature
supermarket has every variety of world cuisine from Thai linguini
to Tex-Mex wraps, with a clutch of haggis nestling in a corner
beneath the International Sausages, like a trap for the unwary.
The newsagent has the same celebrity magazines, soft-core
pornography and tabloid shriek-sheets as in England, the coffee
shops sell the same lattes and espressos, bagels and muffins. One
takeaway stall specialises in Cornish pasties; another in croissants.
On extremely close investigation, you might notice some shortbread in Royal Stewart tartan livery, an 'all-in-one beach towel and
kilt' (also in Royal Stewart) and a variety of tourist kitsch (including
a Viagra Comes To Scotland fridge magnet, a See-You Jimmy
bonnet and an inexplicable keyring of a sexually frustrated Loch
Ness Monster) tucked away like an embarrassing secret.

But beneath the patina of cosmopolitan identikit culture, there
are indications that this is a different place. Suppose you were to
buy something and paid in cash. Your change would look odd. It's
a neat irony that despite the homogeneity of contemporary capi-
talist retail, the circulating medium that sustains it still has a snag of
specific local detail. Just as the euro or the dollar or the yen situate
you outside of England, so too does the Scottish banknote.

Scotland has different banknotes to England, issued by the Bank
of Scotland, the Royal Bank of Scotland and the Clydesdale Bank –
and the novelist Sir Walter Scott appears on every denomination of
the Bank of Scotland notes. He is not there purely in homage to his
ability as a writer. The very existence of the Scottish notes depends
on Scott's journalistic intervention, since, under the pseudonym
of Malachi Malagrowther, he launched a successful campaign to
dissuade the British Treasury from abolishing them in 1826.

In that imaginary transaction where you got a newspaper, or
bottled water, or twenty cigarettes, and a few exchangeable miniature portraits of Sir Walter Scott, you might have noticed that the
representative of Customer Services Personnel had an accent. They
may even have used a word of dialect. This in itself is not unusual:

had you been in Norwich, Exeter or Stepney Green, it's likely that you would have heard a local accent. But North of the Border it's not just an accent, but the visible tip of an iceberg of linguistic difference. You can't buy an accent, but it buys you into a particular community. The Scottish accent can be seen as a subset of Scottish dialect, itself in turn a subset of a *language* called Scots.

What makes this situation unusual is that, unlike the nineteenth-century attempt to regulate Scottish banking, the Scots themselves had tried to expunge their linguistic Scottishness. In the eighteenth century, David Hume implored his London-based publisher to rid his work of 'Scotticisms'. He complained that he and his countrymen were 'unhappy in our Accent and Pronunciation' and 'speak a very corrupt Dialect of the Tongue'. University courses were set up to teach aspiring young Scots proper English; to which end Hugh Blair became the first Professor of Rhetoric and Belles-Lettres at Edinburgh University. A handy primer, called *Scoticisms*, was published by James Beattie: '*we* handle English, as a person who cannot fence handles a sword; continually afraid of hurting ourselves with it, or letting it fall, or making some awkward motion that shall betray our ignorance'.

Two hundred years later and not only is the Scottish accent regularly voted in BBC polls as the 'sexiest' and 'most trustworthy', its status is enshrined by the Scottish Parliament, Westminster and Brussels: 'Notwithstanding the UK Government's and the [Scottish Government]'s obligations under part II of the European Charter for Regional or Minority Languages, the [Scottish Government] recognises and respects Scots (in all its forms) as a distinct language, and does not consider the use of Scots to be an indication of poor competence in English.'

Scots survived the scepticism of the Enlightenment in no small part due to its use in literature. The poetry of Robert Burns showed it could be a medium of sublime lyric expressiveness and outrageous comic potential, and to this day, across the world, people will sing 'Auld Lang Syne' on New Year's Eve and wonder what a syne actually is. But people do not speak in poetry, and Sir Walter Scott's use of vernacular language in his novels ensured its continuing presence. Scott kept a letter, a striking early example of 'fan mail', sent to him by an anonymous shepherd from the Borders, who wrote, 'I cannot help telling you that I am astonished, perfectly astonished, how ye have acquired the Scottish dialect and phrase-ology so exactly. Certainly neither your education nor studies could discover ought of that antiquated language: yet when ye chuse to adopt it ye have it as truly as if ye knew no other.' Through ballad-collecting, the editing and publication of old texts in Scots and above all in the dialogue in the Waverley Novels Scott preserved Scots as a living language and a language with a history.

Then there's the tartan. It can't be avoided that tartan in general and the kilt in particular is the most recognisable and obvious sign of Scottishness. Even the tourism promotion carried out by the Scottish Government in New York each year is called Tartan Week. (Can you imagine a French Expo called Beret Week, or a Dutch Clog Week, or a German Lederhosen Week?) Wedding parties and rugby internationals notwithstanding, it's unlikely that you'd see many people wandering though Waverley Station in full Highland regalia, but it's equally unlikely that there wouldn't be a swatch of tartan somewhere. There is a stereotype about the most blatant Scottish stereotype: that Sir Walter Scott 'invented' the kilt. He categorically didn't, and the whole story, to be unravelled in later chapters, is more bizarre and problematic than casting Scott as the nineteenth century's answer to Mary Quant. Scott's role, however, in the story of tartan is fundamental. In 1746, after the defeat of the Jacobite Rebellion, George II's Government passed the 'Dress Act' which stated that 'no man or boy within that part of Britain called Scotland, other than such as shall be employed as Officers and Soldiers in His Majesty's Forces, shall, on any pretext whatever, wear or put on the clothes commonly called Highland clothes (that is to say) the Plaid, Philabeg, or little Kilt'. The Act was repealed in 1785, and in 1822 Sir Walter Scott persuaded George II's grandson, George IV, to wear a kilt on his visit to Scotland.

All these clues that this is *not England* can be connected to Sir Walter Scott. The ties between the man and the place are not merely a matter of verbal similarity. Theodore Fontane wrote in

Jenseits des Tweed, 'What would we know of Scotland without Scott!' In his posthumous *Memorials of his Time*, Lord Cockburn wrote, 'To no other man does Scotland *owe* so great a debt of gratitude as to *Walter Scott*.' But Scott was not a mere mirror reflecting the place, or an effective public relations expert extolling the unique selling proposition of this small, poor, defeated northern country. Between the political reality of Scotland and the place conjured, imagined and created by the works of a single writer there is a strange overlap; an intersection of the actual, the desired and the concealed; a fraying and braiding of fiction and fact: Scott-land.

Remember the name of the station? This is not Edinburgh, but Edinburgh Waverley. Outside are the Waverley Steps and the Waverley Bridge, the Waverley Gate, the Old Waverley Hotel and, just up the hill, the Waverley Bar. If you were looking in the index of an Edinburgh A–Z, you would also be confronted with Waverley Crescent, Waverley Drive, Waverley Terrace, two Waverley Roads and two Waverley Parks. Waverley itself, if I'm being pedantic, is actually on the A31 near Godalming in Surrey. But since 1814, when Scott chose that name for the prevaricating hero of his first novel, *Waverley, or, 'Tis Sixty Years Since* – a name which latterly came to refer to Scott's entire fictional opus, *The Waverley Novels* – Waverley is inextricably linked to Scotland. It might be difficult to know exactly when or where you start being in Scotland, but it's overwhelmingly obvious when you're in Scott-land.

The Man

Who was Sir Walter Scott? Before we go any further together it would be useful to have a sketch, if not an oil painting, of the man himself.

Sir Walter Scott was born in Edinburgh on 15 August 1771, the fourth child of a farmer's son who had climbed the social ladder to become a lawyer. His mother was the daughter of Edinburgh University's Professor of Medicine. Those with a bent towards astrology might note that on 15 August 1769, a child had been born whose fame would rival Scott's in due course, and of whom Scott would eventually write a biography: Napoleon Bonaparte. Scott was a sickly child, and was left lame by a bout of infantile polio. For his health, he was sent from Edinburgh to grow up on his paternal grandfather's farm, Sandyknowe, in the Scottish Borders, where his nursemaid, in a fit of madness brought on by an illegitimate pregnancy, tried to kill him with a pair of scissors. Although he was schooled at the Royal High in Edinburgh – with a period, again for health reasons, at the grammar school in Kelso – he was from his youth a voracious reader, whose taste, formed on local ballads, tended towards the chivalric romances of Ariosto and Spenser. His lameness was never cured; not even after Dr James Graham – called 'The Emperor of Quacks', and the inventor of an electric-powered Celestial Bed to promote sexual fruitfulness – used a primitive galvanic battery to try to jolt it back into feeling.

Scott's siblings play little role in his life. He remembered his eldest brother, Robert, as a bully who could sing well. Robert failed to thrive in the military, quarrelling with his superior officers and suspected of drinking, and died after two visits to India, in 1787. His elder brother, John, succeeded in the military, but only after Scott was famous enough to secure his promotion to Major. He died in

1816, 'yet a young man'. Scott was closer to his younger brother, Tom, and although Tom disgraced himself financially, Scott eventually made peace with him. The reconciliation happened, in its fullest form, after Tom's death in 1823. His youngest brother, Daniel, who had 'the same determined indolence that marked us all' as Scott said, died on his way back from the West Indies in 1806. Scott's only surviving sister, Anne, died soon after Scott married in 1801. Scott's closest biographer, his son-in-law John Gibson Lockhart, says that she 'had her brother's imaginative and romantic temperament, but without his power of controlling it'. Scott had five other siblings, who died in childhood.

Walter Scott Senior intended that his son should follow in his footsteps. He duly studied law at Edinburgh University, was admitted to the Bar in 1792 and wrote his final dissertation on the disposal of the bodies of executed criminals. A year beforehand he had formed an attachment to Williamina Belsches, whom he wooed with adolescent poetry. She, however, married a financier, Sir William Forbes. The two men's paths would cross again: Scott and Williamina's never did.

Scott was despondent, and girded himself with words from Shakespeare: 'men have died and worms have eaten them, but never yet for love'. He met Charlotte Charpentier, daughter of a French *émigré* and a ward of Lord Downshire, and on Christmas Eve, 1797, after a hasty engagement, they married. They had four children: Walter Jnr, Charles, Sophia and Anne. Lady Scott, as she was to become, first appears as an exotic, foreign beauty, and swiftly disappears into the background of his life, rarely appearing in his correspondence, sequestered in some private sphere of his public life. She could be sharp with people – Lockhart recalls her upbraiding a critic of Scott's saying 'dey tell me dat you have abused Scott in de *Review*', and wondering if the editor 'has paid you well for writing it'. In later life, she seems to have become ill, and, like her husband, took laudanum and opium. There is no hint that Scott ever fell in love with anyone else, and little proof that he ever wholly fell in love with her.

Scott became Sheriff-Depute of Selkirkshire in 1799 and began to write in earnest. His creative endeavours were twofold: translations of avant-garde German writers, such as Schiller and Goethe; and collections of traditional folk-songs and ballads of the Border countries. These bore fruit with the publication in 1802–3 of *The Minstrelsy of the Scottish Border*, a three-volume anthology. The success of *The Minstrelsy* encouraged Scott to attempt an original composition in a similar style. The result was *The Lay of the Last Minstrel*, published in 1805, which sold over 44,000 copies before his death. It transformed Scott into a celebrity. He threw himself into numerous book projects: a complete edition of the works of John Dryden, reviews of Todd's edition of Spenser, *The New Practice of Cookery*, Godwin's *Fleetwood*, Ellis and Ritson's *Specimens of early English Metrical Romances*, Civil War memoirs and a prospective 100-volume 'general edition of the British Poets' which never materialised. Scott even claimed he could create a full-length book of David Hume's poetry – of which there are only four lines – by footnoting every word.

More than any writer before – and perhaps since – Scott's creation of literary texts was intrinsically bound up with the production of physical books. *The Minstrelsy* was printed by a childhood friend, James Ballantyne, who at the time was editing the *Kelso Mail*, and who entered into publishing literature on Scott's suggestion. James was a reserved man, whose personal penchant for ponderous and highfalutin prose belied his precision and clarity as an editor. *The Minstrelsy* was one of the most striking pieces of typographical excellence and elegant design in the history of nineteenth-century book-making, and drew Scott and Ballantyne's work to the leading publishers of the day; especially Archibald Constable. Constable, a portly, shrewd man and inveterate supporter of the Whigs, had graduated from publishing the *Farmer's Magazine* to running the *Edinburgh Review*, and was famous for his generosity towards authors: contributors to the *Edinburgh* were paid an unparalleled rate. In this period, the roles of printer, publisher and bookseller had yet to crystallise into distinct vocations. Scott had a life-long and sometimes vexed relationship with Constable; sometimes removing his works in a fit of pique over politics or bad reviews, often lured back by advances and contracts. James Ballantyne set up a printing and publishing company with his brother John – the black sheep of the family, who had once set up a rival business to his own father – as accountant, and with his youngest brother Sandy – father of the Victorian novelist R M Ballantyne – managing the *Kelso Mail*. Scott was the secret sleeping partner in the business. More often than not, a condition of Constable & Co. getting a Waverley Novel was that Ballantyne & Co. were subcontracted to print it.

The success of *The Lay of the Last Minstrel* was followed by that of *Marmion – A Tale of Flodden Field* in 1808, and then *The Lady of the Lake* in 1810. Scott received an unheard-of 1,000 guineas for *Marmion* from Constable, sight unseen – the first 'advance' in literary history. By 1811 he was able to purchase a farm on the Tweed, which he would transform over the following decade into his estate, Abbotsford. When the hopelessly mediocre Henry James Pye, the poet laureate and Westminster Police Magistrate, died in 1813, the Government immediately offered the laureateship to Scott. He declined – saying that as he already had two lucrative offices gifted by the Crown, he could not in good conscience accept a third 'while so many eminent men remained wholly dependent on their literary exertions' – and magnanimously suggested that Robert Southey be offered it instead. Scott deluded himself that literature 'should be my staff but not my crutch'. If only he had managed to stick by that principle, and treat his income from authorship as an unexpected extra.

Scott's fourth long poem, *Rokeby* (1813), did not replicate the successes of his earlier works; and suffered by comparison with Byron's first two cantos of *Childe Harolde* which appeared the year beforehand. Although he still commanded huge advances – Constable offered £5,000 for the copyright of an unwritten poem called *The Nameless Glen* (which eventually came out as *The Lord of the Isles*) – Scott realised that he was 'eclipsed' by Byron. In a letter to Countess Pürgstall in 1821, Scott wrote: 'In truth I have long given up poetry. I had my day with the public and being no great believer in poetical immortality I was very well pleased to rise a winner without continuing the game till I was beggared of any credit I had acquired with the public. Besides I felt the prudence of

giving way before the more forcible and powerful genius of Byron.'
This influenced Scott's decision to dust down the seven chapters of
Waverley.

Waverley, or 'Tis Sixty Years Since opens a new chapter in literary
history. In Hesketh Pearson's words, it 'changed the direction of
imaginative literature in every civilised country'. Five thousand
copies of the anonymously published book were sold in five
months, an unprecedented achievement for a novel. The novelist
Mary Brunton wrote that it was 'by far the most splendid exhibition
of talent in the novel way which has appeared since the days of
Fielding and Smollett'. Jane Austen, more caustically, wrote 'Walter
Scott has no business to write novels, especially good ones. It is
not fair. He has fame and profit enough as a poet, and should not
be taking the bread out of the mouths of other people. I do not
like him, and do not mean to like *Waverley* if I can help it, but
fear I must.'

When *Guy Mannering, or The Astrologer* was published in 1815, it
was attributed to 'The Author of *Waverley*'. Scott was giddyingly
prolific: accept my apologies for what must be a rather galloping
catalogue. *The Antiquary* appeared in 1816, supposedly as the last of
a trilogy on Scottish manners. His next two prose works, *The Black
Dwarf* and *The Tale of Old Mortality* were published under the title
Tales of my Landlord, as if they were the work of a rival to the 'Author
of *Waverley*'. *Rob Roy* (1817) returned to the 'Author of *Waverley*' fold;
and was followed by the second and third series of *Tales of my
Landlord*, namely *The Heart of Midlothian* in 1818 and *The Bride of
Lammermoor* and *A Legend of Montrose* in 1819. *Ivanhoe* (1819) was his
first venture outside Scotland, although Scott immediately returned
to Scottish themes with *The Monastery* (1820), the failure of which
spawned the only true sequel in the Waverley Novels, *The Abbot*
(also 1820). With the exception of *The Pirate* in 1822, Scott's next
flurry all dealt with English themes: *Kenilworth* (1821) featured
Elizabeth I; *The Fortunes of Nigel* (1822) starred James VI and I, and
Peveril of the Peak (1822) brings in Charles II – who would appear in
a more youthful version for Scott's Civil War novel, *Woodstock*, in
1826. Scott turned to France for *Quentin Durward* in 1823, and

returned to Scotland for his only 'contemporary' novel, *Saint Ronan's Well* in the same year. Scotland was also the setting for *Redgauntlet* the following year. The *Tales of the Crusaders* (1825) contrasted Wales in *The Betrothed* and Palestine in *The Talisman*, and Scott set up yet another series with the first set of *Chronicles of the Canongate* in 1827, with a second set, usually referred to by its tertiary subtitle, *Saint Valentine's Day, or The Fair Maid of Perth* in 1828. *Anne of Geierstein* in 1829 was a Swiss sort-of sequel to *Quentin Durward*, and the long set aside *Tales of my Landlord*, fourth series, was published in 1831, with a tale of Byzantine Crusaders (*Count Robert of Paris*) and a return to home turf in *Castle Dangerous*. To clarify this phenomenal industry: Scott wrote twenty-seven novels in eighteen years, compared to Dickens' sixteen novels in thirty-four years, or George Eliot's seven novels in seventeen years. He wrote more lines of poetry than Shelley and Keats combined.

As if that were not enough, Scott also wrote a number of non-fiction books, most notably his *Life of Napoleon* (1827), an account of the site and battle of Waterloo called *Paul's Letters to his Kinsfolk* (1816), the *Lives of the Novelists* (1821–4) and a child's history of Scotland, *The Tales of a Grandfather* (1827–30, and a supplemental volume on France in 1831). A jaw-dropping total of 4,566 plays, dramatic interludes and theatrical versions of his works exist.

But a life is not just a bibliography. Scott had a genuine gift for friendship: from the ex-poacher, Tom Purdie, whom he met in his lawyerly capacity and subsequently employed as head gamekeeper at Abbotsford, to the Duke of Buccleuch, Scott effortlessly commanded affection and respect. Many of the leading authors of the day were personal friends – even, in the case of Lord Byron, after initial circumspection, or in the case of James Hogg, author of *The Private Memoirs and Confessions of a Justified Sinner* and the so-called 'Ettrick Shepherd', despite frequent slights. He formed a strong, if occasionally tested, friendship with his son-in-law and future biographer, John Gibson Lockhart, who married Sophia Scott in 1820. Lockhart, a vigorous Tory, was such a savage reviewer he earned the nickname 'the Scorpion', and was accused of 'killing' John Keats with his critiques. After turning down the laureateship, he became acquainted with the Prince Regent and future King George IV, whose first act as monarch was to make Scott a baronet. Scott more than repaid the honour by organising the King's visit to Edinburgh – the so-called King's Jaunt – in 1822. The Jaunt was a success for which Scotland has had difficulty forgiving Scott. Scott was an avowed, and at times doctrinaire supporter of the Tory Party. He was also a committed Unionist: though, as a lawyer, he insisted on the exact terms of the Union being upheld, and was quick to act if he believed either side was jeopardising the agreement.

But even the kindness of friends and his proximity to power could not shield Scott from tribulation. Scott may have been a best-seller, but he was also a bestspender, pouring funds into the creation of Abbotsford as a baronial estate. Scott was not alone in rash spending: the first half of the 1820s saw a wave of enthusiasm for shares in countless schemes – railways, South American silver mines, gas companies. It was the equivalent of the dot-com boom, with slower information both about the state of the investments and the extent of the debt. Constable and Ballantyne both fell in the same crash.

Scott drew cash by using 'counter-bills' – in effect, unbanked cheques that passed between creditors. The bubble of speculation broke in November 1825, and the counter-bills were required to be honoured. Scott found himself personally liable for £116,838, eleven shillings and thruppence, with a mortgage on Abbotsford of £10,000. In today's terms, that amounts to £8,830,161.15. Although Scott believed, and Lockhart encouraged the world to believe, that he managed to write himself out of debt, it was only the posthumous sale of copyrights that cleared the outstanding monies due.

Nor were financial concerns the least of his worries. Never wholly as robust as he claimed, Scott had suffered from 'apoplexies' since 1819. Heart palpitations and strokes were to follow, with treat-ments – bleeding, trepanning and large quantities of opium – that must have brought back memories of the electric shocks he was given as a child. He died in 1832, on 21 September, having outlived Byron, Napoleon, Goethe and his wife and his grandson.

Conflate Jeffrey Archer and spin-doctor Alastair Campbell, Hugh Laurie as Dr Gregory House and Stephen Fry as the genial genius host of *QI*, with a dash of Dickens (he was after all, a great novelist), and a soupçon of Indiana Jones (he was once lowered into a dungeon in Hermitage Castle just to retrieve a ring that might identify whose skeleton was there). Even the oil painting of a biography is still mannered by the portraitist, who chooses to focus or smear, highlight or conceal.

Scott's Edinburgh

The Edinburgh that Walter Scott was born into was half the city it was going to become in his lifetime. Its distinctive modern feature – railways stations named after novelists notwithstanding – is its schizophrenia; indeed, the poet Hugh MacDiarmid referred to Edinburgh as a 'mad god's dream'. It exemplified antisyzygy, his preferred creative term, meaning a 'zigzag of contradictions', and originally used by G Gregory Smith as a diagnosis for what was *wrong* with Scottish culture. The Edinburgh I walk through each day is part Piranesi, part Peter Greenaway. I can't tire of its soaring bridges that never cross water, its Tetris blocks of Gothic tenements framed in classical Palladian arches, its tug-of-war between secret vennels and stately locked doors.

Edinburgh's centre is riven, bifurcated: on one hand, the vertiginous, overlapping, haphazard, medieval Old Town, and on the other, the geometric, unfolded, planned, neoclassical New Town. A few years after Scott's death, the American poet and critic Nathaniel Willis wrote that 'a more striking contrast than exists between these two parts of the same city could hardly be imagined. On one side a succession of splendid squares, elegant granite houses, broad and well paved streets, columns, statues and clean sidewalks, thinly promenaded and by the well dressed exclusively, . . . and, on the other, an antique wilderness of streets and "wynds", so narrow and lofty as to shut out much of the light of heaven.' Robert Louis Stevenson described the 'draughty parallelograms' of the New Town and the 'profusion of eccentricities' of the Old; and Edinburgh's most successful modern chronicler, the novelist Ian Rankin, returns to Stevenson's Jekyll and Hyde time and again to capture the city's blend of Gothic and Enlightenment architecture. Perhaps most tellingly, Friedrich Engels wrote about the division in

The Condition of the Working Class in England: 'Edinburgh, whose superb situation, which has won it the title of the Modern Athens, and whose brilliant aristocratic quarter in the New Town contrasts strongly with the foul wretchedness of the poor in the Old Town . . . the prevailing construction of Edinburgh favours these atrocious conditions as far as possible.' The split is not just psychological, but political.

By the middle of the eighteenth century, Edinburgh was increasingly overcrowded and claustrophobic, and not even living in the upper reaches of the tenements could insulate the more affluent classes from the reality of poverty, poor sanitation and crime. Many were relocating to London, so the Lord Provost of Edinburgh, George Drummond, masterminded the creation of a city alongside the city, even extending the burgh boundaries to do so. A design competition was held in 1766, and the winning proposal was the antithesis of 'Edinburgh': spacious, straight-lined, and relying on horizontal rather than vertical expansion. When Scott was a year old, a new bridge – the North Bridge – was opened, linking the now Old Town and the emerging New. It spanned what had been the Nor' Loch, a body of water heavily polluted by the effluent of the Old Town, and which was slowly being drained and reclaimed as part of the transformation of the city. By 1800, just before Scott's first major success as a writer, the first phase of the New Town was complete. By his death, it was recognisably the city it is today.

The New Town was not just novel. It was more than a break with the past, it was a commitment to modernity. A generation before Drummond initiated his scheme, Edinburgh had been occupied by a foreign-led invasion force – the Highlanders loyal to Charles Edward Stuart, working for a restoration of the Catholic monarchy. Not everyone in the capital was unsympathetic to the cause, and, particularly among Edinburgh's women, the dashing Prince struck an immensely attractive figure. Many still resented the Union of Parliaments, which took place only thirty-seven years before the Jacobite Rebellion. The winning design for the New Town, by James Craig, was a simplified version of the Union Jack flag; a testament to the new British state. The names reflect this still: George Street commemorates George III, Charlotte Square for his wife, Princes for his sons, Frederick for his father and Hanover for his family. Running parallel to the main streets are Thistle Street and Rose Street, named to represent the floral symbols for England and Scotland. James Craig's uncle was the poet James Thomson, who had written the words to the song 'Rule Britannia'. The New Town was loyalty in stone. With its wide boulevards and garden spaces, it pre-empted Baron Haussman's radical restructuring of the Parisian streets, with a similar eye on the relationship between urban living and the exercise of state control.

But the New Town reflected a psychological and philosophical as well as a political realignment. In 1696, an Edinburgh student, Thomas Aikenhead, was executed for blasphemy. In 1722, Janet Horne of Dornoch became the last woman executed for witchcraft in Scotland. In 1750 Voltaire wrote, 'We look to Scotland for all our ideas of civilisation', a quote often trumpeted by nationalists despite his satirical intent: if Scotland is leading the world in terms of culture, Voltaire implies, then things really are in a mess. The neoclassical architecture of the new Edinburgh embodied Enlightenment ideals: progress, reason and intellectual openness. The Scottish Enlightenment and the New Town were mirrored in each other. It may have been a prank that led to one street being named 'St David's Street' – it had the home of the freethinker and sceptic David Hume on it, and the chalked-up joke seems to have stuck – but it was no oversight that led George III's ministers to veto the original name of Princes Street – St Giles' Street. In the new Hanoverian Edinburgh, any association with a Catholic saint whose touch – like the Stuart monarchs' – could cure leprosy was not a fortuitous one.

The Enlightenment is not just a category we impose on the past with the hindsight of the present: at the time, there was a feeling of intellectual foment and excitement. The Scottish Enlightenment produced startling new theories in economics (Adam Smith), sociology (Adam Ferguson), statistics (Sir John Sinclair), geology (James Hutton), morality and aesthetics (Francis Hutcheson), epistemology (David Hume), anthropology (Lord Kames), linguistics (Lord

Monboddo), chemistry (Joseph Black), medicine (Alexander Monro *primus* and *secundus*) and historiography (William Robertson). Under the editorship of William Smellie, the *Encyclopaedia Britannica* was begun, reflecting the sense that humanity was close to approaching the point at which everything could be known. From jurisprudence to political theory, human endeavour was reaching a psychological plateau on which contention, rebellion, schism, difference and poverty would level out. 'History' was coming to an end.

David Hume wrote to his friend Gilbert Elliot in July 1757, capturing the surprising swagger and startling self-confidence of the time: 'Really it is admirable how many Men of Genius this Country produces at present. Is it not strange that, at a time when we have lost our Princes, our Parliaments, our independent Government, even the presence of our chief Nobility . . . is it not strange, I say, that in these Circumstances, we shou'd really be the People most distinguish'd for Literature in Europe?'

Hume was using 'literature' in the broadest sense: material to be read. By our definition, the Scottish Enlightenment was sadly lacking in literature. In his letter to Elliot, he cited two examples: Robertson's *History of Scotland* (not then, yet, actually published) and William Wilkie's *The Epigoniad*. Do not feel embarrassed if the name Wilkie means nothing to you: although Hume thought Wilkie a 'Scottish Homer', his reputation did not even last his lifetime – and Wilkie settled down as Professor of Moral Philosophy at St Andrews instead. Hume does not mention in his previously quoted letter his admiration for the dramatist and Church of Scotland minister John Home, whose tragedy *Douglas* was staged the year beforehand. As a minister, it earned him the reprimand of the General Assembly of the Church of Scotland; as a playwright it garnered him the enthusiastic if ephemeral praise of one notoriously patriotic theatregoer – 'Whaur's your Wullie Shakespeare noo?' From posterity he received dusty oblivion and the occasional flutter of purely academic interest. Hume was as entranced with *Douglas* as he was with Wilkie – it was 'one of the most interesting and pathetic pieces that was ever exhibited on any theatre' and Home possesses 'the true theatric genius of *Shakespear* and *Otway*, refined from the unhappy barbarism of the one, and licentiousness of the other', according to the dedication Hume prefaced to his 1757 *Four Dissertations*. The play did not survive its transfer to London, where it was received with such risible derision that Hume's 'critical stocks' were 'reduced to bankruptcy'. To add insult to injury, Hume and Home were both parodied and pilloried in a skit entitled *The Philosopher's Opera* by John Maclaurin.

Hume's high praise seems pretty threadbare with hindsight. In the broadest sense of the period of the 'Scottish Enlightenment', there were Scottish authors of genius. The aforementioned James Thomson, who died in 1748, had a successful career in London, especially with his sophisticated pastoral, *The Seasons*, written between 1725 and 1730, and eventually set to music by Haydn. Thomson applied the most cutting-edge science, particularly Newton's *Opticks*, to the description of landscape. He wrote several successful plays including the masque, *Alfred*, which featured 'Rule Britannia', and the tragedy *Sophobisna*, which has the immortal and pentametrically correct line 'Ah Sophobisna! Sophobisna, ah!'. Less seemly than Thomson, and discouraged from female hands, was the Dunbartonshire-born novelistTobias Smollett, whose rambunctious and alliterative novels *Roderick Random* (1747) *Peregrine Pickle* (1751) and *Ferdinand Count Fathom* (1753) introduced the spirit of Cervantes into the 'English novel'. Smollett, who was also based in London, spent most of the 1750s and 1760s in periodical criticism, literary skulduggery and writing histories and libels. His final work, *The Expedition of Humphrey Clinker* in 1771, was a charming epistolary novel, where much of the humour derives from the various letter writers' rather different perceptions of what they see and whom they meet.

Hume died in 1776, ten years before Robert Burns published his *Poems, Chiefly In The Scottish Dialect*. Had he lived – given his own assiduous excision of Scotticisms – I doubt he would have approved. Nor did he have much to say about Burns's precursors in the use of Scots as a literary language, Allan Ramsay (who died in 1758) and the supremely inventive Robert Fergusson who died, insane, in 1774 at the age of just twenty-four. Wilkie may have been insufferably boring, but at least he wrote in English. There were other poets – the physician John Armstrong, whose immortal line 'Now Muse, let's sing of rats' made Samuel Johnson giggle; the worthy and sensitive James Beattie, author of *The Minstrel* and another Professor of Moral Philosophy. Henry Mackenzie achieved phenomenal (and unrepeated) success with his 1771 novel, *The Man of Feeling*, which, as the title might suggest, was part of the 'Literature of Sentiment', and which was overshadowed by the far more sentimental, indeed practically hysterical, *Sorrows of Young Werther* by Goethe. Edinburgh's literature was politely local: Burns would not reach a European audience until Scott and Byron had carried him over with them.

The year after Hume sent his letter, a young farmer's son and native Gaelic speaker from Kingussie published a rather dull, six canto poem called 'The Highlander', just after he had left his studies at Aberdeen University. It sank without trace. But the author, James Macpherson, provided the Scottish Enlightenment with an invaluable literary service. He did not create a poem so much as create a poet by which Scotland could become the People most distinguish'd for Literature in Europe: Ossian.

Ossian

Had Macpherson died in 1760, at the same age as Fergusson, he might now be remembered as a genius. As it is, his name has become synonymous with literary fraud. It was to John Home that Macpherson gave his first, tentative translations of traditional Gaelic verses he had heard in oral recitations. Home was impressed enough to show Macpherson's work to David Hume, who was 'inclined to be a little incredulous' – but his scepticism, for once, ebbed. Home also showed the work to Professor Blair, who had far fewer doubts. These poems – which, Macpherson had hinted, might be the work of a semi-legendary, indigenous Scottish bard known as Ossian – had the plangent simplicity, the unembellished directness and the stark, uncompromising, melancholic world-view that one might expect from a noble savage at the end of the Age of Heroes. Macpherson was persuaded to publish a selection of these verses as *Fragments of Ancient Poetry collected in the Highlands of Scotland* in 1760. He translated the 'Erse' into sonorous, Biblically cadenced prose: 'Alone I am, O Shilric! alone in the winter-house. With grief for thee I expired. Shilric, I am pale in the tomb. She fleets, she sails away; as grey mist before the wind' is a pretty representative sample. If Macpherson had stopped at the *Fragments*, he may never have been rumbled.

Edinburgh, at that time, was civilised, sophisticated, enlightened and all those qualities, by one theory of literature, militated against it producing a Literary Genius. The qualities of rapturous enthusiasm, divine inspiration and the almost fearful sublime were not what one expected or desired to meet in the street or hear from a pulpit. Thomas Blackwell, the Professor of Greek at Aberdeen – who had died in 1757 – had written a remarkably perceptive book back in 1735 entitled *An Enquiry into the Life and Writings of Homer*, which Macpherson had read at university. Blackwell had argued that

Homer's pre-eminence came less from any individual, semi-divine inspiration, but the precise societal circumstances into which he had been born. The truly sublime occurred in 'the interval between the high liberty and enslavement of a state'. With regards to Homer, Blackwell had written, 'Had he been born much sooner, he could have seen nothing but nakedness and barbarity; had he come much later, he had fallen either in times of peace . . . or in general wars, regularly carried on by civilised states, when private passions are buried in the common order and established discipline.' These sublime fragments seemed to offer proof of Blackwell's theory – as well they might, the theory having, in part, inspired them.

There had been 'bards' like Homer in Scotland's past, whose work was lost in the very Celtic mists of time. Hume had played his card too quickly with poor old Wilkie – but the very fact that he had been so keen to christen someone as a Scottish Homer shows how tinder dry and terribly willing this world was to be set on fire by Macpherson's Ossian.

Ossian was everything the enlightened wanted. He was primitive but eloquent, stricken but honourable: he was even (hadn't they guessed yet?) blind, in both eyes, just like Homer and England's upstart epicist and regicide, John Milton. In 1760, they could only glimpse his genius in *Fragments*, but the feedback loop of theory and creation had begun. In his preface to the *Fragments*, Hugh Blair wrote that 'there is reason to hope that one work of considerable length, and which deserves to be styled a heroic poem, might be recovered and translated.'

Macpherson's later career, as government grub hack and wannabe laird, obscures how terrified that youth must have been. He was, by most accounts, slightly gauche, paunchy and obscure. Suddenly, he was almost famous, and the literati of the day lionised him. He wrestled with himself, and the less secure self won. In 1761, after travelling in the Highlands to source the material, Macpherson unveiled what Blair had tentatively predicted: *Fingal, an Ancient Epic Poem, in Six Books.*

It was an unparalleled success. In later years, Napoleon carried a copy of *Fingal* into battle with him, and Goethe produced long translations in *The Sorrows of Young Werther*. Chateaubriand, Klopstock and Mme de Stael were all enthusiasts – as was Robert Burns. The leading neoclassical painter of the age, Jean Auguste Dominique Ingres, created canvases inspired by the Ossianic mythology, and Schubert set the words to music. Thomas Sheridan told James Boswell that Ossian 'excelled Homer in the Sublime and Virgil in the Pathetic', and used a liking for the poetry as a litmus test for a person's sensibility. The English antiquarian Thomas Gray (author of the poem *The Bard*) wrote to his colleague Horace Walpole in more measured terms about the *Fragments*: 'In short, this man is the very Demon of Poetry, or he has lighted on a treasure hid for ages.' Nobody in Edinburgh was raising so much as an 'either'.

Macpherson wrote in the preface to *Fingal* that critics could decide 'how far it comes up to the rules of the *Epopaea*', while asserting his own belief that it was a 'true epic'. Critics, in the form of Hugh Blair (and Johann Herder in Germany), duly obliged. Blair wrote *A Critical Dissertation on the Poems of Ossian*, where he found that it did indeed measure up to the rules: rules that Blair had already written about, and which Macpherson had read. *Fingal* was actually better than *The Iliad, The Odyssey* and *The Aeneid*. There were plenty examples of lapses of taste in the classical poets – heroes falling in dung, princesses doing laundry, peevish deities who behaved more like teenagers – and there were more significant moral lapses – each epic poem ended with vengeful murder, whether it was Achilles killing Hector, Odysseus slaughtering the suitors and the maids, or Aeneas murdering Turnus. Fingal, however, spares his nemesis Swaran. As Blair put it, 'We find tenderness, and even delicacy of sentiment, greatly predominant over fierceness and barbarity. Our hearts are melted with the softest feelings, and at the same time elevated with the highest ideas of magnanimity, generosity, and true heroism.' In a moment of supreme and inadvertent irony, Blair also wrote that 'Ossian did not write, like modern poets, to please readers and critics'.

One reader and critic who was extremely displeased was Samuel Johnson. *Fingal* was 'as gross an imposition as ever the world was troubled with'. Dr Johnson, who had a lifelong propensity for tweaking the Scots – and who was immortalised as the archetype of

John Bull Englishness by his Scottish biographer, James Boswell – was Macpherson's most vocal opponent. Many of his withering put-downs have a cutting wit similar to that of Oscar Wilde: 'But, Doctor Johnson, do you really believe that any man today could write such poetry?'; 'Yes. Many men. Many women. And many children'; 'Sir, a man might write such stuff for ever, if he would *abandon* his mind to it'; 'A Scotchman must be a very sturdy moralist, who does not love Scotland better than truth.' (Wilde, coincidentally, was named Oscar after one of the characters in *Fingal*.) But the unmasking of Ossian as a forgery was not undertaken by Johnson, whose blunderbuss pronouncements were as ill-considered in their argument as they were accurate in their aim. Rather, it was antiquarians, and in particular Irish antiquarians, who unpicked the intricately stitched text: people like Edmund Burke, Ferdinando Warner, Terence Brady and Charles O'Conor. In Scotland, it was the antiquarian John Pinkerton, author of an *Enquiry into the History of Scotland* (and himself the fabricator of part of the ballad of 'Hardyknute') who saw through Ossian. Pinkerton, like a true Enlightenment scholar, noted the dissimilarities in sources, the anachronisms, the paucity of supporting materials and concluded that the Scotland that Ossian supposedly inhabited never in truth existed. The poems were a 'delicious delusion' and the epic history of Scotland 'a Celtic dream'.

Macpherson made two very big mistakes – well, three if you include his translation of Homer into Ossianic cadences. Firstly, needled by Johnson's demands to see the original manuscripts (although he was well aware that they were purportedly oral documents), Macpherson translated his poetry back into Gaelic. He had, like any good eighteenth-century translator, told his audience that he had accommodated his translation to contemporary taste. But the Gaelic version transpired to be identical to the English: there was no evidence of the 'barbarism' he claimed he had polished away. Then he found *another* epic, *Temora*, which appeared in 1763. Enough was enough. More knowledgeable critics were picking hole after hole in his work, and the rich seam of Gaelic epic abruptly dried up. Macpherson managed to live quite comfortably after the public debunking of Ossian although he lost the support of his erstwhile defenders. In public, David Hume became rueful – 'Men run with great Avidity to give their Evidence in favour of what flatters their Passions, and their national Prejudices'; in private, he was wrathful, saying if fifty bare-arsed Highlanders should say that *Fingal* was an ancient poem, he should not believe them. Nevertheless Macpherson thrived. He was three times elected MP for Camelford, wrote a *History of Great Britain* and on the management of the East India Company, and acted as agent for Mohammad Ali Chan, the Nabob of Arcot. He was so wealthy that on his death in 1796 he could instruct that he be buried, ironically enough, in Poets' Corner in Westminster Abbey. He never backed down over Ossian, or admitted any element of imposture – in 1773, in the Collected Edition, he even used their foreign success as proof of their intrinsic truthfulness, writing: 'Through the medium of version upon version, they retain, in foreign languages, their native character of simplicity and energy. Genuine poetry, like gold, loses little, when properly transfused; but when a composition cannot bear the test of a literal version, it is a counterfeit which ought not to pass current.'

But ghosts, once raised, are notoriously difficult to exorcise. The Highland Society of Scotland, founded in 1784 – that is, twenty-three years after the publication of *Fingal* – had as part of its brief 'the preservation of the language, poetry and music of the Highlands'. The year after Macpherson's death they formed a committee under the chairmanship of the novelist Henry Mackenzie 'appointed to inquire into the Nature and Authenticity of the Poems of Ossian'. It finally reported in 1805, concluding, as had Pinkerton, that there were Gaelic originals – mainly names, incidents and the broadest of similes – for the Ossianic oeuvre, but that Macpherson had freely amplified and constructed a whole narrative around these sparse texts. 'The writer of Ossian's poems was habitually familiar with modern poetry' wrote the anonymous reviewer of the committee's final report in the *Edinburgh Review*. That anonymous reviewer was Walter Scott, who, in the same year, first started to write his own Highland romance in prose: *Waverley*.

What remains of Ossian? Ironically enough, mist. The figures of the *Fragments* flit through mist, and long after the fog of authorial obfuscation had lifted, it was mistiness that remained quintessentially 'Celtic'. It persists in ideas of the 'Celtic Twilight' and in Matthew Arnold's evocation of Celtic literature, typified by magic, melancholy and the natural world. It even becomes philosophical, in the Celt's 'vehement reaction against the despotism of fact', and aesthetic in the impressionistic half-tints and chiaroscuro. Arnold's depiction of the Celt – 'this colossus, impetuous, adventurous wanderer, the Titan of the early world, who in primitive times fills so large a place of earth's scene, dwindles and dwindles as history goes on . . . for ages and ages the world has been constantly slipping, ever more and more, out of the Celt's grasp' – is historical process as mistening. The melancholy is a lachrymose mistiness of emotions. The stereotype lingers: it is through mist that two Americans stumble upon the enchanted village of Brigadoon in the eponymous musical. *Braveheart* establishes its location with mist-covered mountains and the strains of bagpipes. The postcards in Waverley station are rarely of scenes in startling sunshine. Perhaps the most concise combination comes in that novel: 'To speak in the poetical language of my country, the seat of the Celtic Muse is in the mist of the secret and solitary hill, and her voice in the murmur of the mountain stream. He who woos her must love the barren rock more than the fertile valley, and the solitude of the desert better than the festivity of the hall.'

For the young Scott, though, in this newly confident city, Ossian was a problem. It had inflicted a national cringe. It had confused 'should have' and 'must have'. It was the most successful ever version of Scottishness, and it was a fake. The author had become prestigious, and an embarrassment. As Macpherson himself had said: 'He that obtains fame must receive it through mere fashion; and gratify his vanity with the applause of men, of whose judgment he cannot approve.'

Reputation

No author's reputation has ever peaked and pitched like Sir Walter Scott's. 'In the nineteenth century Scott was ubiquitous,' wrote the critic John Henry Raleigh, 'in the twentieth he virtually disappears. Never before or since in Western culture has a writer been such a power in his day and so negligible to posterity.' The 'Great Unknown' became, in his biographer W E K Anderson's phrase, the 'Great Unread'.

With our jaded eyes, it is difficult for us to see how dazzling Scott was. When Byron described his contemporary Parnassus, Scott was securely at the top, and the Waverley Novels were 'a new species of literature'. Goethe claimed that *Waverley* stood 'alongside the best things that have ever been written in the world'. Heine said Scott '*was* Britannia's greatest poet'. Even Stendhal, who voiced a very accurate anxiety – 'In a hundred-and-forty-six years time, Scott will be less esteemed than Corneille still is a hundred-and-forty-six years after his death' – nevertheless recognised Scott as 'our father' who 'invented us all'. Later in the century when Thomas Hardy enthused that the *Iliad* 'was almost in the *Marmion* class', modern readers can't help but feel Hardy was being ironic.

To his contemporaries, and for a century afterwards, there was only one writer to whom Scott could be compared: Shakespeare. Writing to Scott's publisher with her congratulations over *Waverley*, the Irish novelist Maria Edgeworth, whose own work had been an inspiration to Scott, said it showed 'the skill of Shakespeare'. Mary Shelley, in a review of her father's novel *Cloudesley* thought Scott 'unsurpassed, except by Shakespeare, for energy and truth' – the kind of jacket endorsement over which a modern publisher would swoon. The leading critic of the day, and my personal hero, Francis Jeffrey of the *Edinburgh Review*, who notoriously savaged authors (his infamous

review of Wordsworth's *The Excursion* began 'This will never do!'),
wrote in a piece on the first series of *Tales of my Landlord*: 'The author,
whoever he is, has a truly graphic and creative power in the invention
and delineation of characters – which he sketches with an ease, and
colours with a brilliancy, and scatters about with a profusion, which
reminds us of Shakespeare himself.' The poet Swinburne – not, given
his propensity for decadence, ornate expressions and flagellation, the
most obvious enthusiast for Scott – summarised the views of
Emerson, Bagehot and others when he wrote, 'If there were or could
be any man it would not be a monstrous absurdity to compare with
Shakespeare as a creator of men and an inventor of circumstances,
that man would be none other than Scott.'

In his biography of Scott, John Buchan constantly compares the
two: 'when the drama quickens and the stage darkens he attains to a
style as perfect and unforgettable as Shakespeare's'; 'Scott's method is
pre-eminently the method of Shakespeare'; 'He has Shakespeare's gift
of charging our life with new and happier values'. So great was the
identification between Scott and Shakespeare that when critics – like
Hazlitt, or Carlyle – sought to give more critical appraisals, they
tended to do so by anatomising the differences between Shakespeare
and Scott. Scott, for his own part, was wryly curt: 'The blockheads
talk of me being like Shakespeare – not fit to tie his brogues.'

The comparison makes a great deal more sense if we remember
that Scott is being compared to the nineteenth-century Shakespeare.
Late eighteenth- and early nineteenth-century critics praised
Shakespeare for very particular attributes: his profusion and fecundity
of invention, an imagination unfettered by the artificial constraints
of neoclassical unities, and above all his encompassing generosity
of vision. The fact that the plays mixed comedy and tragedy, 'low'
humour and 'high' art, historical figures and imagined characters,
and kings with peasants was seen as Shakespeare's distinctive
breadth and power. All these traits are characteristic of Scott. Just as
Shakespeare could include Theseus and Bottom, or Hamlet and the
gravedigger, or Henry V and Pistol, so Scott would draw together the
Young Pretender and Daft David Gellately, Claverhouse and Cuddie
Headrigg, Queen Caroline and Madge Wildfire.

Shakespeare was also, by the time of Scott, constructed as a national figure. The Jubilee organised by Garrick in 1769 sowed the seed for the coming 'Bardolatry'. August von Schlegel referred to Shakespeare as 'the pride of his nation' and, as Jane Austen wrote in *Mansfield Park*, Shakespeare was 'part of an Englishman's constitution'. Scott, within the new British union, could be read as a Caledonian counterpart to 'Warwickshire Will'.

By 1864, when the Shakespeare Jubilee had been moved from August to April to coincide with Shakespeare's purported birthday and St George's Day, a 'National Monumental Memorial' to the playwright was erected. Scott had been similarly honoured – twenty years beforehand. But the most curious instance of Scott and Shakespeare's connection comes from an account by Robert E Hunter, secretary to the tercentenary committee. At the highlight of the season, a fancy dress ball, alongside Desdemona, Ophelia, Cordelia, Benedict, Owen Glenower and Harry the Eighth, was Edgar Ravenswood – from Scott's *The Bride of Lammermoor*. It's not a unique muddle. A small oil painting by Delacroix is entitled 'Self Portrait (as Hamlet or Edgar Ravenswood)'.

At the beginning of the twentieth century, Victorian veneration of Shakespeare gave way to a more sophisticated critical interpretation, prompted by Shaw's defence of Ibsen's naturalist dramas. Scott enjoyed no such renaissance in reaction to the rise of the modernist novel. In works such as Woolf's *To the Lighthouse*, Linklater's *Magnus Merriman* and Joyce's *Finnegans Wake* (where the 'Author of *Waverley*' is transformed into part of a triumvirate of British bullies, 'scoot, duckings and thuggery') the reading of Scott is a shorthand for a character being behind the times. Joyce seems to have entertained a particular antipathy towards Scott: in 'An Encounter', the 'queer old josser' has all of Scott's works; in 'Araby', the dead priest was reading *The Abbot*; and in *Portrait of the Artist as a Young Man* the students tease an old man with a 'blackish, monkey-puckered face' who is rumoured to be the product of incest. The students' talk has shuttlecocked over the entire Western canon, but the old man only mumbles, 'I love old Scott . . . I think he writes something lovely. There is no writer can touch Sir Walter Scott.' He, and his favourite author, is a symbol of senescence.

F R Leavis excluded Scott from his Great Tradition of novelists worthy to be called literature, dismissing him with the words, 'Out of Scott a bad tradition came.' E M Forster, in *Aspects of the Novel*, sneered, 'Who shall tell us a story? Sir Walter Scott of course,' demoting him from novelist to raconteur. Henry James was more genial, if just as damning: 'He is identical with the fireside chronicler. And thoroughly to enjoy him, we must again become as credulous as children at twilight.' In the face of the new, psychologically inflected novel, Scott was both immature and old-fashioned.

In *Breakfast of Champions* (1973), Kurt Vonnegut uses *Ivanhoe* as an exemplar of irrelevance and the idiocy of the traditional curriculum: pupils 'were told that they were unworthy to speak or write their language if they couldn't love or understand incomprehensible novels and poems and plays about people long ago and far away, such as *Ivanhoe*'. Andrew Crumey's *Sputnik Caledonia* (2008) wittily recommends the same novel as an antidote to bed-wetting and American-comic induced excitement and insomnia. And it gets worse: Irvine Welsh, in conversation with John Mullan at the *Guardian*'s Book Group, not only denied Scott any cultural influence within Scottish writing, but stripped him of any literary significance whatsoever. According to Welsh, Scott was 'just an arse-licker to the Prince Regent'. In less than 200 years, Scott changed from being essential and exceptional to being superfluous and suspect. You might wonder why we are even talking about him.

Monument

Leave Edinburgh Waverley, and almost the first thing you will see is a Gothic folly, a truncated cathedral spire or a steam-punk version of Thunderbird 3, stranded in the middle of Princes Street Gardens: the Scott Monument. In the elegant New Town it strikes a doubly anachronistic note. William Gladstone, in a speech in 1868, commented that 'it is very well that the inhabitants of this island in general, and the Scottish in particular, are not given to idolatry; because the statue, placed as it is, might look, to a person totally unacquainted with the religious beliefs and usages of the country, as if it were placed there to receive the worship of passers-by'. It stands 200 feet and six inches high, with 287 steps leading to a central chamber and higher viewing decks from which you can study the sixty-four statuettes that bristle in their alcoves and the panoramic views beyond. The statue of Scott himself, carved by John Steel from a block of white Carrara marble sits at the base. It is, quite simply, the largest monument to an author in the world. The only potential competition would be with the follies erected by Saparmurat Niyazov, the former president of Turkmenistan and author of the *Ruhnama, or The Book of the Soul*. Scott, however, did not commission his own monument.

A fortnight after Scott's death, a meeting was convened by the Lord Provost of Edinburgh, John Learmonth, in the Assembly Rooms to discuss how Scott should be memorialised in his native city. It was decided that there should be an open competition for the final design, and a separate committee was set up to solicit subscriptions and donations. By the time the Monument was completed fourteen years later, the committee had had to stage extra fundraisers several times to secure the total cost of £16,154, 7 s and 6 d (1,525 roubles were also sent to the committee).

The competition was launched in spring 1836, with a prize of fifty guineas to the winner. They received fifty-four entries, including designs for obelisks, pillars, fountains and statues with canopies. The influential critic John Ruskin did not submit his idea, but later described how he would have preferred to see Scott commemorated: in Holyrood Park, he envisaged that 'a bold and solid mass of mason work be built out from the cliff in gray stone, broken like natural rock, rising some 4 or 5 feet above the brow of the crag and sloping down, not too steeply, into the bank below. At the foot of this, let a group of figures, not more than five in number, be carved in the solid rock, in the dress of Border shepherds . . . On the brow of this pedestal let a colossal figure of Scott be placed, arms folded, looking towards the castle.' Luckily, Scotland avoided having its own Mount Rushmore.

Fourteen of the entries were in the neoclassical style. Given that architectural approach typified Edinburgh's New Town, then still under construction, it might have seemed a logical choice. Had he been alive, Scott would have disagreed. At the very start of his literary career he had vetoed the neoclassicist John Flaxman as illustrator of *The Lay of the Last Minstrel*, preferring the more romantic work of Salvator Rosa. By far the majority of entries were Gothic in conception, and the winner would assuredly have found favour with the author: all of its details were derived from the ruins of Melrose Abbey, close to Scott's home at Abbotsford and a key location in *The Lay*.

In another move that would have appealed to 'the Great Unknown', the winning designer submitted his work under a pseudonym; 'John Morvo', by tradition, the architect of Melrose Abbey. It was not as if his real name would have meant anything to the judges. George Meikle Kemp was unheard-of. He had been born in 1795 in Moorfoot in the Scottish Borders, and worked as a joiner and draughtsman. His architectural knowledge was entirely self-taught, and he had failed to win a similar competition for work on Glasgow Cathedral a few years beforehand.

The foundations were laid in 1840, with a glass jar as a time capsule beneath the foundation stone, containing copies of the local newspapers, a map, a subscription list and a full set of the coin of the realm, all buried fifty-two feet deep. These items were accompanied by a brass memorial plaque, written by the critic Francis Jeffrey:

THIS GRAVEN PLATE
Deposited in the Base of a Votive Building
on the fifteenth day of August, in the Year of Christ 1840,
And never likely to see the light again,
Till all the surrounding structures are crumbled to dust
By the decay of time, or by human or elemental violence,
May then testify to a distant posterity that
His Countrymen began on that day
To raise an Effigy and Architectural Monument
TO THE MEMORY OF SIR WALTER SCOTT, BART.
Whose admirable Writings were then allowed
To have given more delight and suggested better feeling
To a larger class of readers, in every rank of society,
Than those of any other Author,
With the exception of Shakespeare alone;
And which were therefore thought likely to be remembered
Long after this act of Gratitude
On part of this first generation of his Admirers
Should be forgotten
HE WAS BORN IN EDINBURGH
15TH AUGUST 1771
AND DIED AT ABBOTSFORD
21ST SEPTEMBER 1832

The Monument was beset by bad luck. Kemp died, after falling into the Union Canal in 1844, six years before its completion. Financial difficulties beset the Monument as well, with the workers continuing to work in expectation of their wages while the Committee tried to find them, reduced to door-to-door collections. The stone chosen for the 'gew-gaw', as the novelist Sir Edward Bulwer-Lytton called it, was unfortunately a local mined variety called Binnie Shale, which had a tendency to leech oil. The smoke from the nearby and brand new Waverley Station adhered to the oil, making the entire steeple a sooty-black colour. In effect, it immediately started to look older than it was.

Most guidebooks say that the statuettes are all characters from Scott's works. This is not true. The reformer John Knox and Charles I are both there, although they are only alluded to in his books. Fiction and history intermingle: real people like Cromwell, Robert the Bruce, Bonnie Prince Charlie and Elizabeth I sit beside people that never were; Dirk Hatteraik, Minna Troil, Caleb Balderstone and Percie Shafton. Two individuals are depicted twice: Mary, Queen of Scots and George Buchanan are honoured with statues, but their faces also appear at the corners of the four major pillars. It was decided that the pillars should also be decorated with Scotland's other greatest writers – Buchanan, Mary and her two fellow royal authors, James V and James I; Tobias Smollett, James Beattie, James Thomson and John Home; Robert Tannahill, William Drummond of Hawthorden, Sir David Lyndsay and Allan Ramsay; Robert Fergusson, James Hogg, Lord Byron and even Robert Burns float like sulky cherubim around the throne of Scott. William Wilkie is nowhere to be seen. Obviously, there's no Ossian.

At the first level, there is a central chamber, with four stained glass windows depicting St Andrew, Edinburgh, Scotland and St Giles. The glass casts a warm reddish light, throwing shafts of blue and green onto the woodwork, where the names of Scott's published works – even obscure non-fiction ones like *The Memorials of the Halliburtons* and *Letters on Demonology and Witchcraft* – are carved. Above the display cases (sadly devoid of relics these days) are golden bosses of monarchs and legislators. If it were not so secular, and so eccentric, it would seem like a chapel. It feels like a Gothic variant on Dr Who's TARDIS console room, with all the co-ordinates locked on the past.

Outside there is, as you might expect, a statuette of Ivanhoe. Like the other statues he is nowadays covered in light chicken-wire, to protect it from pigeons and to protect passers-by should he fall. He doesn't look like Steven Waddington from the 1997 BBC TV series, or Robert Taylor from the 1952 film, or even like either King Baggot or Lauderdale Templeton, who starred as Ivanhoe in the two competing 1913 films. But Ivanhoe being there is something of an

anomaly. Were you to pore over the statues, only Ivanhoe, Hal o'
the Wynd, Edgar Ravenswood and Jeannie Deans might reasonably
be called the 'lead character' of the novels in which they appear.
There is no statue to Edward Waverley, nor to Henry Morton, Guy
Mannering, Colonel Lovel, Nigel Olifaunt, Darsie Latimer, Francis
Osbaldistone nor Julian Peveril. Hereward, The Earl of Menteith,
Mordaunt Mertoun, Markham Everard, Richard Middlemas,
Quentin Durward, Francis Tyrrel and Roland Avenel were all over-
looked for the accolade of a representation. Whatever the Scott
Monument commemorates or accommodates, it is not his heroes.

The Monument is marred with graffiti these days, and I don't
mind it. It's vaguely depressing that Portuguese teenagers have
chosen to immortalise their love in Tippex; but given, if you look
carefully, you can find scraped names dating back to the 1860s, it
seems churlish to preserve Victorian vandalism and not appreciate
its contemporary version.

If you want my advice and are intent on climbing the Monument,
get there just before it opens. It doesn't exactly take heroism, but it
does require a certain amount of stamina and deep breathing. The
spiral staircases get progressively narrower, and although a score of
people can stand around on the first viewing deck, only four can be
accommodated at the summit. I've been up several times, and several
times more have reached the third platform and decided that's
enough. It's a particularly unpleasant experience to be stuck in a
stone corkscrew, only slightly wider than your body, with the wind
whistling through a balistraria at your foot and your head grazing
the stair above. It's even more unpleasant and claustrophobic when
a class of primary school children are at your back and a corpulent
American is squeezing his way down towards you.

The view from the top is, however gruelling to get there and
clichéd to say, spectacular. From the summit, looking east over to
Calton Hill, you can see the twelve pillars of the unfinished National
Monument overlooking the new Parliament. Started in 1822, and
designed by the eminent Playfair and Cockerell, the National
Monument was supposed to be a replica of the Parthenon in Athens,
in commemoration of the British victory over Napoleon. Funds ran

out and it was abandoned, earning the nickname, 'Edinburgh's Folly'. It seems appropriate that while the National Monument was left unfinished, the Scott Monument was completed. 'Folly' is a delightful double-word – ill-advised foolishness on one hand and a whimsical, purposeless, architectural jeu d'esprit on the other.

Royal Mile

The Royal Mile is longer than a mile, but does link Edinburgh Castle, perched on its volcanic plug, with Holyrood Palace, the Queen's official Edinburgh residence, and now neighbour to the Scottish Parliament. If you were to head up the old *Scotsman* Steps and then down the Mile, you would experience a cacophony of voices, literary and otherwise, insisting on their Scottishness. The Mile is the spine of Caledonian stereotypes, all Saltires and Lions Rampant, tasteful and tacky tartans, whisky shops, bagpipes, artificial thistles, blunted claymores that do not constitute an offensive weapon, ginger wigs, Loch Ness tours, Mel Gibson face-paint, genealogical pseudo-parchments rolling off laser-printers, New Age Pictish mysticism and synthesised bagpipes blaring 'Flower of Scotland' (composed 1967), 'Highland Cathedral' (composed by the Germans Uli Roever and Michael Korb in 1982) and Celine Dion's 'My Heart Will Go On'. You have to wonder about a country where one shop proclaims itself as 'The REAL Scotland SHOP' a stone's throw from another purveying 'Scottish FANTASIES'.

It's an eclectic mixture of local incident, poetic anecdote, political statement and religious exhortation. There's 'Heave Awa House', so named after one Joseph McIvor who survived the former building's collapse in 1861: the rescuers heard him shout, 'Heave Awa Lads, I'm no deid yet.' A Pre-Raphaelite looking bust has his plea modified into more correct English, 'Heave Awa Chaps, I'm no died yet.'

Further down is John Knox's House, where John Knox never definitively lived, a fine example of the architecture of the period with overhanging upper storeys and crow's step gables. A legend in Scots – Lvfe God abvfe al and yi nychtovr as yi self – runs around it. Its own neighbours, appropriately enough, are Scottish Book Trust and the Scottish Storytelling Centre, as well as a kilt manufacturer with the requisite clan logarithms to determine if a Smith is a MacPherson or a Hardy is a Farquharson. Above the kiltmakers, there is no plaque to draw attention to the house where Daniel Defoe stayed, in his capacity as an English spy during the Union of the Parliament negotiations. On the wall of the Scottish Storytelling Centre is a quotation attributed to the novelist Alasdair Gray: 'Work as if you lived in the early days of a better nation.' But again, nothing is quite as it seems. Gray derived the second half of the phrase from the *Civil Elegies* of the Canadian poet Dennis Lee (who, absolutely coincidentally, wrote the lyrics for Jim Henson's *Fraggle Rock*, and co-authored the films *Dark Crystal* and *Labyrinth*).

Religion and literature alternate down the rest of the Mile, as if contrapuntally developing a theme of memento mori. 'Hodie Mihi, Cras Tibi' – 'It is my fate today and thine tomorrow' – reads one solemn reminder. A new statue to the eighteenth-century poet Robert Fergusson, who inspired Burns and died in a madhouse, jauntily strides towards the new Parliament with his thumb keeping place in a book. A plaque is all that remains of the Old Playhouse, where the playwright John Home had his stunning if short-lived success.

At the Parliament itself, the Canongate Wall abuts the Mile. It was decided that this Wall should feature apposite quotations from Scottish authors, engraved into examples of local stone; all of them pertinent to the Parliament and the behaviour of its members. So, for example, it has Psalm 19:14 ('Let the words of my mouth, and the meditation of my heart, be acceptable in thy sight, O Lord, my strength and my redeemer'), a Gaelic proverb ('Abair ach beagan is abair gu math e', 'Say but little but say it well') and Scots ('To promise is ae thing, to keep it is anither'). The words of the industrialist and philanthropist Andrew Carnegie are situated with those of the conservationist John Muir. The Anglo-Irish poet and priest Gerald Manley Hopkins was included, since he worked briefly in Glasgow, and a visit to Loch Katrine inspired 'Inversnaid'. The rest are mostly from historic and contemporary Scottish writers. Alasdair Gray's modern proverb is there – although his name is embarrassingly misspelled Alisdair. Burns, Stevenson, MacDiarmid,

Morgan, Hamish Henderson and others, with a clever mixture of sincerity and humour, lead you to the final stone: Sir Walter Scott.

It is a rather ingeniously chosen quotation that was eventually inscribed there. The Parliament decided to forego the more obvious choices, such as the patriotic paean from *The Lay of the Last Minstrel* ('Breathes there a man, with soul so dead, / Who never to himself hath said, / This is my own, my native land!'). Nor is it the famous lines from *Marmion* ('Oh what a tangled web we weave / When first we practise to deceive') – a bit cynical perhaps. 'Because the Hour's come, and the Man', from *Guy Mannering*, might be a tad too close to manifest destiny and the rationale of dictatorship. ' "That sounds like nonsense, my dear" – "Maybe so, my dear; but it may be a very good law for all that" ', from the same novel, perhaps *ought* to have been carved there. Personally I rather liked Scott's words from his *Journal*: 'But who cares for the whipped cream of London society?' The actual choice was a rueful and wry comment from *The Heart of Midlothian*, set in the immediate aftermath of the dissolution of the previous Parliament: 'When we had a king, and a chancellor, and parliament-men o' our ain, we could aye peeble them wi' stanes when they werena gude bairns – But naebody's nails can reach the length o' Lunnon.' Scott, the arch-Unionist in so many ways, provides via one of his characters a fitting summary of the pragmatics of devolution.

Nation

On 11 September 1997, the Scottish people voted for a devolved parliament with tax-varying powers. On 12 May 1999, after the swearing-in of the Members of Parliament, the oldest member, Nationalist MSP Winnie Ewing said, 'I have the opportunity to make a short speech and I want to begin with the words that I have always wanted either to say or to hear someone else say: the Scottish Parliament, which adjourned on 25 March 1707, is hereby reconvened.' The inaugural First Minister, Donald Dewar, invoked Scott in his speech, saying, 'Only a man with a soul so dead could have no sense, no feel for his native land.' But exactly what that native land *is*, is an ongoing and problematic question. Scotland – rather than the imaginative space of Scott-land – is a persistent square peg in a constitutional theory full of round holes.

Ewing's words neatly summarise the broad realities of Scotland's political status. It was an independent nation until the Union of the Parliaments in 1707, which dissolved Scotland's separate government and incorporated it into a new entity, the United Kingdom of Great Britain. It was already united in terms of dynastic monarchy, since 1603 when James VI of Scotland had succeeded Elizabeth I of England to become James I of Britain; and at least part of the impetus for the later parliamentary union was the fear, after a century of civil war, of Scotland siding with the Jacobite Catholic Pretenders against the now dominant House of Hanover.

But the new Parliament represents only the devolution of power from Westminster, not a separation of Scotland from the United Kingdom. The Parliament was only reconvened in an emotional, not institutional, sense. Devolution, ironically, is a Unionist policy. Certain areas – defence, taxation, foreign policy, biotechnology, broadcasting, energy, immigration, gambling, data protection,

firearms, treason and, most importantly, the future of the constitution – are reserved matters for Westminster.

Having no seat at the United Nations means that Scotland is *de
facto* not a sovereign nation state at present. But calling it an
autonomous, or semi-autonomous, region does not work either –
the Holyrood Parliament has fewer legislative powers than the
average Swiss canton or Kurdistan. Nor is Scotland, despite the
rhetoric of some propagandists, an internal colony, like Tibet or
Chechnya. The Basque Country and Quebec have tried to define
themselves as 'linguistically homogenous territories' – but again
Scotland, with its 'three languages' of English, Scots and Gaelic
(and, for example, more Urdu speakers than born Gaelic speakers)
cannot make a similar claim. Scotland has more powers than a
province but fewer than the partners of the Commonwealth.

The present situation is complicated even further. As of 3 May
2007, Scotland has been governed by a minority administration,
headed by the Nationalist Party. But the correlation between support
for the party and support for its aim – full independence – is still
evolving. Moreover, in terms of political *power*, Scotland – through
the inequities of what has become known as the West Lothian
Question – punches above its weight. Put very simply: Scots are
politically represented by both MPs in Westminster and MSPs in
Holyrood. English voters have only an MP. Therefore an English MP
cannot vote on the non-reserved matters affecting Scotland (health,
education, legal age for the purchase of hamsters) but a Scottish MSP
can vote on non-reserved matters affecting England.

The election in 2007 was – as much as these things ever can be –
thrilling. The Nationalists ended up with a majority of one. In effect,
it meant that the entire shape of Scotland's politics depended on the
final count in the final seat. My father has been a lifelong Nationalist
supporter, with the qualification that as a Church of Scotland elder
he has never allowed optimism to influence his politics: I vividly
remember arguing with him, in my student days, and being taken
aback that he insisted he would gladly pay more tax if Scotland were
independent. It was an article of faith, not a question of fiscal pragmatics. The 2007 election wasn't like the 1997 election, when Labour

took Westminster. There wasn't that tidal wave sense, the foregone conclusion of victory. It was down to the last minute; penalty shoot-out politics. As the Friday waned on, we chatted on the phone about the chance, the slim chance, the getting less slim chance that the SNP would actually win. We both started to use ludicrous arguments, like 'Is there a difference in the air?' and 'Who's smiling?' The win against Labour, as my colleague Kenny Farquharson eloquently wrote, is unique: the SNP's leader, Alex Salmond, as First Minister of Scotland, is effectively in government and in opposition simultaneously.

If the contemporary is confusing, then the past is as vexed. As the historian Michael Fry has commented, in the seventeenth and eighteenth centuries there were a great many separate geopolitical entities, with leaders and representatives and assemblies – the Most Serene Republic of Venice, the Electorate of the Palatinate of the Rhineland, the Kingdom of Savoy – which were assimilated, absorbed or forced into larger political forms; and in which no 'nationalism' now persists. It was the Age of Empire, and even though Scotland became part of a major Empire, its nationalist aspirations were quietened, but not quelled. In the nineteenth century, a resurgence of nationalism quivered across Europe, in Finland, Hungary, Poland and Italy. In each one of those countries, Sir Walter Scott was invoked. Even America looked to Scott as inspiration, model, problem and cautionary tale for a new country. In Scotland, as the Waverley Novels started to smell musty on the shelves, Scott inspired no such nationalist endeavour. When nationalism did return to Scotland, its avowed enemy was Sir Walter Scott.

Geography is of as little use as history when it comes to national identities and notional states. Choose a language and draw your borders: early Cymri might happily carve a line to include Carlisle and Cardiff as a 'once Scottish' space. The Gaelic 'Sassenach' would mean that Sir Walter himself was a southerner and by extension Englishman. Shetland has more in common with Scandinavia, and the Lordship of the Isles only fell in 1493, bringing the archipelago of the west under Scottish regal authority. Shetland was given as a dowry to Scotland by Christian I of Denmark and Norway in 1468, and Orkney (part of the original dowry) was formally annexed in

1472. Berwick-upon-Tweed, just over the contemporary border, changed hands officially thirteen times between Scotland and England, and was occupied by force a great many more. The most obvious indication of its fluctuating status is that Berwickshire does not include Berwick. Not wholly in jest, the Nationalist MSP Christine Grahame asked in Parliament for Berwick to be 'reunified' with Scotland; a call which the Liberal MSP Jeremy Purvis responded to by asking for the Border to be moved a full twenty miles south, to include Berwick Borough Council.

Scotland is an anomaly. It is a country without a nation, a nation without a state, a state without a voice. Scotland is a kind of limbo, a wraith-place. Even in the early nineteenth century, Lord Cockburn wrote of the feeling that he and his companions were living through 'the last purely Scotch age that Scotland was destined to see'. In his polemical essay *Scott and Scotland*, written in 1936, Edwin Muir chillingly described the vacuum of Scotland: Scott, according to Muir, 'spent most of his days in a hiatus, in a country, that is to say, which was neither a nation nor a province, and had, instead of a centre, a blank, an Edinburgh, in the middle of it. But this Nothing in which Scott wrote was not merely a spatial one; it was a temporal Nothing as well'. In a later poem, 'Scotland 1941', he denounced Burns and Scott as 'the sham bards of a sham nation'. The idea of Scotland's *unreality* appears time and again in literature. Robert Louis Stevenson, in *The Silverado Squatters*, asserted that 'Scotland is indefinable; it has no unity except upon the map'. The Glasgow writer Cliff Hanley wrote 'Scotland is not a place, of course. It is a state of mind', perhaps unconsciously echoing Stevenson's idea of a Scottish 'accent of the mind'. In a speech to the Scottish National Party Conference in 1987, the novelist William McIlvanney argued that the Conservative leader Margaret Thatcher would 'remove from the word "Scottish" any meaning other than the geographical', almost reversing Stevenson's dictum by placing the map as the least essential attribute of Scottishness. The title of Donny O'Rourke's anthology of contemporary Scottish poetry was entitled, with all puns intended, *Dream State*.

Yet Scott-land – the imagined Scotland, the recognised Scotland, the *still-different* Scotland – is so obvious (Groundskeeper Willie, Fat

Bastard, Braveheart, John Rebus, James Bond, Mrs Doubtfire, Desmond David Hume, Mr Mackay of Slade Prison, Private Frazer, Scrooge McDuck, Jamie McCrimmon, Connor MacLeod of the Clan MacLeod, 'Raven', Hellboy, Sherlock Holmes) that it sometimes seems as if Scotland *should* exist.

To understand this slippage between a politically intangible entity and a culturally unavoidable set of symbols, between, if you like, the landscape and the mindscape, and to understand Scott's role in it, it's important to remember that Scott wasn't British first and foremost. Nor was he Scottish first and foremost. In James Joyce's *A Portrait of the Artist as a Young Man*, Stephen Dedalus writes on the flyleaf of his geography textbook: '*Stephen Dedalus, Class of Elements, Clongowes Wood School, Sallins, County Kildare, Ireland, Europe, The World, The Universe*', situating himself at the centre of shells of space. Scott's version depends on genealogy as much as geography. He was, as he says in his own autobiographical fragment, the son of Walter Scott, great-grandson of Walter 'Beardie' Scott, great-great-grandson of Auld Watt Scott of Harden, and thus a member of a minor branch of the Scotts of Buccleuch. Scott, first and foremost, was a Scott and a Borderer.

The Borders

In the introduction to *The Minstrelsy of the Scottish Border*, Scott wrote: 'The accession of James to the English crown converted the extremity into the centre of his kingdom.' As far as myths of the union go, this one is the *ne plus ultra*. The Borders is the centre in much the same way as a doughnut has a centre. Geographically, it may be the case that the Border areas became the approximate middle of Britain; but politically power lay in London and Edinburgh, and the Borders remained, as their nickname aptly put it, The Debatable Lands. These were disputed territories even before the ideas of 'Scotland' and 'England' coalesced. Andrew Lang, in his posthumous *Scottish Border Country*, writes how in the Ettrick Valley 'the place-names prove ownership in the past by men of English speech, of Cymric speech and of Gaelic speech. From a single point of view you may see Penchrise (Welsh), Glengaber (Gaelic) and Skelfhill (English).'

That intermittent 's' is intriguing, as if there is some uncertainty as to the exact number of borders there are. The year before Scott's *Minstrelsy of the Scottish Border* appeared, the Revd Richard Warren published *A Tour through the Northern Counties of England and the Borders of Scotland*. In the late medieval period, the whole area – from Carlisle and the Solway to Berwick and the North Sea – was divided into six 'marches', three on the English side comprising Westmoreland, Cumberland and Northumberland, and three on the Scottish side, roughly equivalent to modern-day Kirkcudbrightshire, Dumfriesshire and the 'Scottish Borders' of old Roxburghshire, Berwickshire, Selkirkshire and Peeblesshire. It's just as odd, when you think about it, that we refer to the Scottish, and not the English, Border. It seems to suggest that whereas the limit of England is clear and fixed by its counties, the Scottish one is a more flexible and ambivalent affair.

The Six Marches were jurisdictional areas, and the Keepers or Wardens had an unenviable task. Bartholomaeus Anglicus, a Franciscan encyclopaedist of the thirteenth century, wrote that the inhabitants of the region 'delighted in their own' and 'do not love peace'. For centuries, with royal authority weak or non-existent, the chief Border families on each side conducted guerrilla raids, plundering cattle and provisions, and using extreme violence to monopolise resources in a wild terrain. This persisting conflict was not primarily national in nature, with the families frequently engaged in blood feuds among themselves. Whenever the lawlessness threatened to spill utterly into chaos, authority was restored in a swift, brutal and arbitrary fashion: so-called 'Jeddart Justice' involved the summary execution of suspects, only after which would a court decide on their guilt. That the 'Reivers', as they were called, were more than just a remote inconvenience and local embarrassment can be seen in the 1524 'Great Cursing' of Gavin Dunbar, Archbishop of Glasgow, a truly pyrotechnic piece of rhetoric:

> I curse their heid and all the haris of thair heid; I curse thair face, thair ene, thair mouth, thair neise, thair tongue, thair teeth, thair crag, thair shoulderis, thair breist, thair hert, thair stomok, thair bak, thair wame, thair armes, thais leggis, thair handis, thair feit, and everilk part of thair body, frae the top of their heid to the soill of thair feet, befoir and behind, within and without.
>
> I curse thaim gangand, and I curse them rydland; I curse thaim standand, and I curse thaim sittand; I curse thaim etand, I curse thaim drinkand; I curse thaim walkand, I curse thaim sleepand; I curse thaim risand, I curse thaim lyand; I curse thaim at hame, I curse thaim fra hame; I curse thaim within the house, I curse thaim without the house; I curse thair wiffis, thair barnis, and thair servandis participand with thaim in their deides. I way thair cornys, thair catales, thair woll, thair scheip, thjair horse, thair swyne, thair geise, thair hennes, and all thair quyk gude. I wary their hallis, thair chalmeris, thair kechingis, thair stanillis, thair barnys, thair biris, thair bernyardis, thair

cailyardis, thair plewis, thair harrowis, and the gudis and housis
that is necessair for their sustentatioun and weilfair.

As is almost always the case, this tribalism, criminality and faction-
alism was accompanied by a strict sense of honour. They were the
Klingons of the late Middle Ages. The Reivers, or Mosstroopers, or
Steel Bonnets, have drawn frequent comparisons to the Mafia, and
in one way in particular the comparison is appropriate: sentimentality. Bishop Lesley, in the sixteenth century, commented that they
were 'lovers of eloquence and poetry', and just as the Corleones
could well up at opera, the Reivers cultivated their minstrelsy. As
Scott wrote in the *Minstrelsy*, 'It is not the peaceful Hindu at his
loom, it is not the timid Esquimaux in his canoe, whom we must
expect to glow at the war song of Tyrtaeus.'

The infant Scott, sequestered at Smailholm through illness, heard
many of these old ballads, and was proud throughout his life that he
was descended from robbers, extortionists, bullies, kidnappers, reckless fire-starters and rapists. Like his fellow crippled author, Lord
Byron, his disability was a kind of psychological prophylactic: he was
allowed to thrill at villainy, safe in the knowledge he would find it
physically impossible. But in the late eighteenth century, the Borders
were changing dramatically. James Small's new swing-plough, created
when Scott was a teenager, was revolutionising farming, particularly
in the fertile Merse area around Kelso. David Brewster, the most
important physicist working on light at the time, was living just a
gallop away at Nesbit (and inventing the kaleidoscope in his spare
time). The geologist James Hutton was discovering proof positive of
the ancientness of the Earth by examining the combination of
crumble and steadfastness in the Jedburgh riverbanks. Only a few
years after Scott returned to the Borders, a young boy named James
Wilson would be born in Hawick, and go on to found *The Economist*.
At the same time, just seven miles down the road, James Murray, who
would mastermind the *Oxford English Dictionary*, was born.

Two hundred years beforehand, James VI and I had unleashed a
final reining-in of the Reiving Families, who, with some exceptions,
had skulked through the Civil War, the Restoration, the Glorious

Revolution and the Jacobite Rebellions, with expedience their governing principle, a nose for the deal and an ear close to the ground supplanting an eye for an eye. The Borders were always a singularly plural space, uncertain without being vacillating, ambiguous but still recognisable, ambitious and cautious, sleekit and stieve at once.

The Borders resists dichotomies and it resists the blurring of dichotomies. If the choice is black and white, they refuse even to be grey. It is an Interzone and a 'Gaun-through kindae place', a halfway house that refuses to do things by half, a debatable land indeed.

Scott Country

You can't go by train to the Borders: the National Rail Network has only one region in mainland Britain that has no functional train station, and it's the Borders. As I write, plans are being discussed to open the old (guess what?) Waverley Line, but as things are now, the train just skims the edge of Grantshouse, Eyemouth and Coldingham, never stopping, always heading for somewhere more significant and lucrative. If you don't have a car, then the only way to go is on public transport – and in the smaller villages, like an echo of the old post-chaise, that means in the back of the Royal Mail Delivery Van.

Over the years that I have taken the number 95 back to the Borders from Edinburgh, I have become convinced that, as John Dryden said of Chaucer's poetry, all human life is here. Although on the 95, it is usually left there as well. On one occasion, I sat and chatted with the novelist (and Scott enthusiast) Allan Massie about the future of conservatism in Scotland. The next week I sat next to a late-onset Goth who had just discovered Morrissey and The Smiths. Once, I sat beside a man with swastikas on his knuckles, who did not speak at all. And that was OK by me.

If you were travelling down in a sightseeing mode, you would see a landscape determined to forget itself. At first, Edinburgh thins out through its schemes, and, if you were intent on looking, you'd see on the walls of pebble-dashed houses the names of Scott characters. You'd pass through old mining communities that commemorate their exhaustion and the erstwhile seat of the Lady of Dalkeith and Duchess of Buccleuch, to whom Scott paid almost unironic homage. Dalkeith looks like a town that was hastily rebuilt after terrible bombings, but in actual fact its combination of ruin and Sixties brutalism was entirely planned. My brother always takes a detour to see the house of Scotland's Fattest Man, whose walls were demolished to take out his corpse. Only a brief series of fields and a roundabout stop Dalkeith being the saddest suburb of Edinburgh.

The Borders certainly looks different, and in a sentimental way I suppose I always think it *feels* different. As the comedian Billy Connolly said on his *World Tour of Scotland*, 'The Scottish Borders looks more Scottish in appearance and atmosphere – it is what people think the Highlands look and feel like.' Part of that feeling of change is purely demographic. The Borders has one of the lowest population densities in the country (only Argyll and the Highlands have lower), but it feels more marked because of the proximity to the capital: in the space of twenty miles, you move from Edinburgh – with a population density of 1,725 souls per square kilometre – to Midlothian (231 per km^2), to the Borders (23 per km^2). The geography of the Scottish Borders contributes to its feeling of distinctness and being somehow set apart: the Lammermuirs to the North, the Cheviots to the South, the Lowthers and the Pentlands to the West and the coast on the East keep the region hemmed in, tucked away.

On the way down, through the hamlets of Heriot and Fountainhall, and the village of Stow – all now dormitories of Edinburgh – you can trace the grown-over tracks of the decommissioned railway. You could even, at points and with a very keen eye, see the remnants of the Catrail, a Dark Age ditch and dyke fieldwork stretching some fifty miles, whose significance remains a mystery – another border of sorts, between peoples long vanished? A defensive barrier? A trade route? The hills, thickly forested with pines, seem to resemble a genuine Scottish wilderness, except for the fact that they are mostly modern tax write-offs.

It's a gentler, more rolling landscape than the Highlands, but no less dramatic. The Eildon Hills are especially iconic – a triumvirate of peaks, at times mottled with yellow gorse, at others purplish with heather. The River Tweed meanders in long loops, cutting through red clay soil. As a child, my mental picture of Tolkien's The Shire was, predictably, a mirror image of the Borders.

The closest stop to 'Scott Country' – as it was called by such minor literati as Duncan Montcrieff, the Revd James Baikie, John Geddie and W S Crockett – is the town of Galashiels. Scott himself snubbed Galashiels. His stately home at Abbotsford is closer to Gala (as the locals call it) than any other conurbation, but his headed notepaper carried the address, '*Abbotsford, Melrose*'. Melrose, with its ruined abbey, was a far more sonorous connotation than Galashiels, with its tweed mills, industrial manufacturing and radical 'Weavers' Corporation'. Galashiels has rather suffered in the estimation of writers. Virginia Woolf declared the place 'ghastly', and John and Andrew Lang quoted the 1906 Official Report of H M Stationery Office – 'it would be impossible to find a river more grossly polluted than the Gala as it passes through Galashiels', going on to mention the 'sewage fungus', the frequent reports of dead pigs floating by and commenting that 'he does wisely who stands to windward of the abomination'. The poet Angus Calder, translating Horace into contemporary Scottish references, chose Gala to represent barbaric Scythia. John Ruskin preserved for posterity the nickname given to Galileans (as they call themselves) by outsiders: pailmerks, on account of Galashiels being the last Border town to get sewers (so the denizens might be recognised by the mark of the pail on their posteriors).

In a paler form, the notorious feuding between the families still persists in the rivalry between the towns, mostly on the rugby pitch. As it was notoriously put in a Channel 4 schools documentary on the region, 'There's aye been an awfie lot o' rivalry: Hawick agin Gala, Kelso agin Gala, Selkirk agin Gala.' When the Borders became a council region in 1975, the decision was taken to build the new council headquarters in the neutral and past-less new town of Newtown St Boswells, since it might have seemed dangerously partisan to locate the new offices in any of the older towns. Even today, the local newspaper carries semi-regular grievances about which chain stores have opted to open in Galashiels; about the new train line not extending as far as Hawick; about how little is being done to rejuvenate Jedburgh. When one company moved premises from one town to another – a mere seven miles down the road – many of the workers resigned or retired rather than travel. Almost every town has a variation on its theme of local pride: 'A day oot ae Selkirk's a day wasted.'

I grew up in Gala – in a manner of speaking. I managed to get myself born in Falkirk when my parents were living in Cumbernauld. The family then moved back to the Borders when I was nine months old, to a new council estate on the outskirts of Galashiels called Langlee. It was, in its own way, a New Town; if not *the* New Town. When I was five, we moved out – my parents, being schoolteachers, were sick of seeing their pupils in the pub – to a little village called Lilliesleaf. But I continued to go to school in Gala. The town still had bookshops then, in which I spent all but 12p of my £1 lunch money (12p buying me a cheese roll and a glass of milk). I never bought a single copy of any of Sir Walter Scott's works.

Maybe we all feel an irrational attachment to the scenes of infancy, and maybe with me, Galashiels' bad reputation makes me doubly keen to defend it. It might not be the prettiest town, but it has its loveable quirks. It has the tramp poet Roger Quin, and the only martial war memorial in Scotland (a Border Reiver, sculpted by Thomas Clapperton, showing military valour more than noble sacrifice). Its town song – 'Braw, Braw Lads' – has lyrics by Burns and music by Haydn. The imported fleeces used in the mills were thronging with foreign seeds, teasels and burrs, and even after being doused with sulphuric acid and alkali at 180°∞ Celsius, enough of them survived the purgatorial cleansing to be washed down the lade, into the river, and grow. According to one guide, 348 foreign species of plant grew along the banks of the Gala.

And if Scott chose to turn a blind eye to Galashiels, Galashiels did not sulk at the slight. There's a Scott Street, a Scott Crescent and an Abbotsford Road. Although we lived in the newer part of Langlee, where every street-name was taken from a local flower, the slightly older part was Scott-themed: Kenilworth Avenue, Talisman Crescent, Woodstock Drive and Marmion Terrace (Marmion, incidentally, is a sexual predator, murderer, thief and all-round villain in that poem. It would be a bit like living in Reggie Kray Gardens or Al Capone Villas, and given the unfortunate notoriety of Langlee, it's perhaps an irony too far). Langlee even had one of the three Scott plaques in Galashiels:

AT THIS SPOT
ON HIS PATHETIC JOURNEY
FROM ITALY
HOME TO ABBOTSFORD
AND
HIS BELOVED BORDERLAND
SIR WALTER SCOTT
GAZING ON THIS SCENE FOR THE LAST TIME
'SPRANG UP WITH A CRY OF DELIGHT'

It would be more akin to a shriek of terror if he were to see it now: a quaint market town with an out-of-town style retail park grafted on to it. The view he saw no longer exists. The other plaques are just as unintentionally out of place. Outside my school was a note on a 1960s set of flats, stating: 'Sir Walter Scott of Abbotsford transacted business here with the Leith Banking Company from 1812 to 1832.' For which read: man who went bust got ready cash in here. In a vennel linking the streets of the former centre of Galashiels is another plaque: 'In a building on this site, Sir Walter Scott B^t, was entertained by the Galashiels Manufacturers Corporation after receiving his baronetcy at the hand of his sovereign George IV, 1821, George Walker, Deacon.' Just over the road is a bust of Scott, with a very Ossian-looking minstrel on the pedestal (harp, robes, beard – like someone auditioning for God) and the legend 'O GREAT AND GALLANT SCOTT'. Around the curved wall is one of his couplets: 'The last of all the bards was he / Who sung of Border Chivalry'. This adulatory herm of Scott is positioned right next to the public toilets.

Minstrelsy

As a child, Scott heard ballads from his aunt and grandmother; but he was also a prodigious reader, supposedly having consumed Milton's *Paradise Lost* at the age of six. Although he read Homer in Pope's translation and weighty pious classics like Gestner's *The Death of Abel*, his taste veered more towards the romantic than the neoclassical: the 'first poetry' he remembered by heart was the ballad 'Hardicanute' from Allan Ramsay's *Tea-Table Miscellany*. Through the kindness of a neighbour, Scott had access to a fine library and soon devoured Tasso, Ariosto, Spenser and Ossian (whose 'tawdry repetitions . . . disgusted me sooner than might have been expected'). The book, however, which most entranced him was Bishop Thomas Percy's *Reliques of Ancient English Poetry* (1765). He vividly recollected the sycamore tree under which he read it first, and where he became so engrossed that he missed his supper and was 'sought for with anxiety'. Percy's anthology delighted him so much that it became the first book he bought with his own money.

Percy's *Reliques* collected together traditional ballads – such as 'Chevy Chase', 'The Battle of Otterbourne', 'Sir Patrick Spens', 'Edom o' Gordon' and 'King Cophetua and the Beggar Maid' – alongside lyrics by Shakespeare and other Elizabethan and Jacobean dramatists, and modern imitations of the ballad form. Scott wrote: 'as I had been from infancy devoted to legendary lore of this nature, and only reluctantly withdrew my attention, from the scarcity of materials and rudeness of those which I possessed, it may be imagined, but cannot be described, with what delight I saw pieces of the same kind which had amused my childhood, and still continued in secret the Delilahs of my imagination, considered as the subject of sober research, grave commentary, and apt illustration, by an editor who shewed his poetical genius was capable of emulating the best

qualities of what his pious labours preserved'. Even the title seemed
to pun between the surviving trace of the past, the memorial of
antiquity and the saint's venerated remains.

Both the ersatz Ossian poems and the echt Percy ballads sprang
from the same critical impulse: did Britain have an indigenous
poetic tradition that might stand comparison with the early productions of Greece and Rome, or was it necessarily an imitative and
'second order' culture? Cultural histories tended to pull in very
different directions: broadly speaking, a work like Samuel Johnson's
Lives of the Poets (1779–81) presented a progressive refinement of
taste away from rude and barbarous origins – Johnson's work only
begins with the work of the Caroline poets Cowley and Denham.
Conversely, Thomas Warton's *History of English Poetry* (1774–81) was
more sympathetic to early literature, and sounded the first notes of
romantic primitivism.

Even in the Elizabethan era, critics had been fascinated by poetical
prehistory. Sir Philip Sidney, in his 1579 *Defence of Poesy* wrote that
'never was the Albion nation without poetry' and even though he
must 'confess my own barbarousness, I never heard the old song of
Percy and Douglas [i.e. the ballad of 'Chevy Chase'] that I found not
my heart moved more than with a trumpet; and yet it is sung but by
some blind crowder, with no rougher voice than rude style; which,
being so evil apparelled in the dust and cobwebs of that uncivil age,
what would it work trimmed in the gorgeous eloquence of Pindar?'
In *The Spectator* for 21 and 25 May 1771, Joseph Addison analysed
'Chevy Chase' and found it conforming to the ideals of poetry as
found in Virgil's *Aeneid*. It was 'full of the majestick Simplicity which
we admire in the greatest of the ancient Poets'. Richard Hurd, the
Bishop of Worcester, defended early literature from an antithetical
position. In his 1762 *Letters on Chivalry and Romance*, he argued that
Spenser's *Faerie Queene* was 'not of a classical but Gothic composition', equivalent to the Gothic architecture of the great cathedrals
rather than the Vitruvian neoclassical design.

It does not seem coincidental that at the very moment when the
business of literature was becoming professional and divorced from
aristocratic patronage – the eighteenth century saw the first

Copyright Act passed and the rise of Grub Street 'hacks' and 'scrib-blers' – poets and critics started to investigate the earlier roles and images of poets. The same age that produced Pope's acerbic *Dunciad* and the *Memoirs of Martinus Scriblerus*, also produced Gray's 'The Bard', Beattie's 'The Minstrel', Chatteron's fake medieval poetry, the idealised Scottish Homer of Ossian and the compendious and authoritative *Reliques of Ancient English Poetry*. By the beginning of the nineteenth century, the study of early texts had become more than just an antiquarian concern: it had become fashionable. At the same time as Scott was assembling and publishing *The Minstrelsy of the Scottish Border*, George Ellis published *Early English Poets* (1801) then *Specimens of Early English Romance in Metre* (1805); Joseph Ritson – a cantankerous man who feuded with Percy and used his own unique orthography – produced *Robin Hood: A Collection of all the Ancient Poems, Songs and Ballads now extant relative to that Outlaw* (1795) and *Ancient Engleish Metrical Romanceës* (1802); the politically radical William Godwin wrote a life of Chaucer (1803) and the Revd Henry John Todd produced a critical edition of Spenser (1805). In terms of literary entrepreneurship, a Scottish variant on the predominantly 'English' field seemed inevitable.

Hand-in-hand with the academic reconsideration of early litera-ture was a developing interest in the literature not produced by the literati. In the second edition of *Lyrical Ballads* (1800), William Wordsworth had described the pieces as experiments, 'chiefly with a view to ascertain how far the language of conversation in the middle and lower classes of society is adapted to the purpose of poetic plea-sure' (although the price of the book meant that very few of the lower or middle classes would have a chance to judge the success of the experiment). Johann Gottfried Herder, whose theories of histor-ical evolution would be distantly reflected in Scott's novels, also collected folk-songs in his *Volkslieder* (1778–9), which in turn influ-enced Goethe's use of traditional *Knittelvers* in his epic *Faust*. Earlier, the poets Stephen Duck (a thresher and agricultural labourer) and John Taylor (a London waterboat-man) were briefly lauded as exam-ples of poetic 'naturals'. By far the most significant effort in this line was Robert Burns's work with James Johnson on the *Scots Musical*

Museum (1787–1803), as well as George Thomson's *Select Scottish Airs* (1799–1818, to which Scott also contributed) and the posthumous and bawdy *Merry Muses of Caledonia*. More than that, Burns's original poetic work and public image as 'the ploughman poet' seemed to validate Wordsworth's assertion. In slightly dyspeptic mode, Scott wrote that 'the success of Burns had the effect of exciting general emulation among all of his class in Scotland that were able to tag a rhyme. Poets began to chirp like grasshoppers in a sunshine day. The steep rocks poured down poetical goatherds, and the bowels of the earth vomited rhyming colliers' – although he held a lifelong affection for Burns himself.

Scott's *Minstrelsy of the Scottish Border* stood at the confluence of two notable cultural trends: the vogue for romantic, non-classical, early indigenous poetry and the wealth of traditional work existing in the oral tradition among the 'unlettered' classes. Burns was a model, but not a master; whose own fieldwork proved there was an untapped source of material, untinged by the national embarrass-ment of Ossian. The focus for Burns had been lyric, sing-able poetry: for Scott it would be narrative.

Scott's Minstrelsy

Scott's agenda with *The Minstrelsy of the Scottish Border* was clear: 'by such efforts, feeble as they are, I may contribute somewhat to the history of my native country; the peculiar features of whose manners and character are daily melting and dissolving into those of her sister and ally.' The introduction dedicated itself to 'the manes of a kingdom, once proud and independent', albeit with a 'mixture of feelings', and, in more confident mood, Scott claimed that not just the contents, but the publication of the work carried a subtle patriotic agenda: 'when the book came out, the imprint, Kelso, was read with wonder by amateurs of typography, who had never heard of such a place, and were astonished at the example of handsome printing which so obscure a town had produced'. The Borders was, in Scott's view, saturated with poetry. As he expressed it in a verse epistle in *Marmion*, 'Nor hill nor brook we passed along / But had its legend or its song'.

The book was divided into three volumes; historical ballads, romantic ballads and 'imitations of these compositions by modern authors'. In its final expanded edition, it contained forty-three ballads never beforehand printed, out of ninety-six in total. Although the published book seemed an archetype of scholarship, replete with hefty footnotes, the experience of putting the book together was nothing short of derring-do. Scott may have lapsed, in his dotage, into being a bit of a bookworm, trawling his Abbotsford library for apposite and elusive references, but in his thirties he was something of an adventurer.

Across marshes and moorland, up hills and down screes, Scott actively sought out the poems for the *Minstrelsy*. Rather than relying on manuscript sources, he tried to find oral recollections of the ballad poetry, and that involved going to extremely remote places and working with intransigent individuals. Always over-compensating for his disability, he referred to these expeditions as 'raids', and masochistically rejoiced in the physical punishment involved. 'We have just concluded', he wrote to Ellis, 'an excursion of two or three weeks through my jurisdiction of Selkirkshire' – Scott, lest we forget, was then still employed as Sheriff of the area – and 'in defiance of mountains, rivers, and bogs, damp and dry, we have penetrated the very recesses of Ettrick Forest'. This is both truthful (the area was remote, uncultivated and severe) and boastful – Ettrick has no mountains, nor even a particularly prominent hill. Scott continued in his letter to play up the dangers and stresses, gossiping to his well-connected new friend that they had slept on peat-stacks and eaten a sheep found dead – but had also brought back a 'complete and perfect copy of Maitland with his Auld Berd Graie, referred to by Douglas in his Palice of Honour'. The 'treasures of oral tradition' were also 'copied down from the recitation of an old shepherd, by a country farmer, and with no greater corruptions than might be supposed to be introduced by the lapse of time, and the ignorance of the reciters'. Complete and perfect was also corrupt and ignorant.

The biggest ambiguity, however, about Scott's *Minstrelsy*, is that it is not Scott's alone. On the surface, it is clearly not Scott's. This is Scott's endeavour and passion, but the words are only his through some spit and polish, some footnotes and a bit of creative editing. But it is also a work more collaborative than Wordsworth and Coleridge's *Lyrical Ballads*, with Scott using the project to acquaint himself with the elder statesmen of literary antiquarianism – Ellis, Ritson and Percy – and to seek out new voices and talents. On some occasions he succeeded.

Charles Kirkpatrick Sharpe, who unearthed the ballad 'The Twa Corbies' was a cynical dandy, given to drawing caricatures of his hosts and revelling in the more embarrassing cul-de-sacs of their pedigrees. Robert Surtees, a gentle soul appropriately born on April Fool's Day, sent Scott various ballads (including 'Barthram's Dirge') which he conveniently discovered from an old woman who was weeding his garden. Only after his death, and Scott's, was the hoax exposed. Scott was on surer ground with the formidable John

Leyden. Born in Denholm in the Borders, Leyden was an astonishing polymath who passed his medical exams in only six months and went on to become the Professor of Hindustani and a judge of the twenty-four pergunnahs in India. He had a gift for languages, having learned eight as a schoolboy and mastering several Indian languages in his colonial career before his untimely death in 1811. He was a noted poet in his own right, translating Malay ballads and commemorating his birthplace in a long poem full of local traditions, *Scenes of Infancy*. Leyden was single-minded to the point of eccentricity, once walking nearly a hundred miles just to obtain the missing stanzas of a historical ballad for the Minstrelsy.

Through his friend William Laidlaw, Scott made the acquaintance of James Hogg, the 'Ettrick Shepherd', whose own literary career would be inextricably linked to Scott's. Hogg's mother proved an invaluable source and assistant, able, through an impressively retentive memory, to establish the authenticity of many of the songs. She cautioned Scott that 'there was never ane o' my sangs prentit till ye prentit them yoursel', and ye have spoilt them awthegither. They were made for singin' and no' for readin', but ye have broken the charm now, an' they'll never be sung mair.' It is an iconic anecdote: the gentleman collector and the peasant poet, the competing claims of the textual and the oral, dead print and living tradition. As such, and as always with Scott, there are reasons to be suspicious of such neat paradigms. If the ballads were not supposed to be printed, why would Margaret Laidlaw complain that they were 'nouther richt spell'd nor richt setten down'? She was able to give Scott a full version of the ballad 'Auld Maitland', about which he wrote that 'it is a curious circumstance that this interesting tale, so often referred to by ancient authors, should be now recovered in so perfect a state'. That ambiguity is riddled through the *Minstrelsy*: the 'original' is always unobtainable; the extent of corruption is also the extent of authenticity; the more that something has become illegible, the more that it must be genuine.

Rhymer

One of the most important ballads for Scott was 'Thomas the Rhymer'. The ballad concerns Thomas Learmount of Ercildoune (or modern Earlston), often called 'True Thomas' and popularly supposed to have been blessed with oracular powers. In the poem, Thomas lies on Huntley Bank, near the Eildon Hills, the three peaks that dominate the picturesque centre of the Borders. There are actually four hills – a local legend has it that the thirteenth-century theologian and supposed sorcerer, Michael Scott, commanded the Devil to split the single Eildon into three. After accomplishing the task, the Devil wiped clean his spade, creating the fourth hillock now known as 'The De'il's Spade-fu". Thomas is visited by a 'lady bright' dressed in green silk, whom he erroneously supposes is the Virgin Mary. She is actually the Queen of Fair Elfland, a kind of local version of the Muse. They kiss, and Thomas is fated to serve her for seven years, during which time he may not speak. She shows him three roads – the thorny path of righteousness, the broad way to wickedness and the winding road to Elfland, where there is neither sun nor moon, and all the blood split on Earth flows through its springs. This section of the ballad imitates in part Xenophon's Choice of Herakles parable in his *Memorabilia of Socrates*, where the Greek hero is confronted with the easy route of vice and the arduous ascent of duty. But the ballad breaks this dichotomy, with its third route, representing neither good nor evil. In Elfland, the Queen upsets another ancient fable. In a 'garden green' she plucks an apple from a tree and gives it to Thomas, saying it will make him unable to tell a lie (hence the True Thomas name, although he is confusingly referred to as 'true' before receiving the apple). The Queen undoes Eden: having already given Thomas the knowledge of good and evil, she now reverses mankind's original lie. If

'Thomas the Rhymer' is a metaphor for inspiration, a story about how Thomas came to be a poet and prophet, it is a singularly peculiar one. Thomas is first silenced, then denied the capacity to invent, feign, deceive or make things up. 'Thomas Learmount' was an archetype for poetry; so much so that the Russian writer Mikhail Lermontov would boast of his putative descent from him.

Scott, at the height of his rash acquisition of land and property, extended his estate to include Huntley Bank and the Eildon Tree by which Thomas slipped out of our reality. He returned to Thomas in his final published novel, *Castle Dangerous*, in which Bertram the Minstrel seeks to discover the lost manuscripts of Thomas Learmount. The undead Rhymer supposedly appeared to a previous minstrel in search of the books – 'a tall thin form, attired in, or rather shaded with, a long flowing dusky robe, having a face and physiognomy so wild and overgrown with hair as to be hardly human, were the only marked outlines of the phantom'.

Thomas was both the subject and the creator of poetry. His rhyming prophecies included foreseeing the death of Alexander III, the date of the Apocalypse as reckoned by the tectonic movement of two rocks in the Firth of Tay, and the wonderfully nationalist doggerel 'York was, London is, and Edinburgh shall be / The biggest and the bonniest o' the three' – if Edinburgh were to expand to the size of London, Scott's and Thomas's beloved Borders would be the equivalent of Penge or Streatham – or even the real Waverley.

Bur Scott had other uses for Thomas Learmount of Ercildoune. Under his original plan, the third volume of the *Minstrelsy* would not contain modern imitations at all, but the extant and edited text of Thomas's major work, the romance *Sir Tristrem*. Now, Scott was wrong on almost every count about the poem, its date, its authorship and its provenance. But he was very interestingly wrong.

Gottfried von Strassburg's unfinished 1210 version of the Tristan and Isolde story credited 'Thomas of Britain' as the original author. Brother Robert's *Tristrams saga ok Ísöndar* of 1226 supplied many of the missing sequences. Scott presumed that the lost 'Thomas of Britain' was Thomas the Rhymer, and that the fourteenth-century *Sir Tristrem* was the actual source for von Strassburg and Brother

Robert. This was not sleight of hand on Scott's part: he earnestly believed that the *Tristrem* romance predated all other sources. Given that the author was purportedly out of sync with real time, we can forgive Scott's hasty judgment. But if Thomas *were* the author of *Sir Tristrem*, and time *did* run backwards, then a series of presumptions clicked into place.

The 1066 invasion had made Norman French the predominant language of the court, south of the border. 'It is most probable,' Scott wrote, 'that English poetry, if any such existed, was abandoned to the peasants and menials, while all, who aspired above the vulgar, listened to the lais of Marie, the romances of Chretien de Troyes, or the interesting fabliaux of the Anglo-Norman trouveurs.' In Scotland the case was different, and as Scott surmises, 'those which were chaunted in the court of Scotland must have been originally written in Inglis'. Thus the first poems in English were actually Scottish, and their creators were not peasants or menials, but minstrels of stature and import, whose presence at court showed their high standing. Scotland – or the Borders – created English as a literary language, and the man of the hour was a Border man. Even before the accession of James VI as James I of England and Scotland made the Borders the centre of the kingdom, its minstrels were already outstripping their rivals and pioneering the union in language. As Buchan wrote, when Scott was in his late twenties his 'memory was full of bad models, Augustan jingles, faked Gothick *diablerie* and rococo sentiment, and from them he was delivered by the *Minstrelsy* and restored to the ancient simplicities of earth'.

Last and Latest Minstrel

Scott's first substantial and original literary production was an outgrowth from the *Minstrelsy*, and it is full of bad models, Augustan jingles, faked Gothick *diablerie* and rococo sentiment. Somehow it is also a masterpiece. Taste will never run hindwards, and I can't imagine the *Lay* will ever be as popular as it once was. But it charmed and engaged, was praised and parodied, and was not just of its time, but made its time. It is easier to begin writing about the poem the way that Scott did: with its clever scaffolding of ancientness. (I am drawn to the epigraph in my aging, coverless copy of Scott's poetry: 'to Mrs Foster: In memory of my Father as a token of appreciation for all that she did for him. Victor D' – Dawes? – it is baroque in its flourishes and tremulous in its penmanship.)

The last minstrel is a lonely remnant of his profession, who turns up at the Newark Castle door of Ann Scott, Duchess of Buccleuch and ancestor of the Countess of Dalkeith to whom Scott dedicates the poem and whom he credited, somewhat disingenuously, with the idea for it. The minstrel, like the phony Ossian, is the last of his kind, for whom 'A stranger filled the Stuarts' throne; / The bigots of an iron time / Had call'd his harmless art a crime'. The unnamed last minstrel had kept pegging on to see the Glorious Revolution, and, had he ever existed, was just a generation away from the people who provided Scott with his ballads.

To the point: the Minstrel, who was doing well enough to employ an orphan boy to carry his harp around, told the Duchess of Buccleuch about her family. The tale itself concerns Ann's ancestors, especially the widowed Lady of Branksome Hall. Her daughter, Margaret, is in love with Lord Cranstoun; but unfortunately Lord Cranstoun was part of a group that killed the Lady's husband, so a state of feud, to put it mildly, exists between them. The Lady of

Branksome Hall dispatches a retainer, William of Deloraine, to recover Michael Scott's book of magic from his grave in Melrose Abbey, in the hope of using sorcery to end her daughter's attachment. Deloraine and Cranstoun fight on his way back, and various eldritch shenanigans ensue, inspired by the mysterious goblin page, Gilpin Horner, who seems linked to Michael Scott's book. The Lady's son is lured into the woods by Gilpin and captured by her English foe, Lord Dacre, who besieges the Hall and demands single combat with Deloraine. Through Gilpin's skills, Cranstoun assumes the form of Deloraine and beats Lord Dacre's champion Musgrave, securing his prospective mother-in-law's blessing. At the nuptial feast, Michael Scott's ghost appears and reclaims his book and his bogle-servant Gilpin. The poem concludes with the Duchess of Buccleuch allowing the Minstrel a 'simple bower' where he can 'give the aid he begg'd before'. So there's a double happy ending: the marriage of Cranstoun and Margaret, and the Minstrel's financial independence. At the outset, Scott had stressed that poetry might have a psychologically beneficial motive:

> The present scene, the future lot,
> His toils, his wants, were all forgot:
> Cold diffidence, and age's frost,
> In the full tide of song were lost;
> Each blank in faithless memory void,
> The poet's glowing thought supplied . . .

By the end, it also has a socio-economic benefit. The Duchess of Buccleuch has her sorrows too (her husband was executed for treason in 1685) and she is aware that her ancestors are forgotten: 'fickle Fame / Had blotted from her rolls their name'. In a poem about the literal resurrection of Michael Scott, the Minstrel performs the metaphorical resurrection of the family: 'this old man's verse / Could call them from their marble hearse'. Magic, in the poem, can switch identities, and this is mirrored in the Minstrel's more elaborate exchange: emotional catharsis for property. The end of the first introduction also makes clear that the Last Minstrel is also the Latest Minstrel. By the end, commemorating the past ensures the future, both of audience and author. The subtitle could easily be *The Lay of the Last Minstrel, or, You Too Can Profit From Writing!*

The poem was written in a tripping 'light horseman sort of stanza'. Although there had been metrical experiments in the eighteenth century – most notably in Gray's 'The Bard', the 'Standard Habbie' of Burns, and a few rash attempts at reviving the Spenserian stanza – the predominant verse form was still the heroic couplet. Perhaps the only way to recapture the freshness of Scott's verse would be to read the thumping couplets of William Wilkie's *The Epigoniad* for a few days beforehand. Here is just a sample:

> By War's devouring rage, our martial pow'rs
> Grow thin and waste before these hostile tow'rs;
> While Thebes secure our vain attempts withstands,
> By daily aids sustain'd from distant lands.
> Shall we proceed to urge this dire debate,
> And push, with hostile arms, the Theban state?
> Or by experience, taught the worst to fear
> Consult the public safety, and forebear?

Compare with Scott:

> Then sudden, through the darken'd air,
> A flash of lightning came;
> So broad, so bright, so red the glare,
> The castle seem'd on flame.
> Glanc'd every rafter of the hall,
> Glanc'd every shield upon the wall;
> Each trophied beam, each sculptur'd stone,
> Were instant seen, and instant gone.

This brief contrast shows how Scott, shortening the line to a four stress beat, and introducing alternate rhymes as well as consecutive, gives a far swifter, more free and pleasingly irregular kind of poetry. This is the most difficult thing to appreciate – that reading Scott in 1806 would have been exciting and unpredictable. The plots were not retreadings of classical mythology, or ungainly grafts of pseudo-classical mythology onto British themes (such as the poet laureate Pye's *Alfred*). The verse was breathy and rugged: you can almost feel the wind whistling through, especially the famous stanzas describing Deloraine's gallop to Melrose.

> Soon in his saddle sate he fast,
> And soon the steep descent he past,
> Soon cross'd the sounding barbican,
> And soon the Tevoit side he won.
> Eastward the wooded path he rode,
> Green hazles o'er his basnet nod;
> He pass'd the Peel of Goldiland,
> And cross'd old Borthwick's roaring strand;
> Dimly he view'd the Moat-hill's mound,
> Where Druid shades still flitted round:
> In Hawick twinkled many a light;
> Behind him soon they set in night;
> And soon he spurr'd his courser keen
> Beneath the tower of Hazeldean.

Looking back on *The Lay* in 1830, Scott allowed himself a note of pride. 'It would be great affectation not to own that the author expected some success from *The Lay of the Last Minstrel*. The attempt to return to a more simple and natural poetry was likely to be welcomed, at a time when the public had become tired of heroic hexameters, with all the buckram and binding that belong to them in modern days.'

There had been a few notable attempts at more elastic verse forms: Southey's *Thalaba* (1801) and Coleridge's *Christabel* (1797–1800, published 1816). A great deal of academic controversy raged over Scott's debt to Coleridge: Scott had certainly memorised parts of the poem before it was published. Later biographers and critics have described the relationship between the poems with a whole spectrum of links, ranging from plagiarism, to imitation, to a Zeitgeist synchronicity, to independent experimentalism. Coleridge, it should be said, saw 'no dishonourable or avoidable resemblance'. But that's not to say he actually *liked* it.

The *Lay* tapped into a national mood of bellicosity, while remaining patriotically Scottish – the swelling 'Breathes there a man' speech comes immediately after the minstrel is asked why he does not travel to 'the more generous Southern land'. For all that a conflict between Scottish and English troops is threatened, the single combat resolves this and the soldiers 'pursued the foot ball play' instead; much as they do to this day. Scott himself was always wry about certain imaginative aspects of the poem. The lines on Melrose Abbey

> If thou would'st view fair Melrose aright,
> Go visit it by the pale moonlight;
> For the gay beams of lightsome day
> Gild, but the flout, the ruins grey

he disavowed. 'I had been guilty of sending many persons a-bat hunting to see the ruins of Melrose by moonlight, which I never saw myself,' he wrote. He was asked to copy the speech in autograph for a friend, and changed the final lines of Canto II, Stanza 1 from

> Then go – but go alone the while –
> Then view St. David's ruin'd pile;
> And, home returning, soothly swear,
> Was never scene so sad and fair!

to

> Then go – and meditate with awe
> On scenes the author never saw,
> Who never wander'd by the moon
> To see what could be seen by noon.

Even in this piece of innocuous picturesque, the overlapping of 'real' Scotland and Scott's Scotland, the literary projection and the historical manifestation, grate and become problematic. Above all, as anyone who has seen the Abbey can vouchsafe, the stones, whether in moonlight or lightsome day, are quite clearly red, not grey.

Toponymy

Scott may have got the colour of the Abbey wrong, vexed the eminent Jeffrey with the mixture of supernatural and realistic, borrowed a hint from Coleridge and dressed up the whole media success as a form of vassal-like patronage, but there is one faultless aspect of *The Lay*: place-names. The poem positively bristles with locations. As Deloraine rides to Melrose, Goldiland, the Hawick Moat-hill, Hazeldean, Horsliehill, the old Roman road, Minto-crags, Riddell, Aill, Bowden Moor and Halidon Hill all whizz past. It lends the poem a strange combination of exoticism and familiarity (much the same effect would be achieved in Longfellow's similarly successful *Hiawatha*). Each place comes with a piece of local lore, tradition or memory; whether druids at Hawick, the battle of the Scotts and the Kerrs or the outlaw Barnhill's 'bed of flint'.

As Scott immortalises the Border place-names, the Borders enshrines Scott. Melrose has another statue of Scott (as does Clovenfords and Selkirk, with another bust on the house in Kelso where he first read Percy) situated just outside the Waverley Castle Hotel on Waverley Road. This Scott is rather slumped, with his lurcher Maida at his feet and a book, spine cracked open and discarded at his side. The Clovenfords statue is an upright one, with a rolled-up manuscript in his hand that local lads often paint as if it were a sausage roll. The Selkirk statue is on a much higher pedestal, outside his former court room. There's a George and Abbotsford Hotel in Melrose, a brasserie named after Marmion and even the nursing houses on the site of the old mental hospital were called Woodstock and Ivanhoe. The identification was such that even when Scott disguised Melrose in the novels *The Monastery* and *The Abbot* as 'Kennaquhair' (a Scots pun meaning 'I don't know where') it was immediately recognised. The periodical *Mirror of Literature* for

29 December 1827, provides a full analysis of Scott's literary rendition of Melrose.

By a fortuitous coincidence, the emigration of many Scots occurred at the same time as the exportation of many Scotts. To take just the USA, *The Lay of the Last Minstrel* was published by three different publishers in Philadelphia in 1805, 1806 and 1807; Charleston in 1806; in Boston in 1807; and Baltimore, Savannah and New York in 1811. There are Melroses in California (hence the 1992–9 soap opera, *Melrose Place*), Connecticut, Florida, Iowa, Kentucky, Louisiana, Massachusetts, Minnesota, Mississippi, New Mexico, New York (in the Bronx and in Schaghticocke), North Carolina, Ohio, Pennsylvania, Virginia and Wisconsin. There are also Melroses in Johannesburg, South Africa; Wellington, New Zealand; in the Canadian provinces of Ontario, Nova Scotia, New Brunswick and Newfoundland and in Adelaide and Flinders Range, Australia. Melrose, Scotland, is not a very populous place – either before or after the imperial emigrations – and the only way to account for the geographical spread of the name is via Walter Scott.

Likewise there is a rash of Waverleys across the Scottish diaspora, from Dunedin and Melbourne to Maryland and Ontario; Abbotsfords in Wisconsin, Johannesburg and even an entire Abbotsford City in British Columbia. There's an Ivanhoe Grammar School in Victoria and Ivanhoes in California, Virginia, Texas, Minnesota, North Carolina and even a lost Ivanhoe in Iowa ('For an unknown reason the village died out, and no buildings remain today', according to Linn County's website). At 570 North Rossmore Avenue in Hollywood, Paramount Pictures built an Art Deco hotel called the Ravenswood – after Edgar Ravenswood in *The Bride of Lammermoor*, a novel first filmed in 1909 and subtitled 'A Tragedy of Bonnie Scotland'.

The choice of these names is not just a matter of euphony, but of nostalgia; a deliberate forging of links between birthplace and the new homeland. Like the spread of a species, their survival is subject to natural selection, giving rise to places like the lost Iowan Ivanhoe and even mutation – there are Waverlys and Wavorlys as well as Waverleys. As with so much else, Scott's influence simultaneously promotes the real alongside the fictional: but Scott's influence is indisputable.

Nobody decided to call their newly founded village, suburb, city or county 'Kennaquhair' – as readers, they knew the meaning of the name. Kennaquhair, despite being fictional, has twin towns in the realm of literature. When Thomas Carlyle, in the generation after Scott, was describing the background of his eccentric scholar Diogenes Teufelsdröckh (literally 'God-born Devil's Dung') in *Sartor Resartus*, he named his birthplace 'Weissnichtwo' ('Know-not-where'); and a hint of its persisting influence can be seen in James Robertson's 2006 novel *The Testament of Gideon Mack*, where the eponymous minister lives in the parish of Monimaskit ('many-masked').

The Heights of Parnassus

Scott affected a studied nonchalance over his poetic oeuvre – even his daughter Sophia purportedly replied, 'Oh, I have not read it. Papa says there's nothing so bad for young people as reading bad poetry,' when asked by James Ballantyne what she made of her father's work. His stoic indifference to either praise or censure can appear like false modesty. Even within his lifetime it was apparent that the Waverley Novels far superseded his poetry. In 1825, William Hazlitt wrote in *The Spirit of the Age*, 'It is long since we read, and long since we thought of our author's poetry' – a sentiment that finds an echo in Scott himself, who wrote to Maria Edgeworth in 1818 saying, 'I have not read one of my poems since they were printed, excepting last year *The Lady of the Lake*, which I liked better than I expected, but not well enough to induce me to go through the rest – so I may truly say with Macbeth – "I am afraid to think of what I've done – Look on't again I dare not".'

Hazlitt concluded that Scott's poetry was a 'pleasing superficiality'. Jeffrey, in a surprisingly magnanimous manner, ended his review of *The Lady of the Lake* with the words, 'he has *the jury* hollow in his favour; and though *the court* may think that its directions have not been sufficiently attended to, it will not quarrel with the verdict'.

Scott's poetic reputation gained strength with *Marmion, or A Tale of Flodden Field* (1808) and *The Lady of the Lake* (1810), stalled with *The Vision of Don Roderick* (1811), started to wane with *Rokeby* (1813) and effectively concluded with *The Lord of the Isles* (1815). He also wrote two other long narrative poems, *The Bridal of Triermain* (1813) and *Harold the Dauntless* (1817) which have such a weird provenance that they deserve separate consideration. Lockhart conveniently gives us the critical 'creed now established'; that '*The Lay* . . . is . . . generally considered the most natural and original; *Marmion* as the

most powerful and splendid, *The Lady of the Lake* as the most interesting, romantic, picturesque and graceful'. Scott's own analysis of
the major works was that 'the force in *The Lay* is thrown on style –
in *Marmion* on description – and in *The Lady of the Lake*, on incident',
adding that he hoped *Rokeby* would turn on character.

Criticisms of Scott's poetry soon coalesced into a series of regular
complaints: anachronism, antiquarianism, parochialism, Gothic and
supernatural blemishes, inchoate plotting and morally dubious
central characters. As *The Imperial Review* put it, 'we do not see any
possible good that can be derived from knowing the exact extent,
and all the minute particulars, of the cruelty, robbery, and supersti-
tion of our ancestors'. Coleridge was even more scathing, and in a
letter to Wordsworth dated October 1810 provides a 'recipe for
romances': 'The first Business must be, a vast string of patronymics,
and names of Mountains, Rivers, &c – the most commonplace
imagery of the Bard gars look almaist as well as new by the introduction of Benvoirlich . . . Secondly, all the nomenclature of Gothic
Architecture, of Heraldry, of Arms, of Hunting, & Falconry – they
possess the same power of reviving the caput mortuum and rust of
old imagery – besides they will stand by themselves, Stout
Substantives, if only they are strung together, and some attention is
paid to the sound of the words – for no one attempts to understand
the meaning, which indeed would snap the charm – 3 some pathetic
moralizing on old times, or anything else, for the head and tail
pieces – with a *Bard* (that is absolutely necessary) and Songs of
course – For the rest, whatever suits Mrs Radcliff' (the leading
Gothic novelist of the day). Coleridge even supplements his critique
with a parody.

> Besides, you need not travel far,
> To reach the lake of Vennachar –
> Or *ponder refuge* from your Toil
> By far Lochard or Aberfoil!

Or, as Jeffrey put it when considering *The Lay*, 'to write a modern
romance of chivalry, seems to be much such a fantasy as to build a
modern abbey, or an English pagoda'. Jeffrey's subsequent review of

Marmion was so severe that he showed it to Scott for comment before publication. The two managed to remain friends and Jeffrey credited Scott with 'more magnanimity than others of your irritable tribe' – although in James Hogg's *Familiar Anecdotes of Sir Walter Scott* he maintains that Jeffrey read the review to Scott while boating in the Lake District, and Scott threatened to scupper their vessel in the rapids if Jeffrey did not ameliorate his criticism. Although Jeffrey praises the Flodden battle scenes, calling them the finest since Homer, his meticulous quibbling was paralleled in other attacks. Conspicuously, when Jeffrey came to edit his four-volume *Contributions to the Edinburgh Review* in 1844, he omitted the review of *Marmion*.

Marmion himself is 'not only a villain, but a mean and sordid villain'. Moral laxity, confined to Border free-booters, might be piquant; but in a knight of Henry VIII it seemed *de trop*. The reviewer for *The Satirist* agreed, and his thumb-nail sketch of Marmion conveniently doubles as a plot summary: 'The pretended hero is a bold, bad man, who debauches a nun, practices a forgery, courts an heiress, maintains a lie, combats a real rival and a sham ghost, insults an aged nobleman, fights a tremendous battle, breaks a toledo, receives a home thrust, gets spilt from his horse, swills water, rants, shouts – and dies.'

The Lay had been criticised for its 'exceedingly defective' plot. *Marmion*, by contrast, is almost novelistically replete with plots, counter-plots, forged letters, genuine confessions, disguises, doubles: or, as Jeffrey put it, 'a tissue of incredible accidents' with 'the machinery of a bad German novel'. The complaint which really stung concerned patriotism. Jeffrey railed that 'we must object, both on critical and on national grounds, to the discrepancy between the title and the substance of the poem, and the neglect of Scotish feelings and Scotish character that is manifested throughout. Marmion is no more a tale of Flodden Field, than of Bosworth Field, or any other field in history . . . There is scarcely one trait of true Scotish nationality or patriotism introduced into the whole poem.'

Given the extent to which Scott was to become associated with Scottishness, these words need some explication, over and above a critic's pique. Lockhart's idea that Jeffrey was tainted by party politics – *Marmion*, Lockhart claims, is a martial and patriotic British poem, at a time when the Whigs at the *Edinburgh Review* were arguing for non-engagement and appeasement towards Napoleon – seems convincing. Re-reading *Marmion*, it is striking the extent to which nationality (Scottish or English) plays so little role as a motivating factor for the protagonists. It is not in any profound sense *about* Flodden: Flodden is a setting against which the characters play their roles.

Marmion, in place of a Minstrel, had six urbane and charming verse epistles before each canto (Scott was always a great recycler of materials – these had been initially advertised in 1807 as *Six Epistles From Ettrick Forest*). The epistles make his politics quite clear: there are elegies to the Tory Pitt (reprised at the end) and a balancing tribute to the Whig Charles Edward Fox; both lauded for resisting 'France's yoke'. Scott mounts a defence of the romantic mode, citing Spenser, Milton and Arthurian romance; countering the friends who would have him write a neoclassical epic on contemporary political themes. As he writes to the Latinist Heber, despite his objections to 'the clash of rusty arms / In Fairy Land':

> Of Roman and of Grecian lore,
> Sure mortal brain can hold no more,
> These ancients, as Noll Bluff might say,
> 'Were pretty fellows in their day,'
> But time and tide o'er all prevail
> On Christmas eve a Christmas tale
> Of wonder and of war!

Interesting though the epistles are in terms of the debate between neoclassical and 'Gothic' forms, they also supply part of the reason why Jeffrey thought *Marmion* un-Scottish. The real setting is a chivalric twilight of

> Shield, lance, and brand, and plume, and scarf
> Fay, giant, dragon, squire and dwarf
> And wizard with his wand of might
> And errant maid on palfrey white.

Scott even referred to the mythic 'Albion', a pre-Union notion of British unity. Jeffrey, steeping in Enlightenment values, wanted a poem on Flodden to deal with Flodden. Scott provided instead – with a canny eye to an English market – a poem about valiant reformers on both sides, with nods to Catholic tyranny and duplicity, swaddled in jingoistic rhetoric about the glories of war and combat. No wonder it sold so tremendously well.

Scott was evidently rattled by Jeffrey nonetheless. His next poem, *The Lady of the Lake*, would deal exclusively with Scottish customs and kings, manners and characters. Despite the pose of Olympian serenity, he responded to public criticism. *The Lady of the Lake* has no proto-Byronic anti-hero, and even its fiercest characters are granted nobility alongside their savagery. Even the verse form is smoothed into regular octosyllabics, with inset songs, rather than the spirited variety of *Marmion* and *The Lay*. The plot is simplified: a stranger, James Fitz-James, is given hospitality by a notoriously choleric Highland chieftain, Roderick Dhu. He takes a shine to Ellen, the daughter of Lord James of Douglas, who herself is in love with Malcolm Graeme. Roderick (also in love with Ellen) 'raises the clans' against a threatened attack from Royal forces, and Douglas travels to Stirling to surrender to the King. Fitz-James offers to carry Ellen to safety, which she refuses: in return he gives her a ring that will grant her any boon from the King. He too heads to Stirling and runs in with Roderick; they fight, and Roderick is carried wounded to Stirling. The denouement reveals Fitz-James as James V of Scotland: Ellen presents the ring; James forgives Douglas, Roderick conveniently dies and Ellen marries Malcolm. If you substituted 'offence leading to mortal combat' to 'offence leading to pointed snub'; turned the ring into a lawyer's affidavit, and set the whole thing in Bath it could easily pass as a Regency novella of amours.

The tweaks and concessions worked. *The Lady of the Lake* sold 30,000 copies in its first year (a sum no doubt abetted by the substitution of English Lake for the disconcertingly Scottish Loch). *The Lay* by contrast sold 25,000 after six years and *Marmion*, 17,000 copies in its first year. The reception was ecstatic, and prompted the *New York Observer* to rhyme:

And modern eyes astonished see
The fairy forms of Chivalry.
Hail magic, holy power of song,
To whom all bend the knee,
No gate, hath heaven or earth so strong,
But it shall ope to thee! . . .
Be every maid like ELLEN fair;
And every bard like SCOTT sublime,
Then every maid shall life immortal share,
And every bard outlive the waste of time.

The Lady of the Lake, unlike *The Lay* and *Marmion*, appeared from Ballantyne & Co. rather than Constable (Scott had 'broken' with Constable over the *Edinburgh Review*'s anti-war stance), now self-described as 'Bookseller to the Regent' – the future George IV. James V was Scott's first piece of royal portraiture; and it reputedly went down very well indeed with the monarch-to-be. Not only was James V gallant and honourable (albeit with a weakness for pretty young ladies) his court was an example of Renaissance cultural splendour (again, a retort to Jeffrey's anxieties about 'Scotish nationality'. As John Sutherland observes, this was a court that the Papal envoy referred to as 'the arse of the world'. Scott was giving his readers the history they wanted, not the history they actually had.

The regal flavour ensured *The Lady of the Lake* an unusual afterlife. Like many Scott works it spawned a number of unauthorised derivative works; such as illustrated editions, chapbook versions and dramatic melodramas. One such was staged in London in November 1810, with music by James Sanderson, the conductor of the Surrey Theatre. It quickly skipped the Atlantic, with the musical version of Canto II Stanzas XIX–XX, the 'Boat Song', proving particularly popular. On 4 July 1828, the song was played (without words) by the Marine Band to welcome President John Quincy Adams to the opening of the Chesapeake and Ohio Canal. On 4 March 1845 it was played again, at the inauguration ceremony of President James K Polk, and struck the wife of Polk's successor, John Tyler, so forcefully that it was established that it should be played whenever the

President makes a formal appearance. The opening lines, of course, are 'Hail to the Chief'. It is a minor irony that the song, in the original, welcomes the lawless, bellicose Roderick Dhu.

The Peninsular Campaign against Napoleon continued to cast a shadow over Scott's thoughts and works. He wrote a minor work, *The Vision of Don Roderick*, in 1811, dedicated to the Portuguese War Victims, and the profits (over 100 guineas) from its sale were sent to their fund. Although the historical Don Roderick, 'Last of the Goths', ruled over the end of the Visigothic Empire in Spain – a regime the anti-Semitism of which has drawn chilling comparisons to the Nazis – he was a popular figure in Regency literature, with other versions being sketched by Walter Savage Landor, Washington Irving and Robert Southey. As a glorious failure, he is allowed to predict the liberation of Iberia from Moor and Napoleon alike. Scott's poem controversially omitted all mention of the Whig war hero and martyr, Sir John Moore, drawing further political flak in the literary pages.

It is tempting to think that, having turned down the laureateship in 1813, Scott realised that his poetic career had reached a kind of apex. From unknown to the highest poetic office in a mere ten years is no mean feat; and even the aristocratic refusal seems to indicate a writer sure of himself and his reputation. Given that Scott would spend the end of his life desperately writing to rid himself of his debts, his leisurely disinclination to churn out Birthday Odes mechanically seems poignant. For his fourth work, *Rokeby*, he indulged himself.

The poem was written for his friend J B S Morritt, whose Yorkshire estates at Rokeby Scott frequently visited en route to or from London (Morritt owned the *Venus of Velasquez*, known now as the Rokeby Venus, which he described as 'a fine picture of Venus's backside'). When Morritt mentioned that there was little in the way of legendary lore on which to base a poem, Scott breezily replied, 'Then let us make one – nothing so easy to make as a tradition.' Those words echo through Scott's career, and posthumous reputation. Expectations for the poem were high, and it was even published in a special 'mail-coach' edition: for a higher price, London audiences could be seen reading the book a few days after its Edinburgh publication. Although

Scott reported to Morritt that *Rokeby* was selling 'bobbishly', it failed to exceed, and fell beneath, *The Lady of the Lake*. The poem itself is sweet enough, with especial interest to biographers in that the principal love interest, Matilda, was modelled (according to Scott) on Miss Belsches – so presumably the ineffectual poet Wilfrid is a cipher for one aspect of Scott himself. But the monotony of the four-beat lines, the parochial setting, and some acerbic remarks in the press (especially the poet Thomas Moore's lines in *The Two-Penny Postbag*: he claimed that Scott 'beginning with ROKEBY (the job's sure to pay) / Means to *do* all the Gentlemen's seats on the way') showed that he was no longer in the ascendant. Moreover, the exotic, psychologically penetrating and frisson-inducing *Childe Harold's Pilgrimage* of Byron had taken the market by storm. As Scott ruefully confided in James Ballantyne, 'Byron hits the mark where I don't even pretend to fledge my arrow.'

Scott – as Scott – only wrote one more long poem; *The Lord of the Isles* (1814). It started inauspiciously, with Constable, to whom he had been reconciled, refusing the £5,000 advance Scott thought it worth. He then insisted that Scott's working title *The Nameless Glen* would have to be changed. Despite returning to the irregular style, introducing Robert the Bruce, Bannockburn and a Shakespearian female lover disguised as a page, it was, in the publisher's dread words 'a disappointment'. Scott ended the poem with an elegy for the Duchess of Buccleuch, who had 'inspired' *The Lay of the Last Minstrel*. The harp is hung up; 'one poor garland, twined to deck thy hair, / Is hung upon thy hearse, to droop and wither there'.

Scott's poetry was ably described by Hesketh Pearson as 'the works of a genius, if not works of genius'. Scott did not take his poetry seriously, but he took his literary career seriously enough to know when to quit. In 1814, just prior to the publication of *The Lord of the Isles,* he departed on a cruise around Scotland with the Commissioners of the Northern Lights, including the lighthouse engineer Robert Stevenson, grandfather of Robert Louis. While in Shetland, he records a lovely anecdote, which is not wholly a retreat into his usual dismissal of literary greatness: on Sumburgh Head in Shetland he thought 'it would be a fine situation to compose an ode

to the Genius of Sumburgh-head, or an Elegy upon a Cormorant –
or to have written or spoken madness of any kind in prose or poetry.
But I gave vent to my excited feelings in a more simple way; and
sitting gentle down on the steep green slope which led to the beach,
I e'en slid down a few hundred feet, and found the exercise quite an
adequate vent to my enthusiasm, I recommend this exercise (time
and place suiting) to all my brother scribblers, and I have no doubt
it will save much effusion of Christian ink.'

'Laying a Trap for Jeffrey'

The Lord of the Isles was the last poem by Scott, in that the title page indicated he was the author. But it was not Scott's last long narrative poem. In 1817 a new work, *Harold the Dauntless* was published, described as being 'by the Author of *The Bridal of Triermain*'. That poem had been published anonymously in 1813, having first appeared in 1811 (again anonymously) in the Ballantynes' magazine, *The Edinburgh Annual Register* under the title *The Inferno of Altisidora*. Taxed by both friends and public critics to prove he could write in a vein other than his chosen form, Scott had turned to the Spenserian stanza for *The Vision of Don Roderick*. At the same time he produced works in the style of George Crabbe and Thomas Moore. Bizarrely, he decided he would also write an imitation of himself.

Scott did not deny authorship of *The Inferno*, but certainly spoke of the work as if it were by someone else. To as close a friend as the playwright Joanna Baillie, Scott said that 'the imitation of Crabbe had struck him as good; that of Moore as bad; and that of himself as beginning well, but falling off grievously to the close'. Only Scott's closest friends were allowed in on the secret: William Erskine and J B S Morritt. Scott hoped that Erskine would be taken as the author, and he contributed some scraps of Greek – a language Scott had little sympathy with and little knowledge of – to 'throw out the knowing ones'. He also suggested 'getting up a quizzical review'. To Morritt, Scott was more candid: the whole affair was 'laying a trap for Jeffrey'. Jeffrey, being then on a transatlantic voyage following the death of his wife – and in order to meet his second wife – did not obligingly step into their snare.

The preface to the works again disavowed Scott's authorship: 'nothing burlesque, or disrespectful to the authors, was intended, but that they were offered to the public as serious, though certainly very imperfect imitations of that style of composition, but which each of the writers is supposed to be distinguished'. In the case of his version of himself, this was light rhythms and Pindaric stanzas, oodles of chivalric terminology and copious amounts of place-names; with the major difference being a subject drawn from Arthurian legend. A brief extract shows how well Scott could imitate himself:

> The faithful page he mounts his steed,
> And soon he cross'd green Irthing's mead,
> Dash'd o'er Kirkoswald's verdant plain,
> And Eden barr'd his course in vain.
> He pass'd red Penrith's Table Round,
> For feats of chivalry renown'd,
> Left Mayburgh's mound and stones of power,
> By Druids raised in magic hour,
> And traced the Eamont's winding way,
> Till Ulfo's lake beneath him lay.

In a piece of outrageous nose-tweaking, Scott even has his pseudo-self proclaiming that his lyre – not harp – boasts nothing 'of Border spell' or 'feudal slogan'; that his heroes draw no claymores, and worst of all, it has never won 'best meed to minstrel true, / One favouring smile from fair BUCCLEUCH!'.

Jeffrey may have been indisposed, but Scott's friend George Ellis completely fell for the ruse in the rival *Quarterly Review*. 'It is written,' he argued, 'in the style of Mr Walter Scott; and if *in magnis voluisse sat est* [in great endeavours will suffices], the author, whatever may be the merits of his work, has earned the meed at which he aspires. To attempt a *serious* imitation of the most popular living poet; and this imitation, not a short fragment, in which all his peculiarities might with comparatively little difficulty be concentrated, but a long and complete work; with plot, character, and machinery entirely new; and with no manner of resemblance therefore to a *parody* on any production of the original author;– this must be acknowledged as an attempt of no timid daring.' Poor Ellis may have been misled simply because he did not think Scott would engage in such a scheme of subterfuge without telling him.

But the hoax did not end with Ellis's review of *The Bridal of Triermain*, and its conclusion goes to show that you can push a joke too far. Scott's last attempt at a narrative poem, *Harold the Dauntless*, pretended to be a second work by the anonymous epigone. It is a bizarre tale, indebted to Icelandic skaldic poetry and myths of Viking berserkers, in which the pagan Harold's quest takes him to the underworld, and eventually to Christian baptism. The reviews were not good. *Blackwood's Magazine* called it an 'elegant, sprightly and delightful little poem' but 'generally inferior to the works of Mr Scott, in vigour and interest'. The *Monthly Review* excoriated the 'faults engendered by a servile imitation of Mr Scott's bad grammar and discordant versification'. Most damning of all, the *Literary Gazette* said it had nothing but a 'caricature resemblance' to Scott. Once the critics decide that your new work is actually a weak impersonation of your old work, it's time to call it a day.

'Some satirical flings at Scott'

The Romantic period is often thought of as being especially earnest and sincere – and, indeed, there are very few laughs in Scott's narrative poems, or Wordsworth's *The Prelude*, Shelley's *Prometheus Unbound*, Coleridge's *Biographia Literaria*, Keats's *Hyperion* or Southey's *Thalaba the Destroyer*, except perhaps that title. Byron's monumental *Don Juan* or Hogg's *The Poetic Mirror*, however, are not anomalies in the period, but the visible, 'literary' peaks of a thriving culture of satire, pastiche, burlesque, parody, lampoon and pasquinade. When a writer becomes as famous and widely read as Scott was, it is almost inevitable that this will be reflected in that culture's more irreverent forums.

In his *Life* of Scott, Lockhart mentions this trend.

> About this time several travesties of Scott's poetry, I do not recollect by whom, were favourably noticed in some of the minor reviews, and appear to have annoyed Mr Morritt. Scott's only remark on *The Lay of the Scotch Fiddle*, etc., etc., is in a very miscellaneous letter to that friend:– 'As to those terrible parodies which have come forth, I can only say with Benedict, *A college of such wit-mongers cannot flout me out of my humour.* Had I been conscious of one place about my temper, were it even, metaphorically speaking, the tip of my heel, vulnerable to this sort of aggression, I have that respect of mine ease, that I would have shunned being a candidate for public applause, as I would avoid snatching a honey-comb from among a hive of live bees.'

Scott's pose of phlegmatic hauteur is typical: so too is Lockhart's underestimation.

Lady Anne Hamilton, in *Epics of the Ton, or Glories of the Great World* (1807) was first to have a little dig at Scott (he was a personal friend, and spent the Christmas of 1801 at Hamilton Palace). The poem is mostly an exposé of aristocratic misdemeanours, but she makes space to swipe at poets too:

> Good-natur'd Scott rehearse in well-paid lays
> The marv'lous chiefs and elves of other days.

It's a small but important wryly raised eyebrow: Scott is becoming rich. The poems were generally sold in editions costing around 35 shillings; the equivalent today of £109.54 by the retail price index.

The most famous satirical attack on Scott came in Lord Byron's *English Bards and Scotch Reviewers* (1808).

> And think'st thou, Scott! By vain conceit perchance,
> On public taste to foist thy stale romance,
> Though Murray with his Miller may combine,
> To yield thy Muse just half-a-crown per line?

Byron goes on to call Scott 'Apollo's venal son' with a 'prostituted muse'. That they latterly became friends goes some way to prove that Scott had a certain generosity of spirit; however, at the time, he was splenetic. 'It is funny enough to see a whelp of a young Lord Byron abusing me', he wrote to Southey, 'whose circumstances he knows nothing, for endeavouring to scratch out a living with my pen.' (Scott is somewhat disingenuous here, having already secured several legal positions.) 'God help the bear, if, having nothing to eat he must not even suck his own paws. I can assure the noble imp of fame it is not my fault that I was not born to a park and £5,000 a year, as it is not his lordship's merit, although it may be his great good fortune, that he was not born to live by his literary talents or success.'

The satires tend to reiterate the predominant criticisms found in Jeffrey and other reviewers, with an added element of scepticism about Scott's finances – although Jeffrey himself had ended his review of *The Lay of the Last Minstrel* with the caveat that 'the form of the publication is also too expensive; and we hope soon to see a smaller edition, with an abridgement of the notes for the use of the mere lovers of poetry.' The *Modern Dunciad* (1815) by George Daniel, though complimentary of Scott, still swinges at 'paper-staining', 'venal Scotchmen'. John Taylor's *The Caledonian Comet* (1810) mentions Scott's 'love of lucre' and compares him with another 'flash in the pan', the actor John Kemble. Sir Alexander Boswell wrote a mock-epic version of Scott called *Sir Albon* (1811), which misapplies Scott's manner to mundane subjects. The comedy is sometimes acute, as in these lines:

> De Wodrow! though it mar my tale,
> To sing of thee can minstrel fail?
> For clerk he was, if clerk there be,
> Though little skilled in minstrelsy,
> And less, I wot, of chivalry;
> But I may say, in sooth he knew
> The magic power of two and two,
> And four the wonderful result.

Boswell ends with the familiar jibe. 'I ask but half-a-crown a line – / The Song be yours, the Disk be mine.'

   Some of the satires were simply puerile, such as *The Ass on Parnassus and From Scotland, Ge Ho!! comes Roderigh Vich Neddy Dhu, Ho! Ieroe!!! Cantos I and III of a poem entitled What are Scot's Collops?* (1811) by 'Jeremiah Quiz'. Others use Scott not just as an object of ridicule in himself, but as a vehicle for ridiculing others, much as modern satirical programmes might rewrite the words of a pop-song for humorous effect. It was *presumed* that Scott's work was known. In this category would come George Colman the Younger's anti-Irish *The Lady of the Wreck* (1812); in which 'The stag at eve had drunk its fill' becomes 'The Pig, at eve, was lank and faint', the 'Harp of the North' becomes the 'Harp of the Pats' which 'roused the hopless lover to a rape / Made timorous Tenants knock poor Landlords down' and the famous 'Boat Song' is transformed to

> Hail to our Chief! Now he's wet through with whiskey;
> Long life to the Lady come from the salt seas!
> Strike up, blind Harpers! skip high to be frisky
> For what is so gay as a bag full of fleas?
> Crest of O'Shaughnashane

That's a Potato, plain,
Long may your root every Irishman know!
Pats long have stuck to it,
Long bid good luck to it;
Whack for O'Shaughnashane! – Tooleywhagg, ho!

A surprising number of the satires take the form of a line-by-line parody of the Scott poem. *Marmion Travestied* (1809) by Thomas Hill reapplied the entire narrative, structure and imagery of *Marmion* to send up the *scandale* between the Duke of York and his former mistress (and pioneer of the kiss-and-tell genre) Mrs Mary Anne Clarke.

The Clarke affair had a surprising and unexpected consequence. While the popular press was inflamed with revelations about Clarke's facility in securing pensions and bribes for her friends through the influence of the Duke of York (a situation which became even more farcical when another of her lovers, Colonel Wardle, set a parliamentary investigation in motion), a woman called Mrs Biggs from the Welsh borders (her Christian name has not come down to posterity) wrote to the Lord Chamberlain. She suggested that, in order to 'counteract the pernicious efforts of Mr Wardle', 'his majesty's fiftieth anniversary' would be the ideal time for a 'jubilee or general festival' which 'might excite a spirit of loyal enthusiasm'. This was the first modern jubilee, and its success would be instrumental to Scott's endeavours on behalf of George IV.

The Lay of the Last Minstrel, Travesty (1811) by 'O. Neville' is a burlesque, with a bigamous tailor, his slatternly family and a drunken vagrant replacing the principal characters. Neville says that Scott's 'versification [is] wretched, topography execrable and anachronisms unpardonable', but occasionally hits on a neat joke at Scott's solemnity. 'Breathes there a man . . .' is rendered as the banal 'Is there a man, or is there not?' *Rokeby* spawned *Jokeby* by J. Roby in 1813, which played pretty much the same game, peopling the narrative with characters more reminiscent of Gay's *The Beggar's Opera* and consistently updating into banality – so the 'shaggy mantle' becomes a 'wet umbrella'.

Leigh Hunt wrote satirically about Scott in his 1811 *The Feast of the Poets*, attacking his politics in particular. Apollo calls together the finest writers of the day – Scott, Southey, Campbell, Moore and Wordsworth – though Wordsworth is sent home after showing 'some lines he had made on a straw / Shewing how he had found it and what it was for'. As regards Scott, Hunt writes:

> However he scarcely had got through the door
> When he look'd admiration and bow'd to the floor,
> For his host was a God, – what a very great thing!
> And what was still greater in his eyes – a King!

It might not amuse the radical Hunt that at the outset of his career, Scott had been compared to his political idol and called 'a kind of poetical Godwin . . . call[ing] upon the public to submit to a state of barbarism, by way of arriving at perfection' in the pages of *Le Beau Monde*. Scott's politics were also pilloried in an article in *The Satirist*, which began by talking about second sight and went on to predict Scott's next, ultra-royalist poetic romance, *MacArthur*. Uncannily, the anonymous satirist thought he might address the Jacobite Uprising of 1745.

There were several collections that satirised a number of different writers – James Hogg's *The Poetic Mirror* is the most famous, featuring a Scott parody entitled *Wat O' The Cleugh*. But there were many more: John Agg's *Rejected Odes* (1813), W F Deacon's sublime *Warreniana* of 1824, in which the most celebrated writers of the day all supposedly wrote poems in praise of Warren's shoe-blacking (the company for which the young Charles Dickens worked), and the best known of all, James and Horace Smith's *Rejected Addresses* of 1812. The conceit of the volume is that the poets will all write on the fire at Covent Garden Theatre. Lockhart claims that when 'the whole world laughed over James Smith's really admirable *Death of Clutterbuck* . . . no one laughed more heartily than the author of *Marmion*'. Scott did say that he had 'seldom been so diverted with any thing this long while', but Lockhart manages to get the title wrong – the Scott parody is called *A Tale of Drury Lane* – and although there is a character called Clutterbuck, he does not die (in fact, someone called Higginbottom does). But it must have struck a chord: we will meet Clutterbuck again in Scott's work.

The satire that Lockhart mentions by name, James Kirke Paulding's *The Lay of the Scottish Fiddle* (1813) is actually one of the most astute and interesting of these works. It is remarkable for a number of reasons, but its origin is one of them. This is an American satire on Scott. (An early review in *The Quarterly Review* makes for curious reading, especially for contemporary postmodern theorists: 'The first effort of American wit would necessarily be a parody. Childhood is everywhere a parodist. America is all a parody, a mimicry of her parents.')

The poem claims to be the first American edition of a new work by Scott which has already gone through four editions in Britain, with extra notes for the American audience supplied by Paulding. The action of the poem concerns the retaliation by Warren, Cockburn and Beresford for Madison's incursion into Canada, where they burnt villages in New England. Paulding saw naval action on the American side and introduces Cockburn, the British naval commander, as a stereotypical Scott hero:

> Sir COCKBURN next, a border chief,
> Descended from full many a thief,
> Who in the days of olden time,
> Was wont to think it little crime,
> In gallant *raid* at night to ride,
> And scour the country far and wide;
> Rifle the murder'd shepherd's fold,
> Do deeds that make the blood run cold,
> And cottage fire with burning hand,
> In Durham or in Cumberland.

Paulding offers five proofs that the work is genuinely by Scott. Firstly, it was written in a single week. It features extensive genealogies; an obsession with antiquity but not classicism; inset ballads; and, most of all, places a great deal of importance on locality. This leads to the most linguistically extravagant version of Scott's penchant for topography:

Steady the vessels held their sway,
Coasting along the spacious bay,
By Hooper's strait, Micomico,
Nantikike, Chickacomico,
Dam-Quarter, Chum, and Hiwasee,
Cobequid, Shubamaccadie,
Piankatank, and Pamunkey,
Ompomponoosock, Memphragog,
Conegocheague, and Ombashog,
Youghiogany, and Choctaw,
Aquakanock, Abacooche;
Amoonosock, Apoquemy,
Amuskeag, and Cahokie,
Cattahunk, Calibogie,
Chabaquiddick, and Chebucto,
Chihohokiem and Chickago,
Currituck, Cummashawo,
Chickamogaaw, Cussewago,
Canonwalahole, Karatunck,
Lastly great Kathtippakamunck.

The poem signs off with a very typical attack: 'Yet once again, farewell, Scotch fiddle *dear*, / (For dear thou art, to those who buy this lay).'

The most inventive humour in Paulding's satire comes in satirising Scott's footnotes and editorial material. A couplet which mentions Robinson Crusoe and Sinbad is footnoted 'Here Mr Scott has inserted copious extracts from the romances of these renowned persons, noting all the editions of the *Arabian Nights* that have ever been published, and adding a copious biography of Daniel De Foe.' The footnotes are stuffed with 'original' texts, each lauded by Scott. One is a 'valuable relique . . . communicated to me by my learned friend Mr R Surtees of Mainforth, who had it from his nurse, an old woman, deaf and blind, and therefore more likely to have a good memory'. Another, described by 'Scott' as being better than all classical poetry, reads

Heye dyddle dyddle
Ye catte and ye fythele
Ye keouw yumped over ye moone
Ye leetle dogge laugffed
Vor to zee syche craffte
And ye dysche felle a-lyckynge ye spoone.

Lockhart mentions favourable notices. Although most critics tended to discuss Paulding's politics, *The Monthly Magazine* said not praised \that 'the author has evinced poetical talents of a superior order'. Personally, I agree, and Paulding would cross swords with Scott again, once Scott's fame as a novelist was established. He would also, briefly, be the United States Secretary of the Navy.

Tourism

For every acerbic satire, there were occasional verses of panegyric and encomium. *The Caledonian Comet* spawned *The Caledonian Comet Vindicated* by Martha Anne Sellon. One American aspiring writer, Hugh Henry Brackenridge, originally from Kintyre, wrote an *Epistle to Walter Scott, written at Pittsburgh* which was published in Philadelphia's *Mirror of Taste* in October 1811. He rather over-eggs it: Scott is 'equal with a MILTON'S name; / Or him that sang the fairy-queen, / Or other Southren that has been. / Not SHAKSPEARE would himself disdain / The rivalship of such a strain.' Brackenridge even wrote to Scott to tell him it 'would delight me to have my name alluded to in some of your divine verses'. Fan mail and vanity aside, Brackenridge makes an almost subconscious leap: Scott's poetry can conjure up Scotland to those living far away. And for some readers, the mental transportation of the book was insufficient. The poems encouraged them to see Scott's Scotland for themselves.

The lazy way of describing this is that Scott 'invented' Scottish tourism. The more pedantic definition might be that Scott's picturesque description of Scottish locales and views reached such a vast audience that it led to an increase in the number of visitors to those places. Robert Cadell, Constable's Macchiavellian son-in-law and successor, wrote in his *Memoirs* that when *The Lady of the Lake* was published, 'The whole country rang with the praises of the poet – crowds set off to view the scenery of Loch Katrine, till then comparatively unknown; and as the book came out just before the season for excursions, every house and inn in that neighbourhood was crammed with a constant succession of visitors. It is a well-ascertained fact, that from the date of the publication of *The Lady of the Lake*, the post-horse duty in Scotland rose in an extraordinary degree.' Scott records his amusement that a new inn had been built at Callander, and that a peasant called James Stewart was now making a fine living giving guided tours of 'Ellen's Island'.

In context, the 'discovery' of Scotland as a tourist destination is even more remarkable. Only thirty-seven years beforehand – just over a generation – Samuel Johnson and James Boswell had embarked on their tour of the Highlands and Western Isles. It was conducted in the spirit of an anthropological investigation, an enquiry into barbarism and improvement. Boswell began his account: 'We might there contemplate a system of life almost totally different from what we had been accustomed to see.' Mentioning their forthcoming trip to Voltaire, Boswell noted that the French philosopher 'looked at me as if I had talked of going to the North Pole'. For many English readers, the most immediate stereotype of Scotland would have come from the pages of the English radical John Wilkes's *The North Briton* (1762–71), a scurrilous publication opposed to the Scottish influence in court and parliament, which regularly depicted Scotland and the Scots as impoverished, starving, venal wretches, enthralled to dictatorship and personal advance-ment, and dressed in tartan tatters and rags.

The Revolutionary and Napoleonic Wars had stalled the European 'Grand Tour' of previous generations and led to a gradual increase in domestic travelling for pleasure within Britain, a trend pre-empted by Tobias Smollett's *The Expedition of Humphrey Clinker* (1771). The *Statistical Account of Scotland* (1791–2) by Sir John Sinclair of Ulbster gave a scientific version of the more popular volumes of tours and journeys. The arithmomaniac Sinclair was certainly aware of the influence Scott was having on tourism – he records that his coach was the 297th that season, whereas no previous year had seen more than one hundred, in a letter where he solicited Scott to write a sequel to *The Lady of the Lake* – to be called *The Lady of the Sea* – to popularise his native Caithness. By the 1830s, residents of St Andrews were complaining that it was overlooked by travellers, since it had no connection to the works of Scott, Burns or Byron.

Tourism, of course, existed before Scott: he has a witty account of being shown round Rosslyn Chapel by one Annie Wilson, who recited legends and used a divining rod, long before Dan Brown's *The Da Vinci Code* made Rosslyn internationally famous. Scott chided Erskine for expressing his dismay that Annie would accompany them, saying 'there is pleasure in the song which none but the songstress knows. By telling her we know it already, we should make the poor devil unhappy'.

What differentiates Scott's contribution to the burgeoning tourist trade is the extent to which it encompasses the author himself. Taking Morritt to see Flodden, Scott was astonished to discover at Branxton that the local pub owner wanted to rename his hostelry 'the Scott's Head' and hoped Scott would sit for a portrait. The poet declined, but suggested that the lines from *Marmion* – 'Drink, weary pilgrim, drink, and pray / For the kind soul of Sibyl Grey' – might be amended to 'Drink, weary pilgrim, drink and PAY'. Scott was not just the catalyst for tourism, but the object of it. Washington Irving, who we will meet properly anon, wrote a description of Scott's home Abbotsford within Scott's lifetime, and Lockhart fuelled the curiosity about Scott in his gossipy *Peter's Letters to his Kinsfolk* (1819). Loch Katrine still has a paddle-steamer, now running on biofuel, to carry tourists: the SS *Walter Scott*. Just between Melrose and Bemersyde is a lovely panorama, taking in an oxbow in the Tweed and a fine aspect of the Eildon Hills, which has become known as 'Scott's View', supposedly because the horses pulling his hearse automatically stopped there during the funeral cortege. As we have seen, after his death, Scott is over-written onto the places he described. Scott-land is a palimpsest of Scotland and Scott's works.

Scott and tourism were drummed into me from an early age. In 1982, when I was nine, I won the local newspaper's competition to write an essay to encourage more tourism. Using the technique of an epistle to my older cousin James, I proposed a 'Scott Tour' taking in Abbotsford, Scott's View and his grave at Dryburgh. I won £5, which I spent on a Star Wars PDT-8 troop transporter.

In 1814, as mentioned, Scott set sail on the Lighthouse Yacht *Pharos* to tour Orkney and Shetland. In his diary of the journey he does not mention the advertisement that ran on 7 July in the

Edinburgh Evening Courant, for the tenth edition of *The Lady of the Lake*. It listed other works available – *The Minstrelsy, Sir Tristrem, The Lay of the Last Minstrel, Marmion, Don Roderick, Rokeby* and a volume of *Ballads and Lyrical Pieces*, collecting up his early German translations. No mention, of course, of *The Bridal of Triermain*. A thick black line separates the Scott works from the rest of the advert. It reads:

This day was published,
Handsomely printed in 3 volumes, price 1 *l* 1 *s* boards,
WAVERLEY;
OR
''TIS SIXTY YEARS SINCE'
A NOVEL
'Under WHAT *King? – Bezonian, speak, or die.'*

No one else on the *Pharos*, or in most of Edinburgh, Scotland or Britain for that matter, knew who the mysterious Author of Waverley was.

Heritage

Reading the best part of a year of local newspapers is a strange experience. I'd decided to look for my old article – my first appearance in print – which meant scanning the 1982 editions of the *Border Telegraph* and *Southern Reporter* on microfiche in Hawick's 'Heritage Hub' – a smart, glass-fronted building that houses the local archives and is one of the very few thriving places in town. The total immersion triggers plenty half-forgotten memories: the openings of the Harestanes Woodland Centre, the Teviotdale Leisure Centre (with its spectacularly exotic palm tree), the Galashiels Library lift, David Prowse coming to our school as the Green Cross Code Man (and everyone wanting to really ask him about being the body, if not the voice, of Darth Vader). Some of the moral panics seem dated – there's a lot about glue sniffing, for example. There are lots of appeals, usually to help 'cripples'. Some of it reads as if it's the newspaper for next year, so persisting are the concerns: that supermarkets will make Hawick a 'ghost town'; a rash of nimby-ism about new planning developments in Melrose; the need for cultural tourism. The year 1982 was also the 150th anniversary of the death of Scott, so there's a fantastic number of public lectures (on Scott and Goethe, Scott's legacy, Scott's European context), as well as a rare public opening of Ashiestiel, the house where he wrote *Marmion* (over 200 visitors, the puff-piece proclaims). After two and a half hours of whirring headlines and quaint adverts for long-closed stores, I find the piece. That I won 'joint third' is the first surprise. Memory, with its dispiriting tendency to rose-tint, had misled me to think I'd won the prize outright.

The article reads:

'Dear James, Please come to the Borders for a holiday. Not only would I like to see you, but the Borders is a beautiful and interesting place. Here are a few ideas if you come here. To start with there is Abbotsford and other places connected with Sir Walter Scott. Abbotsford was the last house Scott lived in. It is a huge building full of the great poet's possessions. The Library is a storehouse of information while the dining room shows the area where the poet died. Sir Walter Scott's ghost to this day haunts the room. There are suits of armour and skulls, books and pedestals and even an old church. Following the heritage of Scott there is Dryburgh Abbey where this mighty poet lies. It also shows many secret corridors and many spooky staircases. Lastly (on the trail of Scott) there is Scott's View. It looks over the Tweed and all other beautiful places. He certainly had good taste. On the subject of walks there is Monteviot, home of the Lothians. It has three nature trails which pass the old Cricket Pavilion and an old Dovecote. There is also a loch, a centre and an amazing adventure playground. Bowhill is superb and full of lovely things. It is the home of the Duke and Duchess of Buccleuch. There is a great playground too. I hope that if you come you may see the beautiful countryside which we so often take for granted. – Yours faithfully, Cousin Stuart Kelly.'

I'd certainly forgotten all about the adventure playgrounds, and was slightly taken aback that I referred to Scott as a poet throughout. Did I know he was a novelist? Or did I think that being a poet was somehow more special and interesting?

Waverley

Scott did not set out to be formulaic. He set out to be original, and as his powers waned, he relied on repeating his former successes. Likewise, my reading of Scott had become formulaic. It wasn't a reading at all any more, but the memory of a memory of having read. It was with some trepidation that, after more than a decade, I reopened *Waverley*. Would it seem cruder, gaudier, less assured, less sophisticated? Was my earlier enthusiasm naive, jejune? To try and shock my eyes back onto the page, I bought a new copy – the smart, navy-jacketed hardback in the Edinburgh Edition series, the newest incarnation of an old favourite. (Beforehand I'd read it first in a World's Classics Oxford edition from the library, with my pinky inserted in the endnotes; then in the volume from my own complete set: the late nineteenth-century Melrose edition, embossed with Celtic knots and vizored helmets).

A reproduction of the title page gave me a shudder of recognition and confusion. The line from *Henry IV, Part II* which had appeared in the advertisement was different. It read (more correctly, I realised, after checking my edition of Shakespeare) 'Under which King, Bezonian? Speak, or die!' Nor did it boldly announce itself as 'A NOVEL'. I realised that I had no idea what a Bezonian was. The *Oxford English Dictionary* gives two meanings: primarily, it means a raw recruit, but it can also be used abusively to mean a 'needy beggar, base fellow, knave or rascal'. For those first readers in 1814, the epigraph was already a conundrum. Was *Waverley* about a fresh-faced and ingenuous soldier, or a dangerous scoundrel? The more literate readers might have been aware that Shakespeare uses 'bezonian' twice in that play, the other line being 'Great men oft dye by vilde Besonions'. Did this new *Waverley* hint at political assassinations? Then there was the subtitle – ''Tis Sixty Years Since'. Again, it wrong-foots the reader. Any reader with even the most basic grasp of arithmetic would have considered the book to be set in 1754 – the year in which Hume wrote his *History of Great Britain*, the Royal and Ancient Golf Club of St Andrews set down the rules of golf and the Clandestine Marriages Act turned Gretna Green into a haven for eloping lovers. Even before reading a word of the story, the book seemed less and less predictable.

As for the title itself: Scott relished its vagary in the first chapter. The opening of the novel is a remarkably self-conscious piece of writing. 'The Title', Scott begins, 'of this work has not been chosen without the grave and solid deliberation which matters of importance demand from the prudent.' He goes on to ridicule the 'pages of inanity' of the past half-century with titles like Belmour, Belville, Belfield and Belgrave before, with a flourish, unveiling WAVERLEY, 'an uncontaminated name', 'like a maiden knight with his white shield'. Although coats of arms and heraldry will play important roles in the plot, Scott starts, as a writer, with a metaphorical blank page.

In a similar vein, Scott dissects the business of subtitles. He toys with the different presumptions that would have been occasioned by 'Waverley, A Tale of other Days', 'a Romance from the German', 'a Sentimental Tale' and 'A Tale of the Times'. 'Must not every novel-reader have anticipated a castle scarce less than that of Udolpho', he writes, wittily extemporising, 'of which the eastern wing had long been uninhabited, and the keys either lost or consigned to the care of some aged butler or housekeeper, whose trembling steps, about the middle of the second volume, were doomed to guide the hero, or heroine, to the ruinous precincts?' Then comes the clincher. Scott reveals his chosen subtitle, but states, 'By fixing then the date of my story Sixty Years before this present 1st November 1805 . . .' Now much scholarly ink has been fruitfully spilled in establishing an exact chronology for the composition of *Waverley*. But that doesn't address the interesting question for me. Why would Scott preserve this earlier date, given how easily it might have been changed on the proof sheets? He can't have been that attached to ''Tis Sixty Years Since'.

Scott deliberately makes the reader think that *Waverley* is older than it really is. Having given a wry overview of the fads and fashions of novel-writing, *Waverley* pretends that it has already stood the test of time. Although it was published anonymously, even the earliest adverts made at least a subliminal link to Scott. So in addition to being a work that has, in some way, endured, it is also an earlier work, if we guess the identity of the author. Scott is going back to his original originality – and if the critics don't like it, he can even claim it hasn't aged well. From every perspective, the strange date of *Waverley* acts as a bulwark against criticism.

When I first read *Waverley*, I would show the opening chapter to friends in an attempt to convince them that Scott was worth reconsideration. This wasn't the staid, long-winded Scott of reputation, but a self-aware, exuberant, experimental Scott, the heir to Laurence Sterne and Jonathan Swift and a precursor of John Barth and Italo Calvino. This was Scott the Postmodernist, not Scott the Pre-Victorian. To a great extent, I would stand by those youthful judgements. But reading the novel again, and the first chapter in particular, I'm struck by how tentative, even anxious, Scott sounds. 'Self-consciousness' has a double meaning – and Scott is being both metafictional and acutely, even cripplingly, aware of being observed. The beginning of *Waverley* reads like an author unsure of what he's supposed to be doing. That note of uncertainty is both modern and passé.

It extends to the whole novel. A contemporary author, having decided to write a book about a slightly feckless and unworldly young Hanoverian officer dispatched to Scotland on the eve of the 1745 civil war, would in all likelihood have begun the story with the hero's arrival in alien territories and reveal his back-story through interactions with other characters. Not so Scott. Chapter II – 'Waverley Honour – A Retrospect' – flings us back generations, with Waverley's politically opposed Uncle and Father, a lawsuit of 1670, and by Chapter IV he has even exhumed Wilibert of Waverley, a Crusader ancestor. There are digressions on fly-fishing and Waverley's dubious predisposition to novel reading, a juvenile infatuation and the problems of publishing pro-Catholic sermons. There are also samples of Waverley's attempts at poetry, jostled along side references to *Dyer's Letters*, Scaliger, Bentley, Shakespeare, Milton, Drayton, Spenser, Pulci, Froissart, Brantome, De La Noue, Isaac Walton, Cervantes and Hoppner's *Tale of the Seven Lovers*. It positively twitches and shivers with literary nods and winks. The leisurely tone belies the insistence on bookish pedigree. At one point, Scott defiantly yet almost nervously describes his book:

> I do not invite my fair readers, whose sex and impatience give them the greatest right to complain, into a flying chariot drawn by hippogriffs, or moved by enchantment. Mine is a humble English post-chaise, drawn upon four wheels, and keeping his Majesty's highway. Such as dislike the vehicle may leave it at the next halt, and wait for the conveyance of Prince Hussein's tapestry, or Malek the Weaver's flying sentry-box. Those who are contented to remain with me will occasionally be exposed to the dullness inseparable from heavy roads, steep hills, and other terrestrial retardation, but, with tolerable horses and a civil driver (as the advertisements have it) I will engage as soon as possible into a more picturesque and romantic country, if my passengers incline to have some patience with me during my first stage.

A melancholy footnote to this defence in the later editions states that 'these Introductory Chapters have been a good deal censured as tedious and unnecessary. Yet there are circumstances recorded in them which the author has not been able to persuade himself to retract or cancel.' A confident author, even after decades of success, does not apologise for his apologies.

Scott's use of pacing, plotting and conflict does improve when Waverley reaches the Lowlands of Scotland and becomes assured once he reaches the Highlands. But the indecisive shimmer persists, especially in the psychology of his hero. Waverley meets his uncle's Jacobite friend, Baron Bradwardine, and his daughter Rose in the Lowlands; and ventures on to encounter the Highland chieftain Fergus Mac-Ivor and his sister, Flora. The novel's central peripeteia is Waverley's decision to renounce his commission and throw in his lot with Bonnie Prince Charlie's doomed insurgents. But *why* he would choose to do so is ambiguous. Scott gives many reasons – Waverley is in love with Flora, and wants to impress her; he is piqued by the behaviour of his commanding officer; he is resentful over the Government's treatment of his father; he is dazzled by the glamour of Charles Edward Stewart – but none in isolation nor all taken together wholly explain his decision. It is as if Scott, who at the outset proclaimed 'those passions common to men in all stages of society, and which have alike agitated the human heart, whether it throbbed under the steel corslet of the fifteenth century, the brocaded coat of the eighteenth, or the blue frock and white dimity waistcoat of the present day' actually finds the human heart inscrutable. As a man tutored in the ideals of Enlightenment Edinburgh, Scott knew Adam Smith's *Theory of Moral Sentiments*, with its emphasis on sympathy or fellow-feeling as a natural law as universal as gravitation. But even Smith began his most famous definition of sympathy with the words, 'As we have no immediate experience of what other men feel.' Scott, as much as Flaubert, conceives of the novel as a laboratory for empathetic investigation, and Waverley is subjected to a bewildering array of stimuli to alter his behaviour. But, like another great Enlightenment thinker, David Hume, Scott is wary about assigning causes to effects. Waverley is affected, effected, and even infected: he has many excuses but no vindication.

Waverley's vacillations are not only political. His swerves from Hanoverian to Jacobite to Hanoverian are mirrored in his romantic life. Initially the haughty, dark Flora bewitches him; latterly, the homely, blonde Rose. The transfer of his love is one of the novel's weirdest aspects, and many readers have found a tincture of expedience about it – a reading exacerbated by Waverley's second epiphany: 'he felt himself entitled to say firmly, though perhaps with a sigh, that the romance of his life was ended, and that its real history had now commenced.' But a close reading reveals even stranger undercurrents. Waverley first considers Rose as a prospective wife immediately after Fergus declares an interest in her. Like a parody of Smith's sympathy, Waverley loves her because he imagines someone else loving her. Then, the two take part in a dramatised reading of

Romeo and Juliet. He acts the lover to become one. For all that the 'land of romance and fiction' has supposedly been left behind, it is still through literature that Waverley determines his choices.

The key chapter for Waverley's amorous conversion does not have a title, but a quotation – 'To One Thing Constant Never' – from Shakespeare's *Much Ado About Nothing.* Prefatory quotations are a distinctive feature of Scott's novels – although their invention should be credited to the doyenne of Gothic shockers, Mrs Radcliffe, and she at least never just made them up and attributed them to any 'Old Song'. *Waverley* does not actually have any: there are either chapter titles ('A Nocturnal Adventure', 'Shows That The Loss Of A Horse's Shoe May Be A Serious Inconvenience', 'Rather Unimportant') or quotations. Quotations tend to dominate the latter half of the book, again, as if Scott had hit on the idea midway. But the curiosity of the *Much Ado About Nothing* quote is that it is the second time in the novel Scott has used it. In Chapter XIX, after another fogey-ish aside on 'La Picara Justina Diez – which, by the way, is one of the most rare books in Spanish literature', the recondite allusion comes apropos of the author, Francisco de Ubeda, and his dislike of goose-quills as writing implements. Ubeda's contention is that the goose is 'a bird inconstant by nature, as frequenting the three elements of water, Earth, and air, indifferently, and being, of course, "to one thing constant never" '. Scott, conversely, thinks this makes the goose feather ideal, as his work 'can speedily change from grave to gay, and from description and dialogue to narrative and character. So that, if my quill display no other properties of mother-goose than her mutability, truly I shall be well pleased'. Subliminally, Scott twins the literature-obsessed, hesitant and swithering Edward Waverley with *Waverley* itself.

Waverley still possesses the virtues that previous generations admired. The death of Fergus and the loyalty of his clansman Evan Dhu have a tragic dignity, and Flora's final comment – 'I do not regret his attempt because it was wrong – oh, no! on that point I am armed – but because it was impossible it could end otherwise than this' – encapsulates a whole tragic view of history. Before W C Sellar and R J Yeatman spoofed the notion in *1066 And All That*, Scott had already made the political centres of his novels the contrast between

'wrong but romantic' and 'right but rotten'. The same dynamic
would be played out in Covenanters and Episcopalians; Saxons and
Normans; Roundheads and Cavaliers; Reformers and Catholics;
Tories and Whigs. Scott established his formula with *Waverley*: a
moment of profound historical change, with a liberal hero shuttlecocked between ideologies (Waverley is almost a literal tourist in
Scotland, as well as a political tourist, with Jacobitism as his 'gap
year' dalliance). The contrasting heroines would be reworked in
many novels: as Rebecca and Rowena in *Ivanhoe*, Minna and Brenda
Troil in *The Pirate*, Alice and Fenella in *Peveril of the Peak*, Effie and
Jeanie Deans in *The Heart of Midlothian*.

Waverley ends with a 'Postscript that should have been a Preface',
where Scott analyses his relationship to Scottishness. 'There is no
European nation, which, within the course of half a century, or little
more, has undergone so complete a change as this kingdom of
Scotland', he writes. The purpose of the novel is to preserve this alteration in manners, politics, economy and improvement. Scott explicitly links the depiction of Scottish characters to the methods
employed by Maria Edgeworth in her fictions – a disinclination to
indulge in 'caricatured and exaggerated use of the national dialect'.
Moreover, in this 'mediation' between Irish characters and English
readers, in Scott's opinion, 'she may be truly said to have done more
toward completing the Union than perhaps all the legislative enact-
ments by which it has been followed up'. Scott insists on the factual
basis of fiction, the verisimilitude of the portraits. The most adroit
sleight of hand that Scott uses is to create deliberately fictitious
places – Tully-Veolan, Cairnvreckan, Glennaquoich – that have the
virtue of literally being nowhere and therefore metaphorically representing anywhere in Scotland. Scott can create a novel that explores
the totality of Scotland – Highland and Lowland, feudal and commercial, loyalist and renegade – precisely by *not* sticking to the facts.

In a final twist on the novel's emerging form, the final chapter
ends with a dedication, where the author, evaporating like mist into
'an unknown admirer of his genius', lauds Henry Mackenzie, 'our
Scottish Addison' and the author of the bestseller of 1771, *The Man
of Feeling*. The author's final disappearing trick is to wish that the

entire book did not exist: 'yet heartily I wish that the task of tracing the evanescent manners of his country had employed the pen of the only man in Scotland who could have done it justice . . . I should in that case have had more pleasure as a reader, than I shall ever feel in the pride of a successful author'. Just as Edward Waverley is a 'might have been' of history, *Waverley* is a tactical substitution in the history of literature.

One subtitle Scott did not contemplate is 'Waverley: A Historical Novel'. In shorthand parlance, Scott 'invented' the historical novel. This does not mean that prior novels had not been set in the past – many had, from interminable French romances to Gothic shockers. Scott was not a historical novelist so much as he was a novelist with a theory of history.

'The Author of Waverley'

When Bertrand Russell was attempting to solve a dilemma in Frege's theory of denotation, he turned to Sir Walter Scott. 'A logical theory may be tested by its capacity for dealing with puzzles, and it is a wholesome plan, in thinking about logic, to stock the mind with as many puzzles as possible . . .' he wrote, and presented one conundrum thus: '(1) If a is identical with b, whatever is true of the one is true of the other, and either may be substituted for the other in any proposition without altering the truth or falsehood of that proposition. Now George IV wished to know whether Scott was the author of *Waverley*; and in fact Scott was the author of *Waverley*. Hence we may substitute Scott for the author of *Waverley*, and thereby prove that George IV wished to know whether Scott was Scott. Yet an interest in the law of identity can hardly be attributed to the first gentleman of Europe.' Russell's theory does resolve the logical surface of the puzzle (easily done in symbolic logic, he notes, whereas language is ambiguous). The deeper problems – was Scott Scott? Was the author of *Waverley* also the 'Author of *Waverley*'? – are beyond the remit of philosophy.

The success of *Waverley* was as astonishing as that of the early poems: the first 2,000 copies sold out in two days, and when Scott returned on the *Pharos*, fresh from sliding down hills as an antidote to poetry, *Waverley* was on its third reprinting. The new edition teased even further about the anonymous author, inviting speculation as to 'whether WAVERLEY be the work of a poet or a critic, a lawyer or a clergyman, or whether the writer, to use Mrs Malaprop's phrase, be, "like Cerberus – three gentlemen at once" '. The only people who were apprised of the secret were his friends Erskine and Morritt (who had been in on the 'trap' for Jeffrey) and the Ballantyne brothers, who had to copy out the manuscript in their own hand to conceal his efforts. 'I shall *not* own Waverley; my chief reason is that it would prevent me the pleasure of writing again', he told Morritt, adding, 'I am not sure it would be quite decorous of me, as a Clerk of Session, to write novels.' To Ballantyne, he hinted that more mercantile reasons – the saturation of the marketplace and the concomitant expectations attending an already famous name – were at work:

> No, John, I will not own the book –
> I won't, you picaroon.
> When next I try St. Grubby's brook
> The 'A. of Wa—' will bait the hook –
> And flat-fish bite as soon
> As if before them they had got
> The worn-out wriggler Walter Scott.

Neither Constable, the publisher, nor his London collaborators such as John Murray, were initially allowed in on the secret. Scott, whenever questioned, was evasive. A few years later, when Murray complimented him on *Tales of my Landlord*, Scott wrote back saying, 'I do not claim that paternal interest in them which my friends do me the credit to assign to me' – and, in true lawyerly fashion, it should be noted that not claiming is not the same as not being. Scott would even deny authorship to the Prince Regent – a minor treason.

Even when not directly confronted, Scott missed no opportunity to muddy the waters. He even misled his brother Tom about *Waverley*. 'A novel here, called *Waverley*, has had enormous success . . . the success which it has had, with some other circumstances, has induced people "to lay the bantling at a certain door, / Where lying store of faults, they'd fain heap more". You will guess for yourself how far such a report has credibility.' To Matthew Weld Hartstonge he sent 'a Novel in 3 Volumes, of which the good town of Edinr. give me credit as the Author. They do me too much honor, and I heartily wish I had both the credit and profit.'

With Scott surreptitiously misleading his audience, friends and family about the identity of 'The Author of *Waverley*', rumour swiftly filled the vacuum. Among the candidates were Tom Scott,

Henry Mackenzie (which would make the dedication some kind of triple bluff), Alexander Boswell the satirist, William Erskine, and even Francis Jeffrey – who was supposed to have written it to amuse himself on his recent transatlantic voyage. Despite such speculations – many of which were actively encouraged by Scott – for the vast majority of readers there was little mystery as to who 'The Author of *Waverley*' actually was. 'Aut Scotus, aut diabolus', wrote Maria Edgeworth: 'Either Scott or the Devil'. In 1825, William Hazlitt openly discussed Scott's differences as a novelist and as a poet in *The Spirit of the Age*. *The British Critic* noted that 'the northern literati are unanimous, as we understand, in ascribing part of it at least to the pen of W. Scott. As that gentleman has too much good sense to play the coquet with the world, we understand that he perseveres in a formal denial of the charge.'

Francis Jeffrey – pre-eminent among the literati to which *The British Critic* referred – was actually rather more cautious in his ascription. 'There has been much speculation, in this quarter of the island, about the authorship of this singular performance,' he wrote, 'and certainly it is not easy to conjecture why it is still anonymous. – Judging by internal evidence, to which alone we pretend to have access, we should not scruple to ascribe it to the highest of those authors to whom it has been assigned by the sagacious conjectures of the public; – and this at least we will venture to say, that if it be indeed the work of an author hitherto unknown, Mr Scott would do well to look to his laurels, and to rouse himself for a sturdier competitor than any he has yet had to encounter!'

Jeffrey is being exquisitely shrewd here. He may have heard about the *Bridal of Triermain* hoax, and thought it best to be cautious. But even setting aside any putative, and frankly, out of character anxiety, he still moves in an oddly slant-wise manner around the authorship. He agrees with the public, but does not name the author; then conjures up Scott under a discussion of how he should react were the novel not by him. In later reviews, he maintains the miasma of ambiguity: *Tales of my Landlord* is 'a new coinage from the mint that produced *Waverley*'. There is a kind of cordial conspiracy: if Scott will not admit authorship, Jeffrey will not accuse him of it.

The authorship may have been something of an open secret, but why persist in the secrecy? Scott's various reasons – respectability, a canny sense of literary celebrity, a buried awareness of the perils of mere popularity – do not add up to a reason. The reasons of others are also insufficient: on one hand, Jeffrey is bemused that the author of such a triumph would wish to remain anonymous; on the other, *The British Critic* seems to imply that revealing his authorship after the success would smack of girlish solicitation. Anonymity was not a new conceit; nor is the history of literature devoid of examples of authors who chose to assume anonymity in order to reassure themselves that their work and not their name was the real value – Doris Lessing pulled such a stunt as 'Jane Somers'. But Scott's entanglement with anonymity is deeper, longer and more vexed.

When his authorship was revealed, in the Magnum preface to *The Chronicles of the Canongate*, Scott wrote: 'I can render little better reason for choosing to remain anonymous, than by saying with Shylock, that such was my humour.' It is a definitive non-answer. The line itself from *The Merchant of Venice* reads, 'But say, it is my humour – is it answer'd?' The speech continues:

> Some men there are love not a gaping pig!
> Some, that are mad if they behold a cat!
> And others, when the bagpipe sings i' the nose,
> Cannot contain their urine: for affection,
> (Master of passion) sways it to the mood
> Of what it likes or loathes. Now, for your answer:
> As there is no firm reason to be render'd,
> Why he cannot abide a gaping pig;
> Why he, a harmless necessary cat;
> Why he, a woollen bagpipe; but of force
> Must yield to such inevitable shame
> As to offend, himself being offended;
> So can I give no reason.

What else was going on in Scott's mind when he chose that particular quotation, with its almost surreal image of a man with bagpipe-induced incontinence, to justify his behaviour; a speech, moreover, that insists on the incomprehensibility of whims? 'Because I wanted to' is not an answer to 'Why did you want to hide?'

Although his next two novels, *Guy Mannering* and *The Antiquary* appeared with the legend 'by the Author of *Waverley*', the following novels – *The Black Dwarf* and *The Tale of Old Mortality* – did not. Moreover, they came out with a different publisher (Blackwood, rather than Constable), with a generic title (*Tales of my Landlord, First Series*) in four volumes rather than the customary three. Every effort was made to distance the publication from what were coming to be known as the Scotch Novels if not yet as the Waverley Novels. It worked to the extent that Augusta Leigh, Byron's half-sister, was convinced he had turned novelist to compete with Scott. Scott even reviewed *Tales of my Landlord* for the *Quarterly Review* – in the same letter in which he disavowed authorship to the review's owner, John Murray, he asserted, 'I have a mode of convincing you that I am perfectly serious in my denial – pretty similar to that by which Solomon distinguished the fictitious from the real mother – and that is, by reviewing the work, which I take to be an operation equal to that of quartering the child.' Almost as if to prove his seriousness, he describes *The Black Dwarf* as 'not very original in its concoction, and lame and impotent in its conclusion'.

Scott's review is more than just a literary curiosity. It was part written with his friend Erskine, and it is safe to say that Erskine rather than Scott was responsible for the bedazzled comparisons with Shakespeare. Scott, as he had promised Murray, offered himself no quarter. He complains of the 'flimsiness and incoherence' of the narration, and the 'total want of interest which the reader attaches to the character of the hero'. Waverley, Bertram in *Guy Mannering* and Lovel in *The Antiquary* are all 'very amiable and very insipid sort of young men'. That said, Scott then justifies the passivity of his heroes by discussing how, in order to receive the various impressions of Scotland and Scottishness, it is necessary for them to be somewhat blank as well as bland. The want of 'probability and perspicuity' in the narrative is defended with a favourite quote of Scott's – that of Mr Bays from *The Rehearsal*: 'What the deuce is a plot good for, but to bring in fine things?'

By far the greatest part of the review is taken up with the anonymous reviewer Scott defending the anonymous novelist Scott against the charges laid out in the *Edinburgh Christian Instructor* (and reiterated in the *British Critic* and the *Eclectic*) by the Revd Thomas M'Crie: namely, that Scott had caricatured and vilified the Presbyterians. That Scott's Tory beliefs coloured his depiction is clear from more than just a review by M'Crie, a sympathetic biographer of John Knox. Scott's two chief Scottish rivals, James Hogg and John Galt, both went on to write accounts of the period (*The Brownie of Bodsbeck* and *Ringan Gilhaize*) that took up an antithethical position over the Covenanters and their legacy.

At the beginning of the review, Scott addresses anonymity. 'Why he should industriously endeavour to elude observation by taking leave of us in one character, and then suddenly popping out upon us in another, we cannot pretend to guess, without knowing more of his personal reasons for preserving so strict an incognito than has hitherto reached us. We can, however, conceive of many reasons for a writer observing this sort of mystery; not to mention that it has certainly had its effect in keeping up the interest which his works have excited.' This is as close as Scott gets to confessing to anonymity as a marketing strategy. 'The Author of *Waverley*', by being no one, could be anyone. The review in the *Quarterly* even flaunts the idea that fictional characters, by 'freemasonry', can be recognised by everyone; and Scott gives examples of countless individuals claiming to be the 'original' of certain of his creations.

After the initial *Tales*, Scott reverted to the original form for *Rob Roy* – although the 'Author of *Waverley*' claims to be merely the editor of the first person memoirs, describing himself as a 'phantom' – and returned to the alternative frames for *The Heart of Midlothian*, or *Tales of my Landlord, Second Series*. *Ivanhoe*, in 1819, was supposed to be the first of yet another 'line'.

Since he could not disguise the physical forms of the books, Scott increasingly elaborated on the fictitious narrators of them. *Tales of my Landlord* had introduced the notion that the 'book' was actually written by a local schoolteacher, Peter Pattieson, who got the story from oral sources, and whose papers were arranged by his

successor, Jedediah Cleishbotham. Scott would develop the authorial equivalent of multiple personality disorder, creating pseudo-
authors such as Captain Clutterbuck, Dr Dryasdust, Chrystal
Croftangry and even the mysterious Eidolon of Waverley. It is as if,
in the process of converting Scotland into an imaginary place, Scott
had to make himself into an imaginary author.

A Digression on Secret Identities

'The Author of *Waverley*' was really Sir Walter Scott. Or Sir Walter Scott was really 'The Author of *Waverley*'. To understand the difference, compare these sentences to 'Clark Kent was really Superman' and 'Batman was really Bruce Wayne'. Superman is Kal-El, the Last Son of the planet Krypton, who 'hides' his fantastic powers in the disguise of the hapless hack from Smallville, Clark Kent. Bruce Wayne, on the other hand, was a wealthy orphaned playboy who, by night, assumed the mantle of the Caped Crusader to avenge his parents' deaths. Superman was effortlessly superior; Batman has trained to become extraordinary. Superman pretends to be normal as Clark Kent; Bruce Wayne aspires to be exceptional as Batman. Clark Kent pulls off his civvies to reveal Superman; Bruce Wayne puts on his Batsuit to become Batman. With Superman, *modesty forbids*. With Batman, *necessity demands*. Now which is closest to Scott?

Putting a Country in a Book

In Alasdair Gray's *Lanark*, the aspiring artist Duncan Thaw delivers a speech which has become totemic in discussions of contemporary Scottish literature.

> 'Glasgow is a magnificent city,' said McAlpin. 'Why do we hardly ever notice that?' 'Because nobody imagines living here,' said Thaw. McAlpin lit a cigarette and said, 'If you want to explain that I'll certainly listen.'
>
> 'Then think of Florence, Paris, London, New York. Nobody visiting them for the first time is a stranger, because he's already visited them in paintings, novels, history books and films. But if a city hasn't been used by an artist, not even the inhabitants live there imaginatively . . . Imaginatively Glasgow exists as a music hall song and a few bad novels. That's all we've given to the world outside. It's all we've given to ourselves.'

It was a resolutely Modernist preoccupation that the City is the imaginative locus of the Novel: Gray was widely praised for 'doing for Glasgow what Joyce did for Dublin', or Bely for St Petersburg, or Musil for Vienna, or Dos Passos for Manhattan. Readers might not have imaginatively lived in Glasgow, but they certainly did get a chance to live in Scotland. (Scott, incidentally, only has one major Glasgow scene, with the bourgeois merchant Bailie Nicol Jarvie in *Rob Roy*.) Scott's Scotland is subtly different from the imagined communities of Barsetshire or Wessex that were peopled in the novels of Trollope and Hardy. Although significant locations are metaphors for kinds of Scottish place, they co-exist with the 'real' Scotland of Edinburgh, Stirling, Glasgow and Perth. While Hardy replaced Oxford with Christminster, Scott supplements Melrose with Kennaquhair. In magazine articles, commemorative signage

and even full-length books – latterly, *The Scott Originals* by
W S Crockett and *Illustrations of the Author of* Waverley by Robert
Chambers in Scott's lifetime – readers sought to link the imagined
and actual places, the historical and fictitious characters. Traquair
House in the Borders is like Tully-Veolan (with its bear gates
never to be opened until a Stuart Restoration); David Ritchie of
Peeblesshire is similar to Elshender the Recluse in *The Black Dwarf*;
Tillietudlem Castle in *Old Mortality* is an amalgam of Craignethan
and Bothwell Castles. Just as one fictitious character could be
'recognised' by different people, a fictitious place could be visited in
multiple real locations.

As a young man, Scott began to take such 'escapades' that his
father, no doubt with gritted teeth, 'thought I was born to be a
strolling pedlar'. Before he provided a template for tourists' journeys, Scott was himself a tourist: 'my principal object in these excursions was the pleasure of seeing romantic scenery, or what afforded
me at least equal pleasure, the places which had been distinguished
by remarkable historical events'. He even became a kind of amateur
tour guide, and recollected having 'frightened away' a fellow traveller's sleep with his account of the assassination of Archbishop
Beaton. Scott came to realise he had little ability in art. Like many
other travellers, he attempted to capture the picturesque in drawings and sketches, but was 'totally ineffectual'.

His realisation that he could do in words what he could not in
illustrations has a telling coda. As he wrote: 'Meanwhile I endeav-
oured to make amends for my ignorance of drawing, by adopting a
sort of technical memory respecting the scenes I visited. Wherever
I went I cut a piece of a branch from a tree – these constituted
what I called my log-book; and I intended to have a set of chessmen
out of them, each having reference to the place where it was
cut – the kings from Falkland and Holyrood; the queens from
Queen Mary's yew tree at Crookston; the bishops from abbeys or
episcopal palaces; the knights from baronial residences; the rooks
from royal fortresses; and the pawns generally from places worthy
of historical note. But this whimsical design I never carried into
execution.'

'Whimsical' though this Borgesian scheme to reduce a nation to a chessboard might be, it is also telling; not least in the fact that it was left incomplete. When Scott commenced writing the first series of *Tales of my Landlord*, the intention was 'to give in the four volumes as many tales, each having its scene laid in a different province of Scotland; but this scheme was soon abandoned'. The second series, which eventually was entirely taken up with *The Heart of Midlothian*, was to have had two tales. When Scott's third novel, *The Antiquary*, was published, the prefatory announcement claimed that it 'completes a series of fictitious narratives, intended to illustrate the manners of Scotland at three different periods. *Waverley* embraced the age of our fathers, *Guy Mannering* that of our own youth, and the *Antiquary* refers to the last ten years of the eighteenth century'. As John Wilson Croker observed in the *Quarterly Review,* 'this may be in an occult sense true ... we presume to doubt a little the literal authenticity of the statement'. This does not detract from the genuine feeling of 'signing off', where Scott thanks the public and takes his leave as one 'not likely again to solicit their favour'. The first novels, dealing with living memory, did form a discrete unit. Afterwards, Scott would have to rely on textual sources more than oral ones. It is not coincidental that the switch to his new 'author' – Cleishbotham et al – would entail a more protracted and subtle discussion of how the story came into being.

Scott was continually trying – and continually failing – to find a form in which a comprehensive overview of Scotland, geographically and historically, might be contained. It was evident that a single novel could not accomplish this. With the publication of the Magnum Opus edition, at the end of his life, the Waverley Novels themselves became the grand vision, now including England, Wales, France, Palestine, Germany and Constantinople in the working out of Scottishness.

The Magnum Opus introduced two features which would have a lasting significance to how Scott's novels were read. First, as he had admitted authorship in 1827 with *Chronicles of the Canongate*, this was the edition where Scott as author came centre stage. New prefaces were written, to accompany rather than replace his earlier, wittier prefaces full of wry shadowplay over authorship and authority. In the new prefaces, Scott became his own antiquary: he described the autobiographical genesis of the work – it is from the Magnum that we have Scott's barely credible story of discovering the old manuscript of *Waverley* while searching for fish hooks – and presented the historical evidence on which the fictions are based. Scott assimilates the kinds of readerly speculation about the 'real life' whos and wheres that had surrounded the original publications. The novels become heavily footnoted, further enshrining the idea of a carapace of truth around the Grub Street fiction. Scott is armouring himself. For a nineteenth-century reader, the Magnum Opus was not only a collection of diverting novels, but an eccentric encyclopaedia and prospective itinerary. It was a guidebook as well as a romance. In its accumulation of addenda, it is like the nineteenth-century equivalent of a DVD with Bonus Features.

The second major change was illustration. While the first editions of the novels had appeared unadorned, the Magnum Opus was illustrated throughout, with engravings on the frontispiece and vignette titles. Published concurrently by Robert Cadell was a series of landscapes by James Skene to be bound in with the novels. For the *Poetical Works* and *Miscellaneous Prose Works* published immediately after Scott's death, J M W Turner provided the illustrations. It's hard to overestimate the sea-change illustration brought to the Waverley Novels – they were now, to use an anachronism, multimedia publications. Skene's album, however, is not simply a transcription of places mentioned in the novels. As he says in the preliminary notice, although he had employed 'strict fidelity' in his draughtsmanship, there is one proviso: 'such subjects as are now in ruins, are, where practicable, restored to the state they were in at the particular period assumed by the Author of Waverley'. To recapitulate Gray's frustration about Glasgow, the visitor coming to Scotland for the first time would not be a stranger, but Scotland itself would have become strange. The illustrations are out of time with the world. The imagined Scotland on the pages of the Waverley Novels is found no longer to exist. To complicate matters still further, in the middle of the nineteenth century, preservation undertaken at such sites as

Hermitage Castle and Melrose Abbey restored the ruins to a simulacrum of the image conjured in the novels: not a full restoration but a carefully stalled decrepitude. Scotland was building its own past.

In its obituary, the *Edinburgh Evening Courant* wrote that 'Cervantes has done much for Spain and Shakespeare for England, but not a tithe of what Sir Walter Scott has accomplished for us'. By the 1870s, when many of the 'heritage' sites had been artfully restored, Thomas Cook was running successful 'Tartan Tours', interweaving Scott's life and his works in a package holiday. 'Sir Walter Scott gave a sentiment to Scotland', he wrote, 'as a tourist country, and we have spent twenty-three seasons in attempts to foster and develop that sentiment.' Scott struggled to encapsulate Scotland within a single oeuvre; and that struggle became the wrapping in which Scotland would be packaged.

The Quixotic Nation

A young girl, dressed in swathes of various tartans, implores her father, 'But dinna fash yourself sic a *muckle deal*: come, come, and I will be your *elfin female page*.' But this is not in Scotland, nor the past: the girl, Alice, lives in contemporary London and is the heroine of Sarah Green's wickedly satirical novel of 1824, *Scotch Novel Reading or Modern Quackery, a Novel* **really** *founded on facts*. Alice is devoted to the work of Scott, down to imitating speech and costume. Her father laments that she 'has read them all, or rather skimmed them over, merely to say that she *has* read them; without understanding one half of what she has perused, and scarce comprehending one word of a dialect with which they abound, but which she affects to use on all occasions, generally misapplying every word, as far as my little knowledge of the Scottish dialect goes: but she tells her companions, with an air of consequence, that she never reads any other novels than *Walter Scott's*'. Alice is a caricature, but the caricature is not untethered from reality. Mary Clarke Mohl, a great friend of Florence Nightingale's, in a letter of 3 April 1822, wrote, 'you must read all the works of Scott, my dearest, but not till I return, because I adore them, as I do the whole Scotch nation'.

In the course of the novel, Alice's Don Quixote style infatuation is gradually disenchanted; by meeting a genuine Scots woman who mostly complains about the poverty of Scotland and tells her, sharply, 'Ken ye not weel that 'Tis aw a fable?'; and by falling in love with a Scots soldier. The soldier, who has only a single eye, hand and foot, is actually a disguised Englishman – which raises the curious prospect that to be Scottish is to be a mythical English Nasnas, a half-thing, a cleft-whole. Alice's obsession is, however, far more revealing. This kind of literary monomania is not a new phenomenon – Alice's father notes that they went through a similar phase with her elder sister and

Byron – and the current popularity of the Waverley Novels is compared to the fads for Fanny Burney, Anne Radcliffe and Matthew 'Monk' Lewis. But the voluminous Scott is a more worrying fashion. Readers are 'inundated with showers of Scotch novels, thicker than the snow you see falling', with works 'pouring on us like a torrent from one fertile pen'. It seems to him as if 'there was no another country under the sun worth hearing of than poor, miserable, little Scotland'. Worse, Alice's own mimicry is sanctioned and paralleled by the fact that novelists are already imitating Scott – and these imitators are more blameworthy than the original. Likewise, both the *Edinburgh Review* and *Blackwood's Magazine* (which Alice reads between Waverley Novels) are censured for 'puffing' Scott, and artificially sustaining the hype around his works. Throughout *Scotch Novel Reading* there are attacks on the 'cabals', 'quacks' and 'Scotch Monopoly'. The anxiety is palpable. The worry is not that Scott is a passing fashion, but that he is *not* a passing fashion.

Under such circumstances, it is almost understandable that poor Alice falls so wholeheartedly under the influence of Scott. Alice's impersonation of Scottishness takes two distinct forms: language and costume. These are both derived from the novels, which use multiple linguistic registers and frequently adopt disguises to characterise the difference between the Scots and the English – and indeed, both accent and dress are staples of Scottish caricature to this day. To lampoon the Scots, all you need is a kilt and a distinctive pronunciation of the 'ch' in 'loch'. What is remarkable about such heightened versions is that they frequently began in Scotland. Sir Harry Lauder predates Russ Abbot; and William McGonagall comes before Monty Python's Ewan McTeagle.

Stereotype derives from two Greek words – *stereos*, meaning firm or solid, and *tupos*, an impression, blow or incised mark. Although such depictions can be felt as physical assaults or aggressive blows, the Scottish stereotype seems more like the oxymoronic etymology, a firm impression, both clear and nebulous at the same time. Other groups have advocated the cultural appropriation of former terms of abuse (reclaiming words such as 'queer' or 'nigga', or through dramatising the speaker-specific usage of a word like 'Paki' in

Gautum Malkani's *Londonstani*). Scots cannot enact a similar trans-
formative adoption. Local newspapers in Scotland will happily refer
to 'tartan tat' or 'kitsch kilts' or 'hoots mon' attitudes, but these
stereotypes cannot be reclaimed as they were always ours in the first
place. Alasdair Gray rails about the 'music hall songs and a few bad
novels', but the exportation of a Scottish cliché is not solely about
outdated media and aesthetic inferiority: many of the greatest and
most successful cultural embodiments of Scottishness willingly
embrace the cliché. Sir Walter is at the forefront of both the creation
of that myth and the subsequent fulminating furores around it.

These cross-currents are seen most clearly in the inaugural Donald
Dewar Memorial Lecture given by the former Labour Minister
for Culture, Tourism and Sport, Mike Watson, in 2002. Entitled
'Scotland: A Place for Culture and Culture in Place', with unfortunate
undertones of 'keeping' culture in its place, Watson located Scott at
the interface between tourism and culture: 'Scott's success' was 'in
putting Scotland on the international map'; but, Watson continued, 'I
do recognise too, however, that the cultural images and identity
created by Scott have, in a sense, been too successful.' What does 'too
successful' actually mean? On one hand, it may just be an admission
of the failure of tourism promotions to provide a counter-image as
beguiling and ubiquitous as Scott's. In the same year, VisitScotland,
the Government body tasked to promote tourism, attempted to
'rebrand' away from its former mottoes (including 'Discover the Real
Scotland') with some ill-advised adverts promoting the benefits of
Scotland's rain and mist ('The Scottish weather is perfect for a
romantic break. You won't go out much. In the Scottish Highlands
you may have to stay in and make your own entertainment. Want to
come?' – all puns intended). Stalling critics, VisitScotland assured
reporters that the 'land of the mountain and flood' had not become a
'wet weather knocking shop'. Worse, the chief executive Philip
Riddle, on being asked what united the diverse aspects of contemporary Scotland in a single television advert, was reduced to replying, 'A
strong element of authenticity. It's not staged, it's not Disneyland.'

On the other hand, Watson and others' comments may indicate a
barely suppressed anxiety that Scott's Scotland has, in some vague

world-consciousness, *replaced* the real Scotland. It is akin to the French philosopher Jean Baudrillard's concept of the simulacrum: 'the simulacrum is never that which conceals the truth: it is the truth which conceals that there is none'. Watson is not concerned with Scott as a superior spin-doctor, but with the notion that there is no 'real Scotland' at all. Disneyland is, after all, as 'real' as Auchtermuchty.

Watson's stumbling-block was developed in two works by the former First Minister, Henry McLeish, who after leaving office wrote *Global Scots: Making it in the Modern World* (2006) and *Wherever the Saltire Flies*, with Nationalist MSP Kenny McAskill (also 2006). In their interviews with expatriate Scots and those of Scots ancestry, a tentative accommodation was reached with the international stereotype of Scottishness. Particularly in *Wherever the Saltire Flies*, there was a sense that, if the Caledonian Club of Boulder, Colorado wanted to wear kilts, drink whisky, toss cabers, play bagpipes and eat haggis then indigenous Scots had little or no right to consider their behaviour *ersatz*. This approach towards the marketing of Scottishness reached a kind of culmination in 2009's Homecoming event. Targeting expat, 'diaspora' and 'affinity' Scots, the year-long programme had five principal themes: Ancestry (with special reference to genealogy and by extension, clan tartan); Enlightenment; Golf; Whisky; and, to coincide with the 250th anniversary of his birth, Robert Burns. Although the wheel may have come nearly full circle, with Scots apparently revelling in the very stereotypes that had seemed claustrophobic seven years ago, the significant change from Scott to Burns is central. Burns is (or was) vital, democratic, musical, sexual and inspired, while Scott was (or is) moribund, aristocratic, theatrical, romantic and bookish. It is not a comparison without some truth. I can only blush at Scott's jingoistic parody of the Burns song that was used to open the Scottish Parliament, 'A Man's A Man For A' That'.

> For a' that, an a' that,
> Guns, guillotines, and a' that,
> The Fleur-de-lis, that lost her right,
> Is Queen again for a' that!

We'll twine her in a friendly knot
With England's Rose and a' that ;
The Shamrock shall not be forgot,
For Wellington made braw that.
The Thistle, though her leaf be rude,
Yet faith we'll no misca' that,
She shelter'd in her solitude
The Fleur-de-lis, for a' that.

The culmination of the entire programme was an event called 'The Gathering', billed as 'a celebration of the culture and history of Scotland. Thousands of people from around the globe will come together for the greatest international clan and family gathering the world has ever seen'. Around 140 clans, led by their pipe bands, would parade from the Palace of Holyroodhouse to Edinburgh Castle, where a national pageant would be staged. 'Be a Part of History!' proclaims the advert.

What is unusual is that in all the accompanying bumf and flannel, there is no mention of the previous clan gathering: that master-minded by Sir Walter Scott for the visit of George IV in 1822. When discussing their 2002 'rebranding', VisitScotland pointed the finger directly at Scott. The traditional image was a 'touch bogus', having been 'stamped' on Scotland by him, with the so-called 'King's Jaunt' the crowning vulgarity. When Mrs Sarah Green was satirising the Scotch Novel-obsessed Alice, it is important to bear in mind that she was writing in the immediate aftermath of Scott's incredibly successful public intervention on behalf of the reigning monarch. Questions of Scottish dress, customs, manners, culture and history had become the political issues of the day. Alice's quixotry was not simple a naive confusion between art and life, since life itself had been imitating art. The Waverley Novels continued until 1832, but in some senses their climax was in the 'novel made reality' of the King's visit. But the state visit was not Scott's only such extra-literary interven-tion: there was also the house that the Waverley Novels built.

'Conundrum Castle'

In 1810, flush with the success of *The Lady of the Lake*, Scott started to consider his long-term options. Although the house he was eventually to create was described by H V Morton as 'the rough material of the romantic novel', its genesis was linked to the financial and critical triumph of the poetry. That vein, unbeknownst to the Scott of 1811, was about to run dry. Scott decided to purchase a property on the banks of the Tweed, belonging to the Revd Dr Douglas of Galashiels. To James Ballantyne and Joanna Baillie he referred to the building as a 'cottage', to Morritt a 'bower' and to Byron as 'a gardener's hut', albeit by the 'adjacent ruins of Melrose'. This modesty and caution soon evaporated. The property was acquired for 4,000 guineas and in the first month Scott had spent £1,000 on building work and planting. Within four years, he had acquired five times as much land, by buying up the neighbouring farms of Kaeside and Cauldshiels. By the time of his bankruptcy, his estate was ten times the original size and incorporated the Rhymer's Glen where True Thomas had slipped out of this dimension. Three different architects – William Stark from 1811 to 1812, William Atkinson from 1816 to 1817 and Edward Blore from 1822 to 1824 – worked on the building. It became a destination for literary tourists, the lushly forested seat of a knight of the realm, and a work of art equivalent to and intertwined with his novels. Scott's metamorphosis of the site was nothing short of spectacular: Lockhart remembered the place at first having 'one strip of firs', 'a tract of undulated ground behind, all in a neglected state', a 'small and poor' house with a kailyard and a 'staring barn' and a 'filthy pond covered with ducks and duckweeds'. When William Howitt visited after Scott's death, it was 'a fairy castle', to Andrew Lang, 'hallowed ground'.

The building was, of course, Abbotsford. But legally and technically, Scott never bought 'Abbotsford'. Almost his first action on the site was to rechristen it, based on the moderately spurious premise that the land had once belonged to the Abbey of Melrose, and the Tweed could (with caution) be forded there. The property that Scott bought was called 'Clarty Hole' – 'Dirty Hollow'.

An air of unreality hangs over Abbotsford. Scott often referred to it by other names – it was 'a Flibbertigibbet of a home', 'a kind of Conundrum Castle to be sure', 'a romance in stone and lime'. He compared it to the spun-sugar castles created by Lord Napier and called it a 'museum for living in'. His unpublished guidebook to Abbotsford was entitled *Reliquiae Trotcosienses*, or 'The Relics of Trotcosey' and written under the pseudonym of Jonathan Oldbuck, the eponymous antiquary of his third novel (in which Oldbuck's estate, Monkbarns, was once the property of the Abbots of Trotcosey). 'Flibbertigibbet' is also a character – a vaguely magical vagabond – in his novel, *Kenilworth*. In Scott's lifetime, and more so after his death, Abbotsford became something more than a house. It was a shrine and a source, a thing created by literature in which literature was created. It was a 3D Waverley Novel.

In the Preface to the Magnum Opus edition, Scott actively encouraged a subtle kind of identification between Abbotsford and the Waverley Novels. Although he admits that *Waverley* had been started beforehand, during the move to Abbotsford the manuscript, languishing in an old writing desk, was moved into a lumber garret. 'Thus, though I sometimes, among other literary avocations, turned my thoughts to the continuation of the romance which I had commenced, yet, as I could not find what I had already written, after searching such repositories as were within my reach, and was too indolent to attempt to write it anew from memory, I as often laid aside all thoughts of that nature.' Abbotsford is already a place where things can be hidden, and rediscovered. Looking for fishing tackle for a guest, Scott remembers that the old writing desk was sometimes used to store 'lines and flies' and 'with some difficulty' he retrieves the piece of furniture, and discovers the manuscript as well. The book, in a sense, gestates in Abbotsford. It bides time. The

Preface moves swiftly on to a discussion of Scott's reasons for anonymity, now foregrounded with the idea that the hidden book required a hidden author. The 'Author of Waverley' could be the public disguise and the 'Laird of Abbotsford' could be the public persona. In one of those telling moments where a joke elides with an aspiration, Scott was already half-seriously referring to himself as 'the Laird of Abbotsford' a decade before his regal appointment. *Waverley* ends with the reimagination of old Jacobite castles tended by new Hanoverian hands, for new Hano-Jacobital or Jaco-Hanoverian dynasties, where the past can be acknowledged only in so far as it can be transcended by wealth, security, success and loyalty, and kept sentimentally flickering without ever catching fire.

From the outset, Scott conceived of Abbotsford as an antiquarian project. At Ashestiel he had purchased 'a small lot of ancient armour and other curiosities (Rob Roy's gun among other things) – I defy anyone to say that there is a single article among two hundred which can be of use to a human being, excepting indeed a snuff box, and that is useless to me as I never take snuff'. When clearing the grounds of Clarty Hole, he made much of a 'brazen utensil' he discovered, transforming again an 'ill made coffee pot' into a 'sacrificial Vessel'. In the *Reliquiae* he would send up this propensity, describing a bidding war for some 'gabions', or curiosities: 'it chanced at a sale of household goods by auction, that the present proprietor and a gentleman of rank in the neighbourhood were contending with emulation for possession of what they well knew was, especially from its size, a gabion of great merit . . . when an old woman, after a long look at the countenance first of one bidder then at the other, at length ejaculated with a sigh at the extremity of the contention, "Heigh Sirs! The foundery wark must be sair up in Edinburgh to see the great folk bidding that gate about a kail pot".' A tellingly similar kind of anecdote appears in James Hogg's *Familiar Anecdotes of Sir Walter Scott*.

> Besides having been mentioned by Satchells, the most fabulous historian that ever wrote, there was a remaining tradition in the country that there was a font-stone of blue marble, out of

which the ancient heirs of Buccleuch were baptized, covered up among the ruins of an old church. Mr Scott was curious to see if we could discover it, but on going among the ruins where the altar was known to have been, we found the rubbish at that spot dug out to the foundation, we knew not by whom, but it was manifest that the font had either been taken away, or that there was none there. I never heard since that it had ever been discovered by any one. As there appeared, however, to have been a sort of recess in the eastern gable, we fell a turning over some loose stones, to see if the baptismal font was not there, when we came to one-half of a small pot encrusted thick with rust. Mr Scott's eyes brightened and he swore it was part of an ancient consecrated helmet. Laidlaw, however, fell a picking and scratching with great patience until at last he came to a layer of pitch inside, and then, with a malicious sneer, he said 'The truth is, Mr Scott, it's nouther mair nor less than an auld tar-pot, that some of the farmers hae been buisting their sheep out o' i' the kirk lang syne.' Sir Walter's shaggy eye-brows dipped deep over his eyes, and, suppressing a smile, he turned and strode away as fast as he could, saying, that 'we had just rode all the way to see that there was nothing to *be* seen'.

The origin of all these tales might well be Scott's own, from *The Antiquary*, which features a scene where Oldbuck's disquisition on the vexatious issue of Pictish versus Roman origins of a local ditch ends with the local tramp interrupting with, 'I mind the biggin' o' it' ('I remember when it was built'). In each of these stories, Scott is cast, or self-cast, or his substitute is self-parodied as Don Quixote; fantastically imposing his hopes and dreams onto an intransigent and mundane reality. With Abbotsford, Scott decided to transform his humble windmill into an indisputable giant. He would force and finance and fabricate reality into a more literary mode.

Abbotsford begins outside itself. Around the building, Scott planted acres of trees. 'My oaks will outlast my laurels', he wrote, 'and I pride myself more on my composition for manure than on any composition whatsoever to which I was ever accessory.' The 'strip of firs' turned into an arbour, then a range, then a copse, then a forest of oak, elm and beech. Even today, driving to Abbotsford, you pass through an anomalous, deciduous sprinkle of trees – maybe not ones his own stubby fingers pushed into the soil, but the offspring of ones he cultivated, perhaps. They are unlike the fast-growing and persistent conifers in suburban gardens, designed to screen out the outside and hide the occupants: they are a tangle of glimpses and fretwork of keek-holes. You see bits of Abbotsford before it can be seen entire.

Antiquities were built into Abbotsford like the authenticating footnotes of a novel. The door to the old Tolbooth prison in Edinburgh, and its keys, were removed from its demolition to be incorporated into Abbotsford. As Frances Shelley observed, this was the key which 'had turned the lock on Effie Deans', one of the principal characters of *The Heart of Midlothian*. Scott had Montrose's sword (from *A Legend of Montrose*), a lock of Bonnie Prince Charlie's hair (from *Waverley*), pistols belonging to Covenanters and thumbscrews used upon them (from *Old Mortality*), a portrait of Claverhouse (ditto), Helen MacGregor's brooch (from *Rob Roy*), Cromwell's shirt of mail (from *Woodstock*), Napoleon's pocketbooks (from *The Life of Napoleon*), a crucifix and fragment of dress once belonging to Mary, Queen of Scots (from *The Abbot*), a skull from Waterloo (from *Peter's Letters to his Kinsfolk*), a hunting-bottle of James V's (from *The Lady of the Lake*) and battlefield relics from Flodden (from *Marmion*). His old whimsy of a chessboard constructed from splinters from significant historical sites was becoming a double reality: Abbotsford contained things from the Waverley Novels and the Waverley Novels contained things from Abbotsford. Both were monstrances for history.

The succession of architects reflects Scott's changing desires for Abbotsford, as it progressed from cottage to castellated and crenellated fantasia. ('It will do,' he once said, 'till the Muse and the Masons have made me a better.') Scott disliked the 'modern Gothic' of Atkinson and gave strict orders to Blore to 'Scottify' the place – but whether he meant 'make it Scottish' or 'make it more like Scott' is delightfully ambiguous. The exterior flirted with Border keeps and crow's-step gables, with superfluous defences nodding to a state of war on another continent. It was, as James Macaulay wrote, 'the unsung prototype of Scots-Baronial architecture'. The interior was even more bizarre. Although it is sometimes described as a jigsaw, that image implies a coherent whole carefully unpicked into fiddly, inter-connected fragments. Abbotsford was more like a collage of *objets trouvées*, a Surrealist cut-up and stuck-together artefact. There was no 'picture on the box' that Abbotsford aspired to represent: it was all about effect.

Scott ransacked Scotland's architectural heritage to make Abbotsford. The ceiling of Rosslyn Chapel is copied onto that of Abbotsford's library; the ablutionary piscina from Melrose Abbey is rejigged as a fireplace. John Knox's pulpit, cut in two, is transformed into a pair of window chiffoniers. Oak panelling was modelled on that of the Auld Kirk in Dunfermline; Linlithgow Palace's gateway provides the template for Abbotsford's porch. Mary, Queen of Scots' bedsteads become decorative devices. The main dining table is carved out of oaks from the medieval Drumlanrig Estate, but in the French-Grecian fashion. Time seems to jump tracks between rooms, and even across pieces of furniture – from the mantelpiece that is crowned by skulls that look identical but bookmark Bannockburn and Waterloo, to the jolt from his antique museum to the chinoiserie of the drawing room.

But it was also futuristic, as the tenses collapse again. Abbotsford is a DVD of old mutoscope reels, an iPod full of the hiss, whirr and scratch of needles being laid on old vinyl. Scott had new-fangled gas-lamps instead of candles, so that the imitation past might be seen in the glow of cutting-edge technology. Stained glass is illuminated from inside, rather than outside. In his *Journal*, he writes that 'rain forced me into the Antiquarian Musaeum, lounged there till a meeting of the Oil Gas Committee' and was proud that he had 'all the comforts of a commodious habitation'. This included toilets as well as toile designs. The people of Galashiels would be called pailmerks for a while to come but the family at Abbotsford were so flush with success, they could almost flush.

One of Scott's most flamboyant friends was the playwright and actor Daniel Terry. His reputation now barely warrants a footnote in the history of drama, but in his time he was just a rung below Henry Siddons, whose company he was in, and Siddons's uncle, John Kemble, whom he imitated in reading originals rather than adaptations of the Elizabethan greats. He and Scott met in 1809, and every subsequent encounter between them indicates that their friendship was bizarrely unequal. Scott liked, admired and sought the help of Terry: Terry adored Scott, to the point where, after an accident that had injured his leg, Terry seemed pleased he could now impersonate Scott the better. Terry doted on his friend so much he pioneered adaptations of his work for the stage, a process which Scott referred to as 'Terryfication'. Even the illiterate could experience Scott, and so much the better if the literate and wealthy might pay for it twice. Terry was the stage-dresser for Abbotsford. He brought Stark on board as initial architect, then found Atkinson, then assisted in the final positioning of possessions as props, bric-a-brac as artefacts and anything else as -iana.

Abbotsford was a theatre with no stage and a setting with no story. Each of Scott's novels had tried to make the movement of history inevitable and strived to show that the survivors of their historical turmoils, such as Edward Waverley, thrived on the best parts of the vanquished while embracing the possibilities of being modern. Perhaps the future apathy towards Scott lies in this motion: his novels content themselves to the status quo. Abbotsford was the end of history, to which history had aspired. It presented itself as the story of things being, at long last, over. Napoleon was imprisoned, the radicals were all too busy working, and the Americans were behaving themselves after the ugliness beforehand. The swords and muskets and implements of torture could all stay on the walls, the balistraria and crenellations would offer only picturesque glimpses of a landscape ever growing, always becoming more delightful and enlightened, where no trees would ever be felled to create men-o'-war.

Haunted House

Within less than a generation, Abbotsford was as despised as it had been adored. It was a double folly: an architectural *scherzo* and a piece of reckless stupidity. The historian Thomas Macaulay was succinct about the latter: Abbotsford was typified by 'profuse and ostentatious expense, extravagant waste and rapacious speculation'. For the actor William Macready it was nothing less than the 'the most disagreeable exhibition I have almost ever seen, itself the suicidal instrument of fate, and a monument of his vanity and indiscretion'. As regards the former, the art critic John Ruskin wrote, with wonderful disdain, that Scott 'has some confused love of Gothic architecture, because it was dark, picturesque, old and like nature; but he could not tell the worst from the best and built for himself perhaps the most incongruous and ugly pile that gentlemanly modernism ever designed'.

Abbotsford was Scott's tragic flaw, and its style was Scott's aesthetic failing. 'A plaything' was Nathaniel Hawthorne's dismissive response, and one which applied to the novels as much as the mansion. 'Little better than an oddity and a joke,' wrote Fontane, 'there has been no flash of inspiration sufficiently strong to weld the hostile elements into a unity.' On Scott's death it was decided that the house should remain, as much as possible, as it had been at the moment of his passing. Little wonder that subsequent visitors found it more eerie than quirky, more mausoleum than museum. The difference between accounts of stays at Abbotsford before his death, and visits to it afterwards, is shivering. There is a palpable sense of loss. The soul of the building is gone.

Scott even shattered into his own shrine. His trousers, his walking stick, locks of his infant hair, his quills and his slippers were displayed alongside the historical mementoes and significant trinkets, as if he had been atomised into a series of artefacts. It was Victor Frankenstein's moment of triumph in reverse, a jumble of empty clothes and lifeless implements, held together by haar rather than animated by lightning.

In his biography, Lockhart often used Scott's self-encouraged image of the 'Wizard of the North', no more so than when he had to exculpate his father-in-law from behaviour that might be deemed rash, greedy or feckless: 'He waved the wand of obliterating magic over all besides; and persisted so long, that (like the sorcerer he celebrates) he became the dupe of his own delusions' is just one example. The enchanted palace without the enchanter gave rise to another variation on this theme, as later tourists struggled to make sense of the genius's kitsch castle. Scott was now a different form of sorcerer. Fontane realised that 'while the writer was himself still alive for whom these things had real significance', then the tentative, strenuous suspension was still possible. 'The stones are stone again, and even one who is familiar with Scottish history and song walks through these rooms as though they were a waxwork show.' 'As the fabric of this glorious estate had risen as by the spell of a necro-mancer, so it fell,' wrote William Howitt in 1847. Basil Hall, a close friend in Scott's later years, described how 'at the touch of this bold necromancer, sprung up living forms of the most fascinating grace. The whole public opened eyes of wonder, and in breathless amaze-ment and delight saw this active and unweariable agent call round him, from the brooks and mountains of his native land, troop after troop of kings, queens, warriors, women of regal forms and more regal spirits; visions of purity and loveliness; and lowly creatures of no less glorious virtue.' Scott had 'kept the enraptured public in a trance'. The glamour of both magic and celebrity was gone, and the wizard revealed as a fairground hoodwinker, an avaricious hypnotist, a maleficent meddler who rummaged in tombs.

The connections between Scott and necromancy still resonate. Scott, it was said, had once brought the past to life, in all its colour, vivacity and humanity. Or had he actually just conjured up phan-toms, insubstantial and nebulous and persistent? Or was it worse – a zombie history, with rotting corpses holding rusted reins but still

tugging the bit in the mouth of the knackers' yard-bound, somnolent Scottish public? Was the past ghostly and unsatisfied, treading
over the old boards to achieve resolution; or ghastly, clawing its way
out of a grave towards a world that had happily buried it? Was it
voodoo or spiritualist, undead or unshriven?

Basil Hall, in his hotch-potch memoir, *Patchwork*, had a vision of
Abbotsford in decay, becoming a ruin like the remains of Melrose
and Dryburgh Abbey, all linked together in crumbling glory by the
Tweed. Just as ruins across the country were being improved to capi-
talise on their picturesque attributes, and the Scott Monument was
succumbing to the Industrial Revolution's accelerated ageing, Hall
was hinting at another building's true destiny being not in completion or preservation but in deterioration. Ruskin's criticisms of
Abbotsford stress its 'faked' quality – he took particular exception to
the wood-grained plaster in the library, a modern technique
designed to imitate carpentry without the expense or craftsmanship.
Likewise, the way in which elements lost their original significance –
such as the fireplace purloined from a priestly function – seemed
indicative of the unreality of Abbotsford. Nothing was what it
seemed; nothing did what it should. 'Scott's romance and antiquarianism, his knighthood and his monkery, are all false – and he knows
them to be false,' he railed. The building became, in Freud's evoca-
tive word, *unheimlich* – literally un-homely, metaphorically,
un-canny or eldritch. Without the laird's animating presence, the
willing suspension of disbelief in Abbotsford faltered. Hall's fantasy
of Abbotsford in ruins is almost a wish for sincerity, for it to reflect
that loss; and it tallies neatly with Ruskin's detestation of the
fossilised carnival of the design. In a way, Scott might have agreed
with both men. Abbotsford was, he once wrote, 'one of my air
castles which I am reducing to solid stone and mortar'.

Ghosts

I am sitting in a private sitting room in Abbotsford as tourists mill through the public suites looking for the new cafeteria. Above the fireplace is the worst portrait of Scott I have ever seen. It looks Edwardian, and might have been painted by one of the animators that did 'Silly Symphonies' cartoons. His eyes are too goo-ish-ly large, his hair tousled and his lips are a candyfloss pink. In a grotesque way, he looks cute. This room is the real sanctum sanctorum of Abbotsford, despite the more obvious frisson of Scott's writing room, because this is where the last vestiges of Abbotsford as a home lurk.

On 5 May 2004, Dame Jean Maxwell-Scott died at the age of eighty. She was Scott's last direct descendant. Although Scott conceived of Abbotsford as an estate for future generations, his hopes were blasted. In his lifetime, his beloved grandson Johnny died. His son, Walter Jnr, died without heir in 1847, and the baronetcy became extinct. Abbotsford was inherited by Scott's granddaughter, the daughter of Sophia Scott and John Lockhart, who, on her marriage to Robert Hope, an English MP and barrister, insisted that they take the name 'Hope-Scott' to continue a link between the Scotts and Abbotsford. Their daughter, Monica, married Joseph Constable-Maxwell, the third son of the tenth Baronet Haggerston, and their name changed to Maxwell-Scott. Joseph and Monica's eldest son, Major-General Walter Joseph Constable Maxwell-Scott was made a baronet in his own right, and that baronetcy too became extinct on his death in 1954. Tragedy marked this family as well – the mother of Jean and her elder sister Patricia died when Jean was two years old. Patricia inherited Abbotsford in 1954, and on her death in 1998 stipulated that Jean should inherit, on the condition she take the name 'Scott of

Abbotsford' – a name which Patricia had adopted by deed poll, after marrying Sir Christian Boulton. Although Patricia married, she had no children. Jean never married.

I remember the 'Abbotsford Ladies' from my childhood; two tweed-clad presences escaped from the pages of an Agatha Christie novel, rather than a Walter Scott romance. The private sitting room still has pictures of them from their Edwardian heyday, looking rather more glam than I recollected. The pictures that are *not* of Scott are something of a rarity here: in oils, charcoals, silhouette, marble, etchings, watercolours, the same face is replicated in multiple variations. It must have been an ominously oppressive upbringing. No wonder keeping the name alive, when everything else was gone, seemed so imperative. Although tourists had been visiting Abbotsford since Scott's death, by the mid-twentieth century it had to become a tourist attraction. In melancholy little out-of-date ways they honoured their ancestry: being president of the Dandie Dinmont Breeders' Club, or part owning a horse called 'Sir Wattie' that won a silver medal at the Seoul Olympics. Just after the bicentenary of Scott's death, Abbotsford was attracting 86,000 visitors a year: by the time of Jean Maxwell-Scott's death, the figure had fallen to less than 31,000. The outbreak of foot-and-mouth disease in 2001 and the terrorist atrocity at the World Trade Center were given as explanations, when the real cause was staring everyone in the face. Nobody cares much about Scott.

The house is now managed by a Trust, whose members had kindly agreed to meet me and discuss the plans for Abbotsford's restoration. As I sit waiting for the meeting, a nag in my brain resolves itself. What is different about Abbotsford on this gloomy day compared to all the other times I have visited? No peacocks. There were usually peacocks, and presumably peahens. I remember as a child watching them, and waiting to see the at-any-minute-to-be-revealed tail display. Latterly, it was the eerie, desiccated drag of their unproud feathers and the reptilian clack of their claws on the gravel that I associated with arriving here. Aren't peacocks supposed to be bad luck? I think I remember my grandfather telling me that. The flickering memory sparks the thought of my father, telling me never to scare a peacock, because if they flew away they never returned and cursed the building. A bird that is ill-omened in presence and absence. Bad luck, Abbotsford.

The Trust, which is neither superstitious nor bound by ancient ties of superannuated loyalty, has just successfully completed the first stage of a Heritage Lottery Fund application. It will take in the region of £10 million to complete the project. The roof is being repaired – it was, as Hall predicted, becoming ruinous – and a new Visitor Centre will attempt to put Scott in context. Most of the plug-sockets still take circular pins, which haven't been manufactured for a good thirty years. There is an admirable ambition to strip away the accreted Victoriana from Abbotsford: rehanging the paintings as they were in Scott's lifetime; resetting the dining room; un-furbishing two centuries worth of additional clutter. But we should not mistake this for returning the building to its original, authentic form. It is another fiction, a latest fiction, grafted on to the inherently fictional place. For example, should the death mask of Scott, in its octagonal shrine off his study, be removed? It *definitely* wasn't there in his lifetime. Likewise, there are statues of characters, including the old mendicant Edie Ochietree, in the grounds. Not even the Great Unknown actually lived amongst stookies of his own creations: they are later additions to the 'Abbotsford Experience' and, in a real sense, intrinsic to its atmosphere.

After the meeting, I paced around the public rooms for old times' sake. I must have been younger than ten when we first came here – my youngest brother can't have been born, and I vividly remember my brother and I thrilling at the fact that two coats of arms, with our Christian names, Stuart and Douglas, adorned the east exit of the entrance hall. It was as if Scott had known that we would be here. There is a smell, like the unstirred dust of old books but smothered with furniture polish. The light is strained and intermittent. It feels like a crypt, with so many busts of the dead, skulls (or, weirdly, copies of skulls) of animals and people. There is even a picture of the severed head of Mary, Queen of Scots. The library is all caged up: in Scott's lifetime, I imagine the desk would be piled high with the books he was consulting or cribbing. It is the sort of place that ought to have cobwebs, but there are no cobwebs. Over his desk, the lamp hangs low, and unlit.

I always forget about the weapons room. Every inch of the red walls is encrusted with swords, knives, daggers, guns, muskets, pistols, pikes, axes, instruments of torture – and more exotic items, like Javanese kris blades. Signs say 'Do Not Touch', as if anyone in their right mind would stroke this bristle of savagery. Scott also kept a preserved calf's heart, stuck with pins, a local fetish used in witch-craft. It looks like something out of a Clive Barker horror novel. If any contemporary author had amassed such an arsenal in their home, you would phone the Serious Crimes Unit.

His trousers seem pathetically small and slightly moth-gnawn. Having spent years looking at different portraits of Scott, with his high forehead, sandy hair, bushy eyebrows, quick eyes and usually ruddy cheeks, his death mask strikes me as looking not like him at all. His jowls sag, the eyelids have locked. It looks like a man in pain.

Leaving Abbotsford, I notice on the East Wall of the walled garden that there is yet another bust of Scott, carved in stone, on one side of the gate. It must be of later date as well. This image of Scott, eyes vaguely hooded, mouth downturned, catches my attention because I have seen a near-identical bust, on the door to the old, now closed, Bonnington School in Edinburgh. I pass it on my way to work, and wonder each time why it is there, and who the other figure is. By a piece of complete serendipity, I see the same carved face again that evening. I'd decided to stay the night at my parents' house, and walking round the village I grew up in, spied another version, on the house of my old chemistry teacher. Were they mass-made? Was there once a thriving trade in ornamental Walters? What do they mean? Romantic nationalism or British loyalty? Patriotism or parochialism? They could be a flaunt of cultural capital, displaying the owner's commitment to the idea of literature, if not the business of reading it; conversely, they could be the sign of genuine enthusiasm, like the stickers on cars proclaiming allegiance to a football team.

Around the back of the building, generators are whirring and there's a bustle of bodies. There's also artificial snow on the ground. I'd been warned that a German film crew were using Abbotsford as a location, and told not to discuss it. Although I did wonder what film it might be. Running through the titles of various Gothic novels, I concluded that it must be – given the injunction not to speak of it – a porn movie. And then realised that it was possible that, given Scott's dynasty and lack of dynasty, it might be the only sex to have ever happened in that place.

I remember once hearing an old man interviewed on local radio. He lived in Lauder, just up the road, and had made a museum of sorts. It displayed old agricultural implements, stoneware, glass bottles – at least that is what I presumed, as the snippet gave only a sketchy idea about the museum's contents, concentrating instead on the old man's desire that Lauder should have something for tourists. At the end of the item, the interviewer mentioned that the man had no family to take on the museum after his death and wondered what would happen to it. It might as well all go in a skip, he said, since that's where most of it came from in the first place. The museum: a transient ordering of detritus. An interim salvage. Abbotsford is more than that, or at least, a less temporary version of it.

What would be the best way to describe Abbotsford to someone who has never seen it? I thought about it late into the night. Eventually, I decided it was like the photographs of the Cottingley Fairies. It's obviously fictional, and yet it incarnates and engenders a profound desire to believe. It is a kind of accident that required immense effort. The two girls who took the photographs, Elsie Wright and Frances Griffiths, always maintained that although they had faked the pictures, they also really had seen fairies. The photographs were the only way to convince the grown-ups of that reality. Abbotsford is like that: a forged proof to a supernatural belief.

An American in Abbotsford

A young, bankrupt Manhattanite, with a widow's peak leading to tight curls and an impressive record of publication already to his name, arrived at Abbotsford in 1817. His name was Washington Irving, but he might have been better known in the America of the time as Launcelot Langstaff, William Wizard, Diedrich Knickerbocker or Jonathan Oldstyle. A man with such a propensity for pseudonyms was bound to make friends with Scott: surprisingly, they never discussed the matter. Irving had already caused a sensation with his literary magazine, *Salmagundi*, which he co-wrote with James Kirke Paulding (of *The Lay of the Scottish Fiddle* fame) and which gave the name 'Gotham' to New York and eventually Batman. His first major work, *A History of New-York from the Beginning of the World to the End of the Dutch Dynasty, by Diedrich Knickerbocker* (1809), was a satirical local history and contemporary exposé made even more piquant by the marketing campaign he ran: Irving placed missing persons adverts in the New York newspapers imploring information about the vanished Knickerbocker, concluding with one from an irate hotel owner who insisted that if Knickerbocker did not turn up and pay his bills, he would publish the manuscript left in his room.

Irving left for Europe in 1815, and failed to save the family business, hard hit by the war of 1812. He stayed for another seventeen years, happily out of the family business. He wrote prolifically from the minute he arrived, creating classics like 'The Legend of Sleepy Hollow', 'Rip van Winkle' and 'Philip of Pokanoket'. These were collected together, along with his witty travelogue about being an American in the Old Country, as *The Sketch-Book of Geoffrey Crayon, Esq.*, in 1820. That *Esq.* is part of its delicious cheek – the esquire designation was already an accumulation covering varieties of

gentry, barristers, officers above a major in the forces, holders of
Oxbridge degrees in Britain and landowners. There was a lot of land
being owned in America, without the titles, trappings and etiquette.
In the *Sketch-Book*, Crayon (via Irving) visited sites like Stratford-
upon-Avon and Westminster Abbey, and searched for Falstaff's original Boar's Head Tavern and the London of Dr Johnson. In between
his picaresque amblings, he comments on the state of literature and
publishing generally, with specific reference to Anglo-American
relations. Although Irving went to Abbotsford while writing the
book, he did not include the visit in the finished version, or any
later editions. Only after Scott's death did he write an essay about
Abbotsford.

He guessed that Scott was the Author of *Waverley*, and Scott knew
that he knew and used every bit of legal legerdemain at his disposal
to evade and elude, to answer grammatically if not honestly, to stick
to letter and let the spirit escape. Irving recognised the elegance of
the game, and did not spoil it. His later essay on Abbotsford – an
Abbotsford, by this stage, unrecognisable if Irving were to return – is
still an exceptional first glimmering of Scott-land as a real and
tangible space, partly in the mind and partly on the map.

On arriving, Irving was welcomed and sent away immediately
with Scott's younger son, Charles, to see Melrose Abbey. 'You must
not think our neighbourhood is to be read in a morning, like a newspaper,' chides Scott. Given his working patterns, it is likely he
wanted to write, and did not want an American wag to catch the
Great Unknown unawares. With supreme generosity and selfish-
ness he dispatched Irving, already with the idea that books and
places were both forms of reading matter slyly implanted. At
Melrose, with Scott's spare heir, he met Scott's proxy guide, the old
sexton Johnny Bower. Bower was a precursor of the modern tour
guide. He pointed out the carvings and quoted appositely. He had,
according to Irving, 'gone beyond Scott in the minuteness of his
antiquarian research, for he had discovered the very tomb of the
wizard, the position of which had been left in doubt by the poet.
This he boasted to have ascertained by the position of the oriel
window, and the direction in which the moonbeams fell at night,

through the stained glass, casting the shadow to the red cross on the spot; as had all been specified in the poem. "I pointed this out the whole to the shirra," said he, "and he could na gainsay but it was varra clear." ' 'The fictions of Scott had become facts with honest Johnny Bower,' Irving realises. But this quixotic quaintness leads to broader satire: Bower has also discovered a way to defamiliarise the subject, to borrow a term from Russian literary theory. Bower asks Irving to look at the Abbey from between his own legs ('the "leddies", they were dainty on the matter, and contented themselves with looking from under their arm'.) This gave, Bower claimed, 'an entire different aspect to the ruin'. The climax is Bower's own technological resolution to the poem's aesthetic vagary. The 'sorely puzzled' Johnny, aware that the weather rarely allows for night-viewing the Abbey in ideal conditions, had found a way to imitate the imitation for the 'poetry-struck' visitor. He made 'a great double tallow candle, stuck upon the end of a pole, with which he could conduct the visitors about the ruins on dark nights, so much to their satisfaction that, at length, he began to think it preferable to the moon itself. "It does na light up a' the Abbey at aince, to be sure," he would say, "but then you can shift it about and show the auld ruin bit by bit, whiles the moon only shines on one side." '

Irving was a great foible-cataloguer and his version of Johnny Bower is part recollection and part affectionate caricature. In 1838, the antiquarian Thomas Dibdin wrote about his own 'Scott Tour' and described entering Melrose Abbey ('It would indeed require the keeping-down tint of "pale moonlight" to absorb all these vulgarities in a sort of poetical mist') but was taken aback to see 'the embodied spirit of the GREAT POET sitting upon the *identical spot* which it used to occupy' – only to realise it is Johnny Bower, the 'living genius of the place'; part Greyfriar's Bobby, part body double. Bower then sold him a postcard.

Irving's prose is so effortless and renders the reader so complicit in his knowing attitude that it's useful to scroll back and rephrase this anecdote. Once upon a time there was an author so influential and beloved that an old man chose to believe his words on the page over the evidence of his own eyes. He persuaded people to contort themselves in an undignified and ludicrous fashion like Scottish yogi to better appreciate his master's work, and even created a prosthetic, moveable moon to make the world reflect the text, rather than vice versa. For a smart young American, schooled in the belief that the Old World was the fountainhead of civilisation, this must have been the *ne plus ultra*.

Having survived the trial by parody, Irving was allowed into the inner sanctum. Scott took him on his own tours, where he 'saw a great part of the border country spread out before me, and could trace the scenes of those poems and romances which had, in a manner, bewitched the world'. Scott picked out each famous location, and, if we believe Irving, compared him to Pilgrim in *Pilgrim's Progress* at the Delectable Mountains – which would make Scott either the personification Hopeful who accompanies Pilgrim, or one of the shepherds on the hills who show the wonders of Immanuel's Land to the travellers. Given that Irving had already associated the melancholy of the border ballads with the 'lonely lives' of those who composed them, 'who were often mere shepherds', there seems to be an undercurrent of rivalling ironic allusion at work. But the trump card is Irving's: 'I gazed about me with mute surprise' – the usual, venerating attitude of the Romantic tourist – then 'I may almost say with disappointment. I beheld a mere succession of gray waving hills, line beyond line, as far as the eye could reach: monotonous in their aspect, and so destitute of trees that one could almost see a stout fly walking along their profile; and the far-famed Tweed appeared a naked stream, flowing between bare hills, without a tree or thicket on its banks.'

This was not, as Scott had said, a newspaper, with gossip and adverts and data: it was a novel. It took time to understand. Irving's reaction to the place he knew through books was a double take, twice: first the book supplanted the reality; then the reality was inadequate to the book. 'Such had been the magic web of poetry and romance thrown over the whole, that it had a greater charm for me than the richest scenery I beheld in England,' Irving wrote. Scotland was monotonous and destitute, Scott-land was magical and hidden. It was everywhere around you and nowhere to be found.

Scott helped Irving, with letters of recommendation to publishers and his personal enthusiasm imparted to friends and colleagues. Most of all, after the visit of the creator of Dietrich Knickerbocker, Scott invented Jedediah Cleishbotham as his *nom de guerre*. Irving must have been touched.

Yankee Doodles

Irving's response to Scott, in its ambivalence of awe and scepticism, might stand for the reaction of the entire United States of America. His comrade in periodical arms, Paulding, attempted another satire of Scott when Scott's fame as a novelist eclipsed the sensation of his poetry. *Köningsmarke, or Old Times in the New World*, was published in 1823, and although it began as an out-and-out parody of the Waverley Novels, it evolved into a romance in its own right: it is almost as if, halfway through *Don Quixote*, a real dragon turns up.

Köningsmarke is written in nine books, each being prefaced with a critical disquisition on the art of the novel, which themselves refer to the increasingly self-conscious essays on narrative aesthetics which prefaced the later Waverley Novels. 'We sat down,' Paulding writes, 'to write this history before we had any regular plan, or arranged the incidents . . . it is much better for an author to commence his work, without knowing how it is to end, than to hamper himself with a regular plot, a succession of prepared incidents, and a premeditated catastrophe. This would hold to be an error little less, than to tie the legs of a dancing master, to make him caper more gracefully.' This elegant avowal of dilettantism is actually more significant than it appears. Scott's plots are, perforce, static. The reader can wonder whether or not Edward Waverley will marry the right girl, but can have no doubt over the outcome of the Battle of Culloden. For the American author, there is not yet a 'premeditated catastrophe'. With this freewheeling form, Paulding cherry-picks scenes and character types to satirise. Köningsmarke's sojourn among the Indians replays Waverley in the Highlands (with the extra irony that many Highlanders were cleared off their lands to America); Christina Piper's journey to New York to plead for him is a variation on Jeannie Deans' travelling to London to beg for her sister's life in *The Heart of*

Midlothian. There are sweetly tongue-in-cheek chapter epigraphs –
Peter Piper is introduced with the 'old song', 'Peter Piper picked a peck
of pickled pepper' – and 'translations' of Indian war-songs ('To battle!
To battle! / Hurrah! To battle! / Let them not see us / Let them not
hear us / Let them not fear us / Till they shall feel us') reminiscent of
the Gaelic and Saxon interludes in Scott. Köningsmarke's dark secret
(a trope that links him to Staunton in *Heart of Midlothian* or even
Marmion) is a wonderfully bathetic revelation. He is, apparently,
addicted to pretending to be a literary character. Although the
narrator of the novel grumbles about the 'days of impiety and repub-
licanism', Paulding is sending up Scott's Toryism, as shown by his
sympathetic depiction of William Penn, the democrat founder of
Pennsylvania.

Paulding's exoskeleton of literary theory makes one other very
salient attack on Scott. 'Now, although it is in our power,' he says, 'by
a single flourish of the pen, to account for this singularity, we are too
well acquainted with the nature of the human mind, to deprive our
history at the very outset of the indescribable interest which arises
from the author's keeping to himself certain secrets, which, like
leading strings, as it were, conduct the reader to the end, in hope of
at length being fully rewarded by a disclosure, a hope which, it must
be confessed, he is sadly disappointed, seeing it is much easier to knit,
than unravel, a mystery.' In part, this is Paulding twitting Scott's
transparent anonymity. But more significantly, he is sceptical about
the almost coy artificial creation of suspense. The reader is, to an
extent, cheated by systematic occlusions of motive. This unease
about the 'plottiness' of plots – and how many of Scott's novels
depend on cabals, mutinies, intrigues, secret organisations and
conspiracies! – had a lasting effect: later on, it forms the kernel of a
dispute between Henry James and Robert Louis Stevenson over the
legacy of Scott.

Try as he might, Paulding can't help breaking into a gallop, and
all his ironies and critical caveats can't quite extinguish the thrills. In
the generation after Paulding and Irving, the simultaneous suspension of disbelief and anxiety of influence fissures. On one hand,
there are the Scott imitators, on the other, the Scott iconoclasts.

The first of the great imitators was James Fenimore Cooper. Especially in the *Leatherstocking Tales* – *The Pioneers* (1823), *The Last of the Mohicans* (1826), *The Prairie* (1827), *The Pathfinder* (1840) and *The Deerslayer* (1841) Cooper adopted and adapted the Scott form of the novel for indigenous use. Although they are based around historical events, geography tends to supplant history as the series explores the nature of the frontier (indeed, the chronology becomes slightly muddled and threadbare). More significantly, the 'noble savage', the protector of an outmoded form of chivalry which facilitates the future as much as it elegises the past, derives immediately from Scott's anthropological interests. Natty Bumppo, the woodsman, is a syncretic figure; American with Americans and Indian with Indians, a crosser of borders in the same mould as a Waverley hero switching sides, but fiercely protective of his status as the best of both worlds. American primitivism also typified Henry Wadsworth Longfellow's major work of 1855, *The Song of Hiawatha*. Although Longfellow cites Elias Lönnrot's poem *The Kalevala* – a synthesis of fragments of ancient Finnish poetry into one long, contemporary epic poem – as an influence, he could not read Finnish. Moreover, Lönnrot's work itself was inspired by the ballad-collecting of Scott and the ambitions of Macpherson: by making clear his own role in the construction of the poem and keeping careful transcriptions of the originals, Lönnrot avoided a repeat of the Ossian fiasco. Longfellow had, however, read Scott. The famous Hiawatha rhythm is a development from the 'light horseman stanza' of Scott. The repeated use of place-names and epithets, and the interlacing of the story with inset traditional lore, also put *The Song of Hiawatha* into the same genus of poems as *The Lay of the Last Minstrel*. The overall arc – how Hiawatha moves the tribe towards a more civilised state (as in his practice of exogamy) – again reiterates a Scott dynamic. It is curious to note that the most savage review of *The Song of Hiawatha*, in *The New York Times* (which awarded the poet merit for 'embalming pleasantly enough the monstrous traditions of an uninteresting, and, one may almost say, a justly exterminated race') explicitly linked the preternatural abilities of Hiawatha to those of 'Finn MacCool, that big stupid Celtic monarch'.

Fenimore Cooper and Longfellow enjoyed similarly grand sales, and their works soon spawned dramatic, operatic, satirical, cinematic and later cartoon versions. There is of course another important connection between Longfellow, Fenimore Cooper and Scott: nobody reads them any more either. In an 1836 review of Robert M Bird's *The Hawks of Hawk-Hollow*, Edgar Allan Poe plays a remarkable double-feint. He begins by supposing how he would have reviewed it had the title been *The Hawks of Hawk-Hollow; A Romance by the Author of* Waverley and concludes he would have enjoyed it for 'the sake of Auld Lang Syne, and for the sake of certain pleasantly mirthful, or pleasantly mournful recollections connected with *Ivanhoe*, with the *Antiquary*, with *Kenilworth*, and above all, with that most pure, perfect, and radiant gem of fictitious literature the *Bride of Lammermuir* [*sic*]. His review would have greeted with praise the Author of *Waverley*'s decision to write an American romance, and then consigned it to the second rank of his oeuvre. Bird must have been delighted that Poe seems to be saying he read *The Hawks of Hawk-Hollow* with more enthusiasm than he would have read a new book by Scott. How crushing, then, to find his final opinion is that Bird has no 'pretensions to *originality* of manner, or of style – for we insist upon the distinction – and very few to originality of matter. It is, in many respects, a bad imitation of Sir Walter Scott.'

The arch detester of Scott in the American tradition is Mark Twain. Aside from a penchant for pseudonyms and a fascination with technology (Twain, born Samuel Clemens, was the first writer to compose a novel on a typewriter), few writers have ever stressed their difference from another so assiduously. Twain symbolically discarded Scott when he named the derelict paddle-steamer in *Adventures of Huckleberry Finn* after him; he ostentatiously trounced Scott's aesthetics, politics and imagination when he wrote *A Connecticut Yankee at the Court of King Arthur*. Twain's past was dirty and stupid, not shimmering and noble. But the most extensive demolition came in *Life on the Mississippi* in 1883. It is worth quoting in full:

Then comes Sir Walter Scott with his enchantments, and by his single might checks this wave of progress, and even turns it back; sets the world in love with dreams and phantoms; with decayed and swinish forms of religion; with decayed and degraded systems of government; with the sillinesses and emptinesses, sham grandeurs, sham gauds, and sham chivalries of a brainless and worthless long-vanished society. He did measureless harm; more real and lasting harm, perhaps, than any other individual that ever wrote. Most of the world has now outlived good part of these harms, though by no means all of them; but in our South they flourish pretty forcefully still. Not so forcefully as half a generation ago, perhaps, but still forcefully. There, the genuine and wholesome civilization of the nineteenth century is curiously confused and commingled with the Walter Scott Middle-Age sham civilization; and so you have practical, common-sense, progressive ideas, and progressive works; mixed up with the duel, the inflated speech, and the jejune romanticism of an absurd past that is dead, and out of charity ought to be buried. But for the Sir Walter disease, the character of the Southerner – or Southron, according to Sir Walter's starchier way of phrasing it – would be wholly modern, in place of modern and medieval mixed, and the South would be fully a generation further advanced than it is. It was Sir Walter that made every gentleman in the South a Major or a Colonel, or a General or a Judge, before the war; and it was he, also, that made these gentlemen value these bogus decorations. For it was he that created rank and caste down there, and also reverence for rank and caste, and pride and pleasure in them. Enough is laid on slavery, without fathering upon it these creations and contributions of Sir Walter.

Sir Walter had so large a hand in making Southern character, as it existed before the war, that he is in great measure responsible for the war. It seems a little harsh toward a dead man to say that we never should have had any war but for Sir Walter; and yet something of a plausible argument might, perhaps, be made in support of that wild proposition. The Southerner of the American Revolution owned slaves; so did the Southerner of the Civil War: but the former resembles the latter as an Englishman resembles a Frenchman. The change of character can be traced rather more easily to Sir Walter's influence than to that of any other thing or person.

One may observe, by one or two signs, how deeply that influence penetrated, and how strongly it holds. If one take up a Northern or Southern literary periodical of forty or fifty years ago, he will find it filled with wordy, windy, flowery 'eloquence', romanticism, sentimentality – all imitated from Sir Walter, and sufficiently badly done, too – innocent travesties of his style and methods, in fact.

Too harsh? The relative number of deaths of Confederacy and Union commanders in the Civil War seems to bear out Twain's contention. The Southerners tended to lead from the front, on horseback. The Northern leaders stayed safely behind their heavy artillery. Chivalry led straight into the mouths of cannon. Twain's argument is not a reductio ad absurdum, but rather an inflation of criticisms that were already current. From the opening, when he raises the necromantic Scott again, through the attack on the 'sham' Scott – a severer version of Ruskin's already tetchy dismissal of the false and fake taste evident in Abbotsford – to Coleridge's and Byron's irritation at Scott's antiquated diction: all these attacks on Scott had been made before. Yet at the same time, the former slave and campaigner for abolition, Frederick Douglass, had his surname suggested by a friend who had been reading *The Lady of the Lake*.

In fact, the South found solace in Scott. The Waverley Novels, with only minor interpretative tweaking, proclaimed the 'Wrong but Romantic' myth: the Confederacy could align itself with the Jacobites and the Cavaliers as movements that were impossible rather than reactionary – that were, in a way, too noble for this world. It is this air that suffuses not only Allen Tate's Southern-agrarian novel, *The Fathers*, in 1938, but the most famous mythology of the South which appeared on the silver screen the following year: *Gone with the Wind*. Scarlett is the haughty Flora: Rhett is a vacillating Waverley who finally grows a backbone. The restoration of the family seat, even in defeat, is a triumph.

Sir Walter Scott, a year before his death, flanked by his beloved Shakespeare and his beloved deerhound, Maida. Portrait by Sir William Allan © National Portrait Gallery

TOP. The Scott Monument, the largest monument to a novelist on the planet. © Cornell University Library

ABOVE. Clarty Hole, Conundrum Castle, Abbotsford: Scott's home and 'romance in stone and lime'. © Abbotsford Trust

RIGHT. Sir Walter Scott's collection of weapons and instruments of torture, a testament to his thwarted ambition to be a soldier. © Abbotsford Trust

Napoleon adored the works of the ersatz Gaelic bard, Ossian. Note that these Highland heroes are surprisingly unbekilted. *The Apotheosis of the French Heroes who Died for their Country during the War For Freedom*, 1800–1802 (oil on canvas), Anne Louis Girodet de Roucy-Trioson (1767–1824). © Giraudon/The Bridgeman Art Library

Elizabeth Taylor as Rebecca and Robert Taylor as Ivanhoe in the 1952 MGM movie. Like William Thackeray and others, the producers thought the real story was the impossible love between the Jew and the Crusader. © Apic/Getty Images

Sir Walter Scott's son-in-law and biographer, John Gibson Lockhart – a critic so severe he was nicknamed 'The Scorpion' – and his wife, Charlotte Sophia Scott. Lockhart was painted in after Charlotte's death. The painting is by Robert Scott Lauder (after 1838). © National Galleries of Scotland

The Hawick Common Riding in the Borders, when the region reconnects to its Reiving heritage. © Rob Gray/digitalpix.net

A scene from *Aisling's Children*, the historical pageant that concluded the 2009 'Homecoming' celebrations. © Scotsman Publications

An idealised version of George IV – as Highlander, Jacobite heir and slender – by Sir David Wilkie. Wilkie removed most of the jewellery along with several pounds and the King's pink stockings. *George IV in Highland Dress*, 1830 (oil on canvas), Sir David Wilkie (1785–1841). © The Bridgeman Art Library

A less idealised version of George IV, when he was Prince Regent, by James Gillray (entitled 'A Voluptuary under the Horrors of Digestion') from 1792. Scott's 'fat friend' came to Scotland during a personal, domestic, national and international crisis.

Different versions of Scott: the comic, the Gothic and the sentimental.

There is, finally, one other Walter Scott that deserves to be mentioned – Walter E Scott, also known as Death Valley Scotty. He was a friend of Buffalo Bill, a railroad entrepreneur (the 'Scott Special' shaved nine hours off the Los Angeles–Chicago run, setting a new record) and the promoter of a number of fraudulent mining schemes. A play about him opened in 1906, and the subject was arrested immediately afterwards. A rogue, con man and publicity-seeker, he shared with his namesake an interest in building projects. 'Scotty's Castle' in Death Valley is neither a castle, nor did it belong to Scott. He constructed the two-storey Spanish villa for one of his dupes (after various shenanigans over who actually owned the land), and is buried overlooking it. The main door is constructed as a cylindrical tower with crenellations, completely out of keeping with the ranch style of the rest of the building. It is a picture book version of a castle, a piece of made-up history brought to life. The original Walter Scott, that friend of poachers, reivers and vagabonds, would probably have been proud.

Where Did It All Go Wrong?

The traditional view among critics is that Scott's best work is not the entirety of the Waverley Novels. It is a pleasant irony that the term adopted by twentieth-century academics for the quintessential Scott is a resurrection of an old term – the Scotch Novels. Scott, they argue, increasingly wrote for money rather than through inspiration, and it is on the handful of novels with Scottish themes and Scottish settings that his worth as a novelist rests. It's still a flexible category, but broadly speaking the 'quality Scott' runs from *Waverley* in 1814 to *The Bride of Lammermoor* in 1819, with *Redgauntlet* in 1824 and the *Chronicles of the Canongate* in 1827 seen as a late return to form. Within that time frame, few make grand claims for *The Black Dwarf* and the only person I have heard of promoting the excellence of *A Legend of Montrose* was the novelist Robin Jenkins. This distillation down to Scott's 'real' novels is not wholly a nationalist whim: the two novels dealing with the Reformation, *The Monastery* and *The Abbot* are usually excluded (indeed, Scott only wrote *The Abbot* because *The Monastery* was such a disaster), nor does it include his Shetland romance, *The Pirate*, nor his odd tragi-comedy of manners, *St Ronan's Well*. *The Fair Maid of Perth* has some advocates, and his final completed novel, *Castle Dangerous*, very few. The core canon of Scott – a view promoted by writers as different as Virginia Woolf and the Marxist critic Georg Lukács – comprises *Waverley, The Tale of Old Mortality, Rob Roy, The Heart of Midlothian* and *The Bride of Lammermoor*, with honourable mentions to *Guy Mannering* and *The Antiquary*. It is a neat sweep from the Protestant Covenanters in 1679 in *Old Mortality* (which ends with the Glorious Revolution and the removal of the Catholic Stuarts) to the 1707 *Bride of Lammermoor* (with Jacobite agitation, Whiggish cabals and the path to parliamentary union in the background), through the first Jacobite uprising in

Rob Roy to the 1736 Porteous Riots under the absentee George II in *The Heart of Midlothian*, concluding with the first novel and the end of the Jacobite adventure in *Waverley*. *Redgauntlet*, set during a fictitious third Jacobite uprising, deals with the same thematic concerns: who should govern Scotland and how should Scotland be governed? What is the relationship between religion, politics and authority? What is loyalty?

The Bride of Lammermoor is a useful biographical hiatus. It was the first novel for which Scott 'found it necessary to employ the hand of another'. John Ballantyne and William Laidlaw acted as amanuenses during the period when Scott's 'apoplexy' (his own term) had incapacitated him. Lockhart says that he 'lost a great deal of flesh . . . his countenance was meagre, haggard, and of the deadliest yellow of jaundice – and his hair, which a few weeks before had been but slightly sprinkled with grey, was now almost literally snow-white'. Lying on a sofa, and occasionally pacing the room when he had the strength, Scott dictated most of *The Bride of Lammermoor* and all of *A Legend of Montrose*, interspersed with 'a groan of torment'. Another account is given by Ballantyne, who later brought the printed proof sheets to Scott: 'when it was first put into his hands in a complete shape, he did not recollect one single incident, character, or conversation it contained . . . "For a long time," he said, "I felt myself very uneasy in the course of my reading, lest I should be startled by meeting something altogether glaring and fantastic" . . . "Well," I said, "upon the whole, how do you like it?" – "Why," he said, "as a whole, I felt it monstrous gross and grotesque; but still the worst of it made me laugh, and I trusted the good-natured public would not be less indulgent." '

It would be critically convenient to see the book, begotten in agony and composed like surrealist experiments in automatic writing, as a watershed in Scott's career. The manuscript evidence tells a different story, as by far the greater part of *The Bride of Lammermoor* appears in Scott's autograph. The myth of the composition of the novel is recognisably Romantic in nature: Scott is unshackled from reason by illness; his subconscious alone dictates the work, freed from the internal editor, played on only by his own sense of inspiration.

Lockhart's legend aligns Scott with his contemporary Mary Shelley, to whom *Frankenstein* came in a troubled dream; or Coleridge's opium-induced 'Kublai Khan'. In terms of later aesthetic judgements, the illness both facilitates the creation of Scott's first truly tragic novel and tragically exhausts the author of any future work of equal merit. His next book lent weight to the idea that *The Bride of Lammermoor* marked a transition. That novel was *Ivanhoe*.

The 1819 Introduction purports to be from one Laurence Templeton, an antiquary in Toppingwold, near Cumberland, and is dedicated to Dr Jonas Dryasdust, a friend of Jonathan Oldbuck, the eponymous antiquary of Scott's third novel. The epistolary Introduction deals with the feasibility of a 'Scottish Novel' that was not Scottish. The gentlemen had been discussing the 'cause of the popularity these works have attained in this idle age, which, whatever other merit they possess, must be admitted to be hastily written, and in violation of every rule assigned to the epopeia'. Dryasdust had advanced the notion that their success lay in 'art with which the unknown author had availed himself, like a second M'Pherson, of the antiquarian stores which lay scattered around him, supplying his own indolence or poverty of invention, by the incidents which had actually taken place in his country at no distant period, by introducing real characters, and scarcely suppressing real names'. After all, 'it was not above sixty or seventy years, you observed, since the whole north of Scotland was under a state of government nearly as simple and as patriarchal as those of our good allies the Mohawks and Iroquois'. The English had no equivalent rapid transition into modernity. The 'Author of Waverley' therefore, 'was, like Lucan's witch, at liberty to walk over the recent field of battle, and to select for the subject of resuscitation by his sorceries, a body whose limbs had recently quivered with existence, and whose throat had but just uttered the last note of agony . . . The English author, on the other hand, without supposing him less of a conjuror than the Northern Warlock, can, you observe, only have the liberty of selecting his subject amidst the dust of antiquity, where nothing was to be found but dry, sapless, mouldering, and disjointed bones, such as those which filled the valley of Jehoshaphat.'

Undeterred, Templeton has attempted to work a similar magic on English materials. But having to set the action in a more distant period necessitates a further fictionalising: while the language of the Scotch Novels was broadly intelligible, the English of his period (1194, during the reign of Richard the Lionheart) would be utterly alien to the modern reader. It is therefore necessary to find a register that is just archaic enough to convey the remoteness of the age while remaining comprehensible to the reader. It is a crucial difference. The new Waverley Novel is edging away from realism. *Ivanhoe* is a story written *as if* it were historical. There can be no anachronisms in terms of the future – the knights cannot wear pocket-watches – and there can be no verisimilitude in terms of the past – the knights cannot speak Anglo-Norman. The England that appears in the Waverley Novels, by the author's own admission, never existed. It is a wry touch that Scott has Templeton claim that the story of *Ivanhoe* came from a manuscript in the collection of Sir Arthur Wardour, Oldbuck's rival and antagonist in *The Antiquary*. Not only, as an 'English' 'Scotch Novel', could it be seen as a form of rival publication, the alert reader might well remember that in *The Antiquary*, the gullible Wardour was the character most taken in by the fraudster Dousterswivel.

In the 1830 Magnum Preface to *Ivanhoe*, Scott's motives for attempting a new 'line' were made even more explicit. 'It was plain, however, that frequent publication must finally wear out the public favour, unless some mode could be devised to give an appearance of novelty to subsequent productions', he wrote. 'Scottish manners, Scottish dialect, and Scottish characters of note, being those with which the author was most intimately, and familiarly acquainted, were the groundwork upon which he had hitherto relied for giving effect to his narrative. It was, however, obvious, that this kind of interest must in the end occasion a degree of sameness and repetition, if exclusively resorted to, and that the reader was likely at length to adopt the language of Edwin, in Parnell's Tale: "Reverse the spell," he cries, "And let it fairly now suffice. The gambol has been shown" . . . Nothing can be more dangerous for the fame of a professor of the fine arts, than to permit (if he can possibly prevent it) the character of a mannerist to be attached to him, or that he should be supposed capable of success only in a particular and limited style.' In other words, it was not commercially viable to continue producing the same kind of work. Not only did he run the risk of becoming predictable to his audience, his popularity had flooded the market with inferior imitations.

> In a highly polished country, where so much genius is monthly employed in catering for public amusement, a fresh topic, such as he had himself had the happiness to light upon, is the untasted spring of the desert; – 'Men bless their stars and call it luxury.' But when men and horses, cattle, camels, and drome-daries, have poached the spring into mud, it becomes loath-some to those who at first drank of it with rapture; and he who had the merit of discovering it, if he would preserve his reputation with the tribe, must display his talent by a fresh discovery of untasted fountains.

Writing after Scott's death, Lockhart was at pains to undo his father-in-law's embarrassing revelations. *Ivanhoe* was written with an eye to commercial success and written in a style more self-consciously artificial to his previous works. *The Bride of Lammermoor*, therefore, became the perfect opportunity to account for this change in sensi-bility. *Ivanhoe*, needless to say, was one of Scott's most popular works in his lifetime. The popular disenchantment with Scott's works came later.

Regalia

When, in 1817, Scott was in the process of writing *The Heart of Midlothian*, and was still unsure of the exact extent of the work, he toyed with the idea of filling out his latest opus with another tale, *The Regalia*. The rediscovery of the crown, sceptre and sword of state of Scotland would, he said in a letter to his friend, the formidable Lady Louisa Stuart in January 1818, make a 'capital' tale for Jedediah. The fiction was never written, but on 4 February 1818 Scott went one better. He rediscovered the Regalia in reality.

The Scottish Regalia had been sealed away by order of the last Scottish Parliament before the Union in 1707: the very Act of Union specified their right to place them in secret safekeeping, both as a sop to national pride – the Regalia, unlike the Stone of Destiny, would not be transferred to London as a visible symbol of Scotland's subaltern status – and as preventative measure: the Regalia was under clandestine protection, so that it did not become a focus for quasi-nationalist resistance to the Union. The ruse worked, despite rumours that the crown, sword and sceptre had been surreptitiously removed to London. When Charles Edward Stuart occupied Edinburgh, he made no efforts to reclaim the Regalia and announce himself the legitimate Jacobite monarch of Scotland with all the symbolic trappings of the kingship – the Castle being in Hanoverian hands throughout Charles's stay in Edinburgh may have been a factor, but it could not have been an overwhelming obstacle had it been deemed politically advantageous to reclaim the Regalia by stealth.

Scott's unwritten story, in which the widow of the minister of Kinneff would discover the Regalia hidden beneath her late husband's pulpit and succeed in entrusting it to a member of the Scottish aristocracy, made one major alteration to history. In the sketch for the tale, outlined in his correspondence, the Regalia is lost during the Commonwealth period, rather than being legally deposited by the Parliament. It is a far more high-spirited, adventurous affair in comparison with the reality of the situation, and reveals Scott's dissatisfaction with the mundane truth. The whole romantic story of the rediscovery of the Regalia is more than slightly undermined by the inconvenient fact that everyone knew where they were anyway.

Henry Cockburn's account in his *Memorials* is perhaps the most vivid account of the recovery: 'they found the Regalia sleeping beneath the dust that had been gathering round them ever since the Union. It was a hazy evening, about four o'clock, when a shot from the Castle and a cheer from the regiment drawn up on the Castle Hill announced to the people, that the Crown of their old kings was discovered.' You can almost visualise the dust-motes and twilight, hear the exhaled breaths and crack of the broken chest-lid. Scott's daughter Sophia said that at the moment of opening the chest, she almost fainted. One of the group, 'not quite entering into the solemnity with which Scott regarded this business', made to place the crown on the head of one of the young ladies: 'By God, no!', he shouted – the tone 'something between anger and despair'.

The whole description is gloriously stagey, and the verb used by Sophia in her eye-witness account is curiously telling. The gauche young man had not 'entered into' the spirit of the proceedings. There was no natural reverence for the moment – indeed, I doubt the workmen with crowbars who broke open the two padlocks and were then instructed to fit a new iron grating to the chimney and new shutters to the windows thought of it as anything other than another job of work. Sophia also remembers that her fainting fit was precipitated by 'her father's conversation' which 'had worked her feelings up to such a pitch'.

Scott had been badgering people about the Regalia ever since he first met the Prince Regent in 1815. Moreover, he was fully aware that a previous Commission, in 1794, had breached the 'Crown Room' but had decided that the precise wording of their warrant did not allow them actually to open the chest. The whole palaver gets even better: Lockhart neatly smudges the chronology of events to make it appear as if Sophia's moment of being overwhelmed happened at the very point where the long-lost jewels were revealed to the light. In fact, Sophia's visit occurred on 7 February. The Commission formally relocated the crown jewels three days earlier. (So Sophia would have heard no crack of padlocks or creak of crowbars at all: the chest was already unlocked and opened.) The first opening is a dress rehearsal, and a wise precaution. Had they opened the chest with all due pomp and circumstance, only to discover that the rumours were true and the English had spirited the Regalia away on the sly, the entire pageant would be ruined.

None of this invalidates Lockhart's claim about 'the profound seriousness with which Scott's imagination had invested this matter'. It could be argued that the closet preparations and quiet stage-managing show how seriously he took the affair. Accidents would not happen; everything would proceed as planned. Subsequent biographers and critics have used the rediscovery of the Regalia almost as a metaphor for Scott's entire aesthetic and personality. He is the person who brought back Scotland's glory, who asserted Scotland's equal partnership within a British monarchy. But it was also part of Scott's occasionally indiscreet lobbying for preferment. As his correspondence shows, he was much exercised with the possible vacancy for the role of the Knight Marischal, 'the official keeper of the regalia'.

In the aftermath of the reclamation of the Regalia, Scott wrote the newspaper account for the *Edinburgh Evening Courant* and circulated a pamphlet description of the proceedings; the story was greatly amplified by Lockhart in his biography. Scott had taken the precaution of bringing along four official artists; in part to create scale drawings of the Regalia to satisfy the Prince Regent of their authenticity. One of them, Andrew Geddes, created a massive oil painting, *The Discovery of the Regalia of Scotland* (1821), which failed to sell at the Royal Academy and was eventually cut up into portraits: all that remains are his rather more immediate black chalk sketches.

In many ways, the whole saga of the Regalia was a dry-run for the far more elaborate, sophisticated, successful and contentious staging of the interface between propaganda, celebrity, royalty and

loyalty, history and fiction that took place when George IV visited
Scotland in 1822. Although a biographer like Buchan can describe
the rediscovery of the Regalia as proof of Scott's 'burning reverence
for the past', Cockburn provides evidence of Scott's more self-
conscious and ironic attitudes. When he was asked by the actor John
Kemble, 'Was the Crown not splendid?', Scott purportedly replied,
'The last time I saw you as Macbeth, you had a much grander
one.' Scott may be criticised for romanticising history or making a
dramatic spectacle to distract from *Realpolitik*, but we cannot ignore
that what he truly achieved was making a convincing dramatic spectacle and a tenaciously romantic history. It is not the fact of his
fictionalising, but the quality of his fictionalising that matters.
Scott's pamphlet *Description of the Regalia of Scotland* (1819) is, in
effect, a brochure to accompany the public display of the crown,
sword (albeit without scabbard or hilt) and sceptre, and Scott's
tightrope act of balancing national pride and Unionist pragmatism
was never more eloquently expounded.

> We look upon the Regalia of Scotland, venerating at once the
> gallantry of our forebears, who with unequal means, but with
> unsubdued courage, maintained the liberties and independence
> of Scotland through ten centuries of almost ceaseless war; and
> blessing the wise decrees of Providence, which, after a thou-
> sand years of bloodshed, have at length indissolubly united two
> nations, who, speaking the same language, professing the same
> religion, and united in the same interests, seem formed by
> GOD and Nature to compose one people . . . the feelings with
> which we now view these venerable national reliques are of a
> nature less agitating than those of our forefathers, to whom
> they conveyed the remembrance that Scotland had lost her
> place among the independent states of Europe, and that her
> national consequence was merged in the wealth and power of
> an ancient rival. We who now reap the slow, but well ripened
> fruits of the painful sacrifice made at the Union, can compare,
> with calmer judgement, the certain blessings of equality in
> laws and rights, extended commerce, improved agriculture,

individual safety, and domestic peace, with the vain, though generous boast of a precarious national independence, subject to all the evils of domestic faction and delegated oppression.

Such stirring sentiments almost occlude the true nature of a slogan like 'improved agriculture' – cleared farms, forced migration, and the invention of a romantic wilderness.

The Regalia played a major role in the King's Jaunt and now sit in a museum display in Edinburgh Castle. They are behind thick sheets of bulletproof glass. Would anyone bother to steal them? I've never met anyone in Scotland overcome with awe for the Regalia. They are there for tourists, not for Scots, except for the occasional busload of schoolchildren doing history projects. Contrast them to another artefact, now sitting in the same case, and the extent to which Scott resurrected and neutralised these symbols becomes clear: the Destiny Stone.

The Stone of Scone, or Stone of Destiny, was used in the coronation of Scottish kings from Kenneth MacAlpin in the ninth century onwards. Its mythological origins are brilliantly baroque: it was the Dalriada Gaels' stone of kingship, brought from Ireland; it was the travelling altar used by St Columba, it was the pillow on which the patriarch Jacob slept. In 1296 it was captured by Edward I of England as spoils of war, and integrated into St Martin's Chair, used for English coronations: even had Edward not referred to it as a 'turd', the inescapable image is of an English regal arse squatting on the Scots' symbol while an English crown was placed on his head. After its move southwards, more rumours started that the *real* Stone of Destiny had been hidden by the monks of Scone – a theory still advanced by the current First Minister of Scotland, Alex Salmond. Although the Stone's return was agreed in 1328 in the Treaty of Northampton, it remained in Westminster Abbey until 1996, when it was considered a good piece of public relations by the then-unpopular Conservative Party to return the Stone in the face of growing dissatisfaction in Scotland with their government.

That is, except for its most famous escapade. In 1950, on Christmas Day, four students – Ian Hamilton, Gavin Vernon, Kay

Matheson and Alan Stuart, all Scottish Nationalists – stole the Stone
from Westminster Abbey. They discovered it had been cracked,
although press reports of the time blamed the four conspirators
for the damage. It was hidden for sixteen months before being
'found' on the altar of Arbroath Abbey. This was not the first ploy
to seize back the Stone: in 1934, the Modernist poet, Communist
and Nationalist Hugh MacDiarmid plotted a similar repatriation,
but the plan was never carried to fruition. More rumours started:
that the Stone had been copied by stonemasons during its sixteen-
month Scottish sojourn, and that the current Queen was ordained
monarch on a fake. It was an idea widely promulgated by Johnny
McAvoy's song, 'The Magic Wee Stane'. As a child, driving round
the Borders with my dad in a brown Maxi car the size and smell of
a hearse, he taught my brother and me to bellow out the last verse:

> So if ever ye cam' on a stane wi' a ring
> Just sit yersel' doon and proclaim yersel' king
> There's nane will be able tae challenge yer claim
> That ye've crooned yersel' King on the Destiny Stane
> Wi' a too-ra-li-oo-ra-li-oo-ra-li-ay

As a teenager, I remember a local stonemason, a Second World War
Polish refugee named Eddie Laub, holding forth in one of the local
bars in Lilliesleaf (where every young man, then, had to have their
feet dipped in paint and imprinted on the ceiling the night before
their wedding) that he had been one of the forgers. He certainly did
sculpt the stone that stands on the bleak Carter Bar border road
between England and Scotland, and he was the kind of man whose
eyes always twinkled at getting one over on authority. I would like
to think that he did participate in the hoax.

Nobody dreamed of stealing back the crown jewels of Scotland.
The stories of the Stone of Scone though are the kind of yarns a postmodern Walter Scott would adore: if all the later myths are true,
then it's a forgery of a forgery now sitting in Edinburgh. The Stone's
capacity to foment dispute and generate narratives is undiminished.
As part of the deal for its return, it must go back to Westminster for
the next coronation. When Charles III or William V or Arthur II or

Harry IX comes to the throne, there is no guarantee that the future administration will abide by the agreement. When Elizabeth II oversaw the reopening of the Scottish Parliament in 1999, she did not wear the Regalia; they were toured up the Royal Mile a few hours before her. Indeed, Winston Churchill was adamant that when she visited in 1953, she must not actually wear the Regalia, as this might be considered as a second coronation in a separate country. Since its re-presentation, no monarch has actually *worn* the Regalia.

Ivanhoe

What connects the former British Prime Minister Tony Blair and the Vietnamese revolutionary Ho Chi Minh? Bizarrely, they share a favourite novel: *Ivanhoe*. Paradoxically, of the two, Blair's profession of admiration is perhaps the more surprising.

Although his friend James Hogg wrote that 'the only blemish or perhaps I should say foible that I ever discerned in my illustrious friend's character was a too high devotion for titled rank', Scott became the darling of classical Marxist literary critics. Pre-eminent among these was the Hungarian scholar Georg Lukács. Although he readily admitted Scott's 'personal, petty, aristocratic-conservative prejudices', Lukács believed that these 'psychological-biographical' traits not only failed to invalidate his theses, they actively facilitated Scott's unique insight into historical materialism. 'That he builds his novels around a "middling", merely correct and never heroic "hero" is the clearest proof of Scott's exceptional and revolutionary epic gifts', wrote Lukács. In *The Historical Novel*, Lukács argued that Scott's novels embodied a Marxist view of history: the clash of cultures lead inevitably to bourgeois progress; feudalism gave way to emergent capitalism; history was driven by class struggle, not the whims of great men. Lukács wrote his influential study in Russia in 1936–7. At the same time, Ho Chi Minh – having worked as a waiter in Crouch End, petitioned the French Prime Minister Raymond Poincaré to outlaw English terms in sports reporting and been declared dead in Hong Kong – was recovering from tuberculosis in the USSR. For any young revolutionary, the works of Walter Scott were essential, and indeed approved, reading.

Tony Blair's love of *Ivanhoe* was revealed on BBC Radio 4's *Desert Island Discs* in 1996. He claimed not to have truly 'savoured' a novel since reading *Ivanhoe* at school and described it as 'one of the greatest love stories in British literature'. It was a canny choice. In the run-up to the 1997 election, Blair chose a novel that ostentatiously lauded national unity. It featured a leader committed to progressive reconciliation and could even be read – in its synthesis of Norman, Saxon and even Jewish elements – as an allegory of a multicultural Britain. Blair carefully described it as a British novel: a Scottish author's recreation of an English past. It also contrasted with the choice of Blair's political opponent and Conservative predecessor, John Major. On the same programme in 1992, Major's choice was *The Small House at Allington* by Antony Trollope – a *sotto voce*, quintessentially English novel mostly concerned with the unrequited love of a junior tax clerk John Eames for the impecunious Lily Dale. At an almost subliminal level, the association between Major and the decent but ineffectual Eames and between Blair and the returning hero Richard the Lionheart was striking.

That Scott created a new, popular vision of Scotland and Scottishness is unquestionable and widely acknowledged. That he did the same for England and Englishness is less well documented; but *Ivanhoe* initiates a series of national stereotypes that persist to this day. The most significant innovation was the character of Robin of Locksley, or Robin Hood. Joseph Ritson had written an important academic work on the legends of Robin Hood, hitherto collected by Percy in the *Reliques*, but it was Scott's version that took hold in the popular imagination – even the Disney film version includes the famous scene where Robin's arrow splits his rival's in the bull's-eye. Robin of Locksley is a yeoman in Scott's version, but later adaptations of the story graft Wilfrid of Ivanhoe's story – a dispossessed nobleman returning from the Crusades – on to Robin. The idea of the 'loyal rebel' became important in political discourse: Thomas Carlyle, in *Past and Present*, imagined 'a Robin Hood, a William Scarlet and others have in these days, put on Lincoln coats, and taken to living in some universal-suffrage manner, under the greenwood-tree'. John Henry Newman said Scott 'first turned men's minds in the direction of the middle ages', and *Ivanhoe* was the novel which most clearly signalled this bearing. The idea of a rural, freedom-loving, chivalrous Englishness contributed a great deal to nineteenth-century 'medievalism'. It is not too great a leap to suggest that a direct line may be drawn from the publication and popularity of *Ivanhoe* to the decision, in 1835, that the new House of Commons in the Palace of Westminster should be built 'in the national style . . . Gothic or Elizabethan' rather than the neoclassicism of Scott's home town.

Scott also contributed a lasting perspective on Englishness in that he christened one of its most famous periods. In 1964, the acclaimed directors Peter Hall and John Barton staged Shakespeare's two historical tetraloges – Henry VI Parts I, II and III and Richard III; Richard II, Henry IV Parts I and II and Henry V – under the title *The Wars of the Roses* for the Royal Shakespeare Company. The same name was given to Michael Bogdanov and Michael Pennington's 1987 version of the plays for the same company. Although Shakespeare invented the actual scene – in Act II Scene IV of Henry VI Part I – where the nobles pick red or white roses in the Temple garden to signify their allegiance to York or Lancaster, it was Scott – in *Anne of Geierstein* – who called the ensuing civil war, 'The War of the Roses'.

(And if one were looking for a clichéd English name, one could do far worse than suggest Cedric, which first occurs in *Ivanhoe*. And yet the name itself is, as H H Munro quipped, is not a name but a misspelling: a metathesis of the original Saxon name Cerdic.)

Ivanhoe is perhaps Scott's most enduring novel, and the one that inspired most adaptations. In his own lifetime, Scott saw the operatic version by Gioachino Rossini (and noted in his *Journal* that 'it was an opera, and, of course, the story sadly mangled and the dialogue, in part nonsense'). Further operas based on the story were composed by Otto Nicolai and Heinrich Marschner, as well as an operetta by Sir Arthur Sullivan. It has spawned three TV series: a 1958 version with Roger Moore, *Young Ivanhoe* in 1995 and *Darkest Night* in 2000, as well as four television mini-series and the famous 1952 film starring Robert Taylor and Elizabeth Taylor. Thomas Dibdin created a dramatic version in 1831, William Kitchiner and Alred Bunn both did the same in 1820, and Joanne Mattern retold the whole story through the eyes of a dog called Wishbone in her 1997 *Ivanhoe*. Hazlitt complained after seeing the two 1820 competing versions at Drury Lane and Covent Garden that 'it argues little for the force or redundance of our original talents for tragic composition when our authors of that description are periodical pensioners on the bounty of the Scottish press'. It is *Ivanhoe* that Jem read to Mrs Dubose in *To Kill a Mockingbird*, and it is *Ivanhoe* that inspired Louis L'Amour, author of *Hopalong Cassidy*, who called it the first Western. Even in *Finnegans Wake*, 'the lionses of Lumdrum hivanhoesed up gagainst him'.

Many people had doubts about Tony Blair's tenure as Prime Minister, not least because of the Iraq and Afghanistan Wars (it is curious to note that the pre-9/11 Robin Hood film, *Prince of Thieves*, had a 'Saracen' – and one conspicuously similar to Saladin in Scott's *The Talisman* – among the Merry Men). Personally, my doubts set in when he called *Ivanhoe* 'one of the greatest love stories'. *Ivanhoe* is many things: stirring, rip-roaring, dramatic, adventurous, but *romantic*? I think not. Scott himself was sanguine about the conventionality of his love plots, and Stendhal perceptively wrote, in his essay comparing Scott and Mme de Lafayette's *La Princesse de Clèves*, that 'the movements of the heart, which, to begin with, are so difficult to discern and so difficult to describe with precision and without either timidity or exaggeration, would scarcely furnish a few lines' in Scott. *Ivanhoe* reiterates the familiar Scott pattern of the dark, dynamic, alien, dangerous and unattainable woman (the Gaelic Flora McIvor, the Jewish Rebecca in this novel) and the blonde, boring, second-best wife-material (Rose Bradwardine, Rowena here). Ivanhoe dutifully ends up with Rowena. The ending so angered William Makepeace Thackeray that he wrote one of his wittiest burlesques, *Rebecca and Rowena*, to redress the story. 'Nor can I ever believe,' he wrote of Rebecca, 'that such a woman, so admirable, so tender, so heroic, could disappear altogether before such another woman as Rowena, that vapid, flaxen-haired creature, who is, in my humble opinion, unworthy of Ivanhoe, and unworthy of her place as heroine. Had both of them got their rights, it ever seemed to me that Rebecca would have had the husband, and Rowena would have gone off to a convent and shut herself up, where I, for one, would never have taken the trouble of inquiring for her.' 'That icy, faultless, prim, niminy-piminy Rowena' is promptly killed off, and Rebecca and Ivanhoe enjoy 'some sort of happiness' of which 'melancholy is a characteristic'. Even while ostensibly correcting Scott's amatory infelicity, Thackeray partakes of his curiously unsentimental view of romance. Perhaps both Ho Chi Minh and Tony Blair, at some level, understood that the story of *Ivanhoe* is not about liberation, enlightenment or progress, but steely pragmatism.

For all of the liberal virtues of *Ivanhoe*, it contains in embryo a darker vision of history. The Templar Knight, Bois-Guilbert, attempts to rape Rebecca, and finds her ability to fend him off an even greater attraction. He goes on to 'woo' her with his delusions of power: if he becomes Grand Master of the Templars he 'shall ascend their throne, our gauntlet shall wrench the sceptre from their gripe. Not the reign of your vainly-expected Messiah offers such power to your dispersed tribes as my ambition may aim at. I have sought but a kindred spirit to share it, and I have found such in thee.' The flip-side of the progressive, multicultural, gradually syncretic version of history – the marriage – is the conspiracy, here uniting two groups who would feature prominently in paranoid nightmares ever after: the Jew and the Templar. Without *Ivanhoe* there would be no Dan Brown.

British Literature

After *Ivanhoe*, Scott returned to Scottish history with *The Monastery*. His original intention was for *The Monastery* to be published simultaneously with *Ivanhoe*, as if they were rival and competing works by different authors. The scheme never came to fruition – and no doubt his publishers were relieved that Scott's increasingly thrawn fixation with anonymity did not split their potential profits. *The Monastery* is Scott's own avowed failure and the only novel that required a remedial sequel. Set during the Reformation, its fundamental structural error is a totally credulous piece of supernaturalism, the White Lady of Avenel. In the novels of Mrs Radcliffe, and even in his own previous works, spirits were raised to be explained away rationally (the kind of revelation now unfortunately familiar as the *Scooby-Doo* Closure). Prophecies were introduced alongside a psychological realism that made them self-fulfilling: knowing the prophecy predisposes the character to enact the prophecy. But the White Lady of Avenel is a 'real' ghost, and a slightly ludicrous one at that, who veers between solemnity and slapstick. *The Abbot* is a better novel, though generally thought not to be of the first rank. Constable, with an eye to sales, thought it should be called *The Nunnery*, with its quasi-erotic undertones.

Part of the problem with both novels is the setting. Scott was, according to Hogg, 'no religionist' and told him

> There is nothing in this world to which I have a greater aversion than a very religious woman. She is not only a very dangerous person but a perfect shower-bath on all social conversation. The enthusiasm of our Scottish ladies about religion has now grown to such a height that I am almost certain it will lead to some dangerous revolution in the state. And then

to try and check it would only make the evil worse. Hogg if you ever chuse a wife for God's sake as you value your own happiness don't chuse a *very* religious one.

It is telling that the Catholicism of Charles Edward Stuart plays little part in *Waverley*, and that Scott's previous visions of religious conflict – *The Tale of Old Mortality* in particular – dealt with the fusion of ecclesiastical and political factions. By the time of *The Antiquary*, Oldbuck's Presbyterianism and Wardour's Episcopalianism were just another set of hair-splitting opportunities with which the old eccentrics could needle each other. But religion was the ideological battlefield of the Reformation, and it was one with which Scott singularly failed to empathise.

Scott's depiction of Mary, Queen of Scots in *The Abbot* is a little masterpiece of judicious selection. Her imprisonment in and subsequent escape from Loch Leven Castle forms the principal action of the novel – her incarceration in Fotheringay would have tended towards Mary as the Tragic Heroine; the murders of Darnley and Rizzio would have sketched her as Villainous Lamia. Although the critic John Sutherland has written that '*The Abbot* glamorized posterity's image of Mary, Queen of Scots to the point where it can now never be deglamorized', this seems to me to overstate the case. Scott was ambiguous about Mary. He later said, 'I cannot think of any biography that I could easily do excepting Queen Mary, and that I would decidedly not do because my opinion in point of fact is contrary both to the popular feeling and to my own'; again showing his canny eye to audience reaction. Scott's version is markedly less sympathetic than either Schiller's 1800 drama *Maria Stuart* or William Robertson's account in his 1794 *History of Scotland*. Here, for example, is Robertson's cadenza on her.

> Polite, affable, insinuating, sprightly, and capable of speaking and of writing with equal ease and dignity. Sudden, however, and violent in all her attachments; because her heart was warm and unsuspicious. Impatient of contradiction; because she had been accustomed from her infancy to be treated as a queen. No stranger, on some occasions, to dissimulation;

which, in that perfidious court where she received her education, was reckoned among the necessary arts of government.
Not insensible of flattery, or unconscious of that pleasure with
which almost every woman beholds the influence of her own
beauty. Formed with the qualities which we love, not with the
talents that we admire, she was an agreeable woman rather
than an illustrious queen. The vivacity of her spirit, not sufficiently tempered with sound judgment, and the warmth of her
heart, which was not at all times under the restraint of discre-
tion, betrayed her both into errors and into crimes. To say that
she was always unfortunate will not account for that long and
almost uninterrupted succession of calamities which befell
her; we must likewise add, that she was often imprudent.
Humanity will draw a veil over this part of her character which
it cannot approve, and may, perhaps, prompt some to impute
some of her actions to her situation, more than to her disposi-
tions; and to lament the unhappiness of the former, rather than
excuse the perverseness of the latter. Mary's sufferings exceed,
both in degree and in duration, those tragical distresses which
fancy has feigned to excite sorrow and commiseration; and
while we survey them, we are apt altogether to forget her frail-
ties, we think of her faults with less indignation, and approve
of our tears as if they were shed for a person who had attained
much nearer to pure virtue.

Scott, however, introduces her by saying that

her face seems at once to combine our ideas of the majestic,
the pleasing, and the brilliant, leaving us to doubt whether
they express most happily the queen, the beauty, or the accomplished woman. Who is there, that, at the very mention of
Mary Stewart's name, has not her countenance before him,
familiar as that of the mistress of his youth, or the favourite
daughter of his advanced age? Even those who feel themselves
compelled to believe all, or much, of what her enemies laid to
her charge, cannot think without a sigh upon a countenance
expressive of anything rather than the foul crimes with which

she was charged when living, and which still continue to shade, if not to blacken, her memory . . . We know that by far the most acute of those who, in latter days, have adopted the unfavourable view of Mary's character, longed, like the executioner before his dreadful task was performed, to kiss the fair hand of her on whom he was about to perform so horrible a duty.

But turning to her personality rather than her features, the first word that Scott uses is 'sarcasm'. Fundamentally, Scott would not have wanted Mary pardoned, or in power.

It seemed natural to move from Mary to her arch-rival, Elizabeth I of England. Again, Constable interfered over titles. His choice was *The Armada*; Scott's *Cumnor-Hall* and the compromise was *Kenilworth*. It was to be Scott's last 'English' novel. Thereafter, his cycle of historical novels set in England would chart the reigns of James VI and I, the Commonwealth and Charles II, and would concentrate on the emerging 'British' identity. The three 'British' novels – *The Fortunes of Nigel*, *Peveril of the Peak* and *Woodstock* – are united by concerns over London's financial supremacy and underground criminality; the moral laxity of the court; the persisting divisions between Parliamentarians and Royalists, Roundheads and Cavaliers, Catholics and Protestants. They also explore the relationship of the regions (Derbyshire, Oxfordshire, the Isle of Man) to the capital, and the idea of the court. It is worth noticing that while Scott created memorable portraits of Mary, Queen of Scots, Elizabeth I, James VI and I, Cromwell and Charles II, and even Charles Edward Stuart, he never depicted a ruling Hanoverian monarch in his novels (Queen Caroline in *The Heart of Midlothian* comes closest). The novels, by this stage, were firmly historical: his endeavours on behalf of the dynasty took place in reality instead.

Scott's Englishness was always more self-consciously and even blatantly fictive, which accounts for some of the more negative comments on his switch away from Scottish topics. Hazlitt, in his early reviews of the stage versions of *Ivanhoe* remarked that 'in fact, we conceive, as a point of speculative criticism, that the genius of the author of *Waverley*, however lofty, and however extensive, still has discernible limits . . . on his native soil, within that hallowed circle of his warm affections and keen observation, no one will pretend to cope with him. He has there a wide and noble range, over which his pen "holds sovereign sway and masterdom" . . . But on this side of the Tweed we have others as good as he. The genius of that magic stream may say to him "Hitherto shalt thou come, but no further".' Henry Beers, in his survey of the Romantic period, concurs: 'This Antaeus of romance lost strength, as soon as he was lifted above the earth.' It became a critical commonplace. Elizabeth Lady Holland wrote in 1823 that Scott 'should never cross the Tweed: he has rarely done so with impunity, tho' *Ivanhoe* is all countries, being I suspect the manners of no one'. Sarah Green's Scott-obsessed Alice is practically traumatised that the Great Unknown is setting novels anywhere other than Scotland; even her father rues the fact that he 'certainly writes better when he lays his scenes in Scotland'.

Anachronism, deemed essential for *Ivanhoe*, became pervasive in the later novels set in England. Amy Robsart, the heroine of *Kenilworth*, had been dead for fifteen years by the start of the novel; and Ralegh is congratulated on a military campaign in Ireland that would take place in five years time. But chronological errors are less significant than Scott's aesthetic temporal meddling. *Kenilworth* derives its atmosphere from the poetry of Spenser and Shakespeare – characters quote *The Tempest* even though Shakespeare is only eleven years old at the date of the tale. Likewise, for the atmosphere of his Jacobean novel, *The Fortunes of Nigel*, Scott used 'city comedies' such as Shadwell's 1688 *The Squire of Alsatia* and Dekker's *Shoemaker's Holiday* of 1600, for a work set in neither period. *Woodstock* sets up a dialogue between admirers of Shakespeare and Milton, despite Milton's significant poetic output coming after the Restoration. In each novel the predominant cultural references that shore up the text are discontinuous with the literature which the characters might have (in reality) been reading. In a strange feedback loop, Scott uses literature to mould English history novelistically and creates a representation of reality by using prior representations of reality. In his excellent study, *Englishness*, Simon

Featherstone discusses how writers as diverse as J B Priestley (*English Journey*), H V Morton (*In Search of England*), Edward Thomas (*The Heart of England*), C E Montague (*The Right Place*) and H J Massingham (*Through the Wilderness*) embark on journeys in the twentieth century to 'rediscover' England. 'Never before have so many people been searching for England,' began Morton, and each author, in their own manner confronts a nebulous, frustrated quest: Massingham found a country 'adrift from its landmarks, set in the void, an expressionless mask'. His comment brings to mind Edwin Muir's sullen insistence that Scotland had a 'blank' instead of a centre, and raises the possibility that these disappointed seekers-after-England were so because the England that they sought was, and always had been, a fictional construct.

Common Ridings

Scott's famously wry retort to Morritt when they were contemplating the plot for *Rokeby* – 'nothing so easy to make as a tradition' – might have been uttered with the Border Common Ridings in mind. These unique events, described by one travel guide as combining 'the thrills of Pamplona's Fiesta de San Fermin with the concentrated drinking of Munich's Oktoberfest', are integral to the identity of the Borders as a whole and to the individual town's distinctiveness. Although some of the Common Ridings were happening in Scott's lifetime, Scott's life would latterly become embroiled in the evolving, mutating traditions. In Andrew and John Lang's *Highways and Byways in the Border*, the brothers wrote, apropos of Selkirk but applicable to every town, that 'there are many traditions to which the inhabitants . . . cling tenaciously. Some, I fear, will not bear too close investigation. Traditions are mis-chancey things to handle; it does not always do to enquire too closely if one would retain one's faith . . . it is an ungrateful task to rake among the dead cinders of time-honoured traditions.'

The Ridings take place between June and August, with the traditional first Riding taking place in Hawick in the second week of June. It dates, in some form, to the late thirteenth and early fourteenth century, when each town's leading denizens would ride, on horseback, around the established boundaries of their locales to ensure their security. Its modern incarnation is rather more formalised and bacchanalian at the same time. The calendar is fixed: Hawick, Selkirk, Melrose, Peebles, Galashiels, Jedburgh, Duns, Langholm, Kelso, Musselburgh, Lauder, Coldstream. Each town elects its 'principals' – called the Cornet in Hawick, Peebles, Langholm and Lauder, the Standard Bearer in Selkirk, the Braw Lad in Galashiels, the Kelso Laddie in Kelso, the Callant in Jedburgh, the

Reiver in Duns, the Honest Lad in Musselburgh and the Melrosian and Coldstreamer in Melrose and Coldstream. The rules for election have had to slacken recently: beforehand, the Principal had to be born in the local cottage hospital or town. Since the opening of the Borders General Hospital, a period of residency has had to become sufficient. The male Principal also had to be unmarried, and remain unmarried for the year, then for the following two years when he would take the honorific role of Right-Hand Man then Left-Hand Man to future Principals. Each Principal also has a female companion, usually called the Lass. At each town's Common Riding, the Principals from all the other towns are present, almost like ambassadors. During the Common Riding Week, the town is bedecked by bunting in the town's colours (usually the same colour as the rugby team: black and yellow in Melrose, blue and white in Kelso, maroon in Galashiels – the exception being Selkirk, where the Standard Bearer can choose his colours). Each town has its own set of songs: 'Teribus ye Teri Odin' in Hawick; 'Jethart's Here' in Jedburgh; 'Ride on Kelso Laddie' in Kelso; 'Hail Smiling Morn' in Selkirk.

There are multiple local variations around the central theme of ride-outs, but the core of the Common Riding is, well, riding. Most of the rides before the major foray on the Saturday take in local villages that have a time-honoured relationship with the town, and many of the villages have their own rituals and Principals to welcome their quasi-feudal overlords: the Bari Gadgi and the Bari Manushi in Yetholm, the Whipman in West Linton, St Ronan and his monks in Innerleithen. There are 'dances' – dances that are, to all intents and purposes but never called so, céilidhs. Wreaths are laid on war memorials; the Principals promise to protect the town's standard (or flag); drinks are ceremonially and then copiously taken. Everything is taken very seriously.

As a child in the Borders, the Common Ridings frightened me into sarcasm. It helped that I could not participate: I'd been born in Falkirk to Borders parents; I was violently allergic to horses; and my early treatment for asthma had meant I was a fat, unsporty little pudding. The 'children's sports' was a sheer nightmare, as I waddled along to lose another egg-and-spoon race. Moreover, I lived in Lilliesleaf and went to school in Galashiels: what this meant, in effect, was that none of my schoolfriends lived near me, and none of my village friends went to the same school. We were stranded, outside the *esprit de corps*. Even worse, Lilliesleaf was, in the famous words of Sir Robin Day, 'seven miles from everywhere'. No town really claimed 'The Leaf', as we called it, as their own. Or rather, Hawick once had, but my piano teacher saw a man widdling in a grit-bin during the festivities and they were asked not to come back. The Common Ridings seemed to me to encapsulate everything backward, boorish and parochial. It took me a long time to realise what was admirable about them. They don't just preserve local colour and difference: they create identity, community, fellow-feeling. As a teenager I loathed what I thought of as a macho, Philistine spectacle: as an adult I came to cherish the idea that there are social connections not based on a mutual appreciation of the poetry of the Romantic period.

There is a keen rivalry among the towns about the earliest Common Riding, so much so that those with a more recent provenance vie for an earlier founding myth. Historically, the Common Ridings of Selkirk, Lauder, Hawick and Langholm are the oldest. Selkirk commemorates the supposed return of one 'Fletcher' from the Battle of Flodden, with a captured English flag. He was the only Souter (as Selkirk people cry themselves) to return out of over seventy who left, and every year the Standard Bearer swirls and leaps around the flag in a ceremony that seems to transform a town pageant into a pagan ceremony. Hawick has a similar myth, with less loss: the year after Flodden, 1514, a group of Hawick youths found some English soldiers at Hornshole and took their flag. Lauder can point to Town Council minutes from 1686 to establish their seniority and admit that it 'fell into abeyance' before a revival around the coronation of George V in 1910. Langholm's Riding is enshrined in a 1760 legal dispute, where the Court of Session awarded the Ten Merk Lands to the local burgesses over rapacious landlords. They still announce the (almost) original proclamation:

There is a muckle Fair to be hadden in the Muckle Toon o'
Langholm, on the 15th day of July, auld style, upon his Grace
the Duke of Buccleuch's Merk-Land, for the space of 8 days
and upwards; and a' land-loupers and dub-scoupers, &
gae-by-the-gate swingers, that come here to breed hurdrums
or durdrums, huliments or druliments, hagglements or brag-
glements; or to molest this Public Fair, they shall be ta'en by
order o' the Bailie, & their Lugs nailed to the Tron wi' a
Twapenny nail; & they shall sit doun on their bare knees and
pray 7 times for the King and 3 times for the Muckle Laird o'
Ralton, & pay a groat to me, Jamie Fergusson, Bailie o' the
aforesaid Manor, and I'll away hame & hae a bannock an' a
saut-herrin' to my denner by way o' the auld style.

The greatest Scottish poet of the twentieth century, Christopher
Grieve, was born in Langholm in 1892 – although he became famous
under the far-more Scottish pseudonym, Hugh MacDiarmid. He
pioneered the bricolage of Scots, science, political analysis and
commitment, translated inserts and local memory in truly Modernist
poetry: I would like to imagine he once stood listening to the
Langholm Festival and Eureka'd the moment when he realised the
potential of the Scots language.

There is some residual hauteur from these festivals towards the
'new festivals': the rest were instituted between 1897 (Peebles) and
1952 (Coldstream), with the majority dating from the 1930s. In that
decade, one town – Eyemouth, the Borders' only fishing town and
coastal area – started its own non-Common Riding Festival. They
called it the Herring Queen Festival, and the skippers of each ship
used to elect a girl to be part of the Herring Queen's court. That so
many decided to create a festival in the 1930s is telling, and explains
why even the older festivals include a visit to the local war memorial. The world had changed, and was still changing, and even the
past had changed in the meantime: the past that they had hoped
would be a possible future had fallen as well. The Great War had
many casualties, but hypothetical hopes outnumber corpses in
every war. Most Common Ridings would desist during the next war,

to revive even more ardently after it. A blithe young queen was on the throne; a generation that could remember their grandparents forced from farms to factories were returned to a different place; now both rural and modern. In schemes like Langlee and Burnfoot and Philipburn a traumatised remnant met a grieving legacy.

No one denies that some of the Common Ridings are of more recent date. That does not invalidate the fact that they have now been happening for over seventy years: they have, in effect, become traditional. During the outbreak of foot-and-mouth disease in 2001, when the movement of animals had to be curtailed to prevent the spread of the infection, Melrose substituted a cycle ride; which then continued in later years as part of the tradition. Even the long-established rides have changed. It is startling to read in the Langs' book (published in 1913) that in Selkirk 'the custom as yet gives no sign of waning in popularity; indeed, as the years pass, it seems to rise steadily in favour, and where one rode fifty years ago there must now be a good half-dozen who follow the cavalcade'; especially since now over 500 riders participate. The Langs also mention that the date of the ride changed from August to June: 'Why . . . I do not know, – unless it was to permit of the introduction of those immense and very famous gooseberry-tarts which are so conspic-uous a feature in Common Riding rejoicings.' I have never seen a single gooseberry-tart at the Common Riding, either in Selkirk or elsewhere. Indeed, I had never heard of them before reading the Langs' volume.

Traditions mutate and at the same time insist on their immutability. The Galashiels Common Riding, founded in 1930, commemorates (although that word seems wrong) an event in 1337, when some Gala folks discovered some English soldiers stealing and eating 'soor plooms', and killed them. The idea of a triumphant victory over English soldiers incapacitated by stomach cramps and possibly diarrhoea almost seems deliberately parodic of the founda-tion myths of older festivals. There is a darker side, however, to the necessary fiction of unbroken traditions.

In 1996, two women, Mandy Graham and Ashley Simpson, took part in a Hawick ride which had hitherto been exclusively for men.

After announcing their decision to participate they had drinks poured over them, were called 'slags' and 'whores' and were attacked in the street. The town divided between the 'Lady Riders' Association' and the 'Supporters of Hawick, its Traditions and Customs'. One opponent of the female riders said, 'It is something more complicated than sexism. It is in your blood. It is about that day when the young lads of the town scored that victory over the English. And, quite simply, there were no women there.' On the actual day of the ride, men on rooftops in the village of Denholm threw roofing slates at the female riders and their horses. It was an ugly confrontation, and confirmed many of the worst stereotypes about the region. Although Sheriff Principal Gordon Nicholson ruled, in 1997, that the ban on women riders breached European human rights legislation, and, for the most part, the participation of women riders is now accepted, the genuine anguish that split the town has not wholly healed. In 2008, a young man was sentenced to three months in prison after an assault precipitated by long-running antipathies over the women riders. The awful irony of the whole saga was the revelation that women had actually taken part in the ride up to 1932 (when one was injured, leading to the then-Cornet's crypto-chivalric decision). And to go even further back, into Scott's lifetime, the Common Ridings were occasionally censured and attempts were made to suspend them; not because of their conservatism, but their radicalism. The Common Ridings were thought to be hotbeds for emergent trade unionism and a dangerous forum for working-class solidarity. There might be nothing easier to invent than a tradition, and nothing more intractable when it comes to reinvention.

Scott is now woven into the Ridings. The Braw Lad of Galashiels pays an honorary visit to Abbotsford, fording the Tweed outside the house, and is now greeted by the building manager in the absence of any distant descendants. Melrose includes a pilgrimage to the Rhymer's Stone, recently refurbished to stress the area's links with Thomas of Ercildoune. Innerleithen has its 'St Ronan's Festival', with medieval legends like artificial fossils surrounding the spa which Scott wrote about in his 1824 novel, *St Ronan's Well*, and which was built in 1828.

The Common Ridings are a kind of meta-Scott-land. The means by which the towns have retained and sustained their identities – pride, costume, song, custom, history – replicate in heightened miniature the same strategies we see in the wider country. The struggle between self-consciously invented tradition and its nevertheless sincerely held emotional resonance is likewise similar. The Borders manages to transcend irony, and does so very knowingly.

Shivered Timbers

The Pirate, published in 1822, interrupts Scott's Elizabethan-Jacobean sequence. Constable had again attempted to influence the direction of the Waverley Novels by suggesting *The Bucanier*, in which three of the regicides who signed Charles I's death warrant – John Dixwell, Edward Whalley and William Goffe – would be captured by pirates en route to New England. Constable had come to think he knew the market even better than his author: his son-in-law recalled him bellowing, 'By G—, I am all but the author of the Waverley Novels!' This would have followed naturally from the Jacobean setting of *The Fortunes of Nigel* and had the added incentive of flattering the increasingly important American market. Scott, however, retained nothing except the rough idea of piracy. It seems as if he had been stung by the accusations that his non-Scottish novels lacked a certain *élan*, and had retrenched with a return to his Scottish settings. If he hoped this would recapture the public acclaim, he was sorely mistaken.

Writing to Francis Jeffrey, the Revd Sydney Smith said, 'It is certainly one of the least fortunate of Sir Walter Scott's productions. It seems now that he can write nothing without Meg Merrilies and Dominie Samson [*sic*]! One other such novel, and there's an end; but who can last for ever? Who ever lasted so long?' Throughout *Scotch Novel Reading* there are pointed criticisms of the derivative nature of *The Pirate*, with the conclusion that 'the GREAT UNKNOWN is beginning to get rather stale'. Even a friend and supporter, such as Maria Edgeworth could write to her mother, 'I fear the repetition of Meg Merriless [*sic*]', although she recanted five days later, calling Norna 'quite new' to her friend Sophy Ruxton, adding that 'only common readers will all say this is repetition'.

After the novelty of the non-Scottish settings, the return to familiar territories with *The Pirate* also revealed the extent to which

Scott's construction was becoming mechanical. The novel has the familiar blonde and dark heroines, Brenda and Minna Troil, with the novel ending with Brenda married, and the unfortunate Minna unmarried. There are two heroes, the 'middling' Mordaunt Mertoun and the eponymous pirate, Clement Cleveland, taking the Byronic anti-hero role. As the commentators above suggested, Norna of the Fitful Head is another insane female prophetess in the mould of Meg Merrilies (and with a similar background of sexual victimhood) and the 'eccentric' comic relief role is provided here by the improving farmer Triptolemus Yellowley, a character in the 'stock' form of Dominie Sampson. James Kirke Paulding's *Köningsmarke*, discussed earlier, also plays up these stereotypes; with Bombi of the Frizzled Head and Lob Dotterel in the respective roles.

Nevertheless, *The Pirate* had the 'bookish' air of the more historically distant fictions. Set in Shetland, which Scott had briefly visited during his trip in 1814, the description of the island relied, more than in any other 'Scottish' novel, on secondary literature to create the atmosphere. In particular, Scott used the maritime sections of Smollett's *The Adventures of Peregrine Pickle* to lend authenticity to the Pirate's background (Scott was always more comfortable on horseback than on boats). The library air to the novel so infuriated one of Scott's greatest admirers, James Fenimore Cooper, that he specifically wrote *The Pilot* (1824) to 'present truer pictures of the ocean and ships than any that are to be found in *The Pirate*'.

Scott did not return to Scottish novels in such a formulaic manner until his precarious financial situation meant that the pressures of the market outweighed the pressures of his carefully constructed authorial reputation. When he did go back to Scotland, it was to experiment with modern social tragi-comedy in *St Ronan's Well*, and for his ambiguous, haunting late masterpiece *Redgauntlet*. The *Chronicles of the Canongate* series also show him looking more askance at notions of heroism and chivalry (a feature of all the late novels), and breaking away from his triple-decker forms in favour of shorter and more concentrated narratives (such as *The Two Drovers* and *The Highland Widow*).

The Pirate, along with *The Bride of Lammermoor* and *Ivanhoe*, is one of the three candidates for the novel where Scott shifted gear; when the books became encores to a career rather than pioneering performances. With *The Bride* he was stricken by the first intimations of the strokes that would kill him; with *Ivanhoe* he revealed a streak of what some might call perspicacity and some might call venal crowd-pleasing. With *The Pirate* his mind was elsewhere.

The Jaunt

At the Union of the Crowns in 1603, when James VI travelled from Edinburgh to London to be crowned as Elizabeth I's successor to the English throne, he promised that he would return to Scotland every three years. He managed to return once, in 1617, during his eighteen-year reign. Since the Union of the Parliaments in 1707, no reigning British monarch had come to Scotland at all, and the only member of the ruling dynasty to set foot north of the Border had been George II's younger son and uncle to George III, William, Duke of Cumberland; sometimes called 'Sweet William' but more often referred to as 'Butcher' Cumberland, who brutally enforced reprisals after the failure of the Jacobite uprising in 1745. That George IV visited Scotland at all was due to an intricate alignment of *Realpolitik*, discomfiture, Machiavellian manoeuvring, stifling etiquette, propaganda and rampant bibliophilia.

The period around George's coronation, on 19 July 1821, had been fraught. The King was, frankly, unpopular. Now a bloated, ailing parody of his once glamorous and dashing younger self, he was profligate, lecherous, sentimental and vain, slicked in powders and rouge and sporting a red wig. (A red wig? A foreshadowing of future parodic Scottishness!) His unpopularity had soared during the final throes of his acrimonious estrangement from his wife, Caroline of Brunswick. Determined to prevent her from attending his coronation as Queen Consort, he had been advised not to press for a divorce and instead organised for the introduction of the Pains and Penalties Bill 1820 to legally dissolve their marriage. It was, in effect, a public trial of the Queen to determine her adultery. If George had hoped that a Parliamentary Bill, rather than a divorce hearing, would draw a discrete veil over his own marital failings, he was sorely disappointed: Caroline's defence attorney, Henry

Brougham (one of the founders of the *Edinburgh Review*) threatened in the House of Lords to bring evidence of the monarch's own frequent affairs. The trial descended into farce, with one witness, Theodore Majocci, being required to demonstrate a suggestive dance; another, Pietro Cuchi, testifying about the use of chamber-pots and a chambermaid, Barbara Kress (in a scene now weirdly reminiscent of Bill Clinton's impeachment) cross-examined about the specific nature of 'stains' she had seen on bedclothes. Although *The Times*, with phoney piety, lamented being obliged to report 'filth of this kind', the press had a field day, with increasingly salacious and pornographic details circulating in numerous satirical prints and broadsheets. Percy Shelley wrote an entire burlesque based on the play of Oedipus, *Swellfoot the Tyrant*, satirising the proceedings, while privately referring to Caroline as a 'vulgar cook-maid' whose sole redeeming quality was the nature of her opponents. The affair ended in a muddled stalemate: the Lords initially voted 123–95 in favour; then, after the divorce clause was dropped, 108–99 in favour, but the Prime Minister Lord Liverpool then withdrew the Bill in the face of public unrest. The Queen's party declared a victory, to scenes of public rioting where pro-divorce newspaper offices were set alight and windows smashed.

The more serious side of the 'solemn farce' was Caroline's tactical alliance with the Radical cause. Brougham, like his Whig allies in the *Edinburgh Review*, was pro-Reform; but Caroline became a figure-head for the more thorough-going proponents of democracy. William Cobbett, later to become famous as the author of *Rural Rides*, acted as a speech-writer. It was most likely he who penned her most famous endorsement of the Radical position: 'If the highest subject in the realm can be deprived of her rank and title – can be divorced, dethroned and debased by an act of arbitrary power, in the form of a Bill of Pains and Penalties – the constitutional liberty of the Kingdom will be shaken to its very base; the rights of the nation will be only a scattered wreck; and this once free people, like the meanest of slaves, must submit to the lash of an insolent domination.' Likewise, she declaimed, 'All classes will ever find in me a sincere friend to their liberties, and a zealous advocate of their rights' and

The Times reported her as saying, 'A government cannot stop the march of intellect any more than they can arrest the motion of the tides or the course of the planets.' Her defence lawyers made a point of comparing George to Nero, the most autocratic of the early Caesars. As a figurehead for the Radicals, she did not survive her eventual capitulation to the Government's offer of £50,000 per year; nevertheless, at the height of the trial over 800 petitions totalling over a million signatures in her support were delivered to the Government. Scott, no friend to the Radicals and well aware of the King's shortcomings, was wryly detached and disinclined to take sides over the 'Queen-fever', as he called it. 'I should not be surprised to see her fat bottom in a pair of buckskins, and at the head of an army, God mend all!', he quipped.

The years in the approach to the Coronation were pierced not just by Radical discontent, but Radical activism. On 16 August 1819, a crowd of around 70,000 workers met in St Peter's Field, Manchester, to demand parliamentary reform and universal suffrage. The crowd was charged on the orders of the magistrate William Hulton by members of the Cheshire Yeomanry and the 15th Hussars, leading to the deaths of fifteen protestors (including four women) and around 600 serious injuries. On 23 February 1820, Bow Street Runners arrested the ten men behind the 'Cato Street Conspiracy'. By the use of double agents and *agents provocateurs*, the Government had learned of a plot to invade the home of Lord Harrowby, Lord President of the Council, and execute the entire Cabinet. Five of the guilty men were transported, and five were executed. Among the grislier details to emerge during the trial was that the men had drawn lots to see to whom the honour would fall of slitting the throat of the hated Foreign Secretary, Castlereagh – immortalised by Shelley in *The Masque of Anarchy*

> I met Murder on the way –
> He had a face like Castlereagh –
> Very smooth he looked, yet grim;
> Seven bloodhounds followed him
> All were fat; and well they might

> Be in admirable plight,
> For one by one, and two by two,
> He tossed them human hearts to chew
> Which from his wide cloak he drew.

and by Byron, after Castlereagh's death

> Posterity will ne'er survey
> A nobler grave than this:
> Here lie the bones of Castlereagh:
> Stop, traveller, and piss.

More pressing as far as Scott was concerned were the events that stretched between April and September 1820. Depending on the political hue of the historian, these events are variously now known as the Weavers' Revolt or the Radical War.

The spark which ignited the conflict was the publication of a draft proclamation, on 2 April, from the 'Committee for Organising a Provisional Government', formed on 21 March. The Committee comprised educated weavers, elected by the local workforce, most of whom had read Thomas Paine's *The Rights of Man* and one of whom, John Baird, had served in the army and took over drilling the militants. The proclamation demanded universal suffrage, and called for a general strike and the 'taking up arms for the redress of our common grievances'. Although a Glasgow police officer named Mitchell claimed that members arrested before the strike confessed 'their audacious plot' was 'to sever the Kingdom of Scotland from that of England and restore the ancient Scottish Parliament', the Proclamation included references to Magna Carta and the English Bill of Rights, and ended with an appeal to 'Britons'. A celebrated elderly radical, James Wilson, when the insurrection came, carried a banner with the legend 'Scotland Free Or A Desart' [*sic*], creating the popular impression that the Radical War was not only a class conflict, but a national conflict. Wilson had previously edited a radical magazine, with the title *The Black Dwarf*, co-opting a title from the country's most famous Tory. On the Monday following the proclamation, over 60,000 workers went on strike, mostly in

Glasgow, Stirlingshire, Dunbartonshire, Renfrewshire, Lanarkshire and Ayrshire. The next day, one John King (who was most likely a double agent) gave half a torn card to John Baird, and the other half to one Andrew Hardie, who both marched on the Carron Ironworks in the belief that they would be able to acquire guns, bayonets and ammunition there. Despite their hope that there would be a 'small army' for the operation, a mere thirty men participated. At Bonnymuir, the party skirmished with the 10th Hussars, and the revolution petered out. Indeed, it seems as if the entire debacle was in part encouraged by agents provocateurs. The aforementioned Mitchell wrote that 'if some plan were conceived by which the disaffected could be lured out of their lairs – being made to think that the day of "liberty" had come – we could catch them abroad and undefended'.

Wilson was found not guilty of three charges of treason, but guilty of 'compassing to levy war against the King in order to compel him to change his measures'. Although the jury recommended compassion and mercy, he was nevertheless sentenced to death as well. A crowd of 20,000 in Glasgow watched the execution of the sexuagenarian on 30 August. Hardie and Baird were executed on 8 September in Stirling. They were forbidden from making speeches, unless of a religious nature, on the scaffold by the Sheriff of Stirling, Ranald MacDonald of Staffa. They were hanged, and then beheaded by a medical student who had volunteered as executioner. He was heard to say, 'I wish to God I had not had to do it' after ceremonially lifting up the severed heads and announcing, 'This is the head of a traitor.' Eighteen other men were sentenced to transportation.

Scott, with all his naive enthusiasm for matters military, was permitted to raise a volunteer regiment (all bedecked in uniforms he designed himself) and offered their services to Viscount Melville, the First Lord of the Admiralty and the Tory administration's manager of Scottish affairs – who politely declined. His letters at the time are full of hawkish fulminations: to Walter Jnr, then serving with the 18th Dragoons, he wrote: 'the Radical scoundrels had forgot there were any men in the country but their own rascally adherents . . . I am sure the dogs will not fight and I am sorry for it.

One day's good kemping would cure them most radically of their radical malady & if I had anything to say in the matter they should remember the day for half a century to come.'

Scott had been impressed by the King's coronation (he invited James Hogg to attend with him, but Hogg declined as it would mean him missing the St Boswell's Fair) and wrote a description of it for Ballantyne's newspaper. It was a magnificent affair, costing nearly a quarter of a million pounds more than his father's. Queen Caroline had attempted to attend, and George had posted Bow Street Runners at the doors to forbid her entry: when she managed to gain access via Westminster Hall she was witnessed being held back with a bayonet to her throat. She was eventually dissuaded by Sir Robert Inglis and returned home. She fell ill that night and never recovered, dying three weeks later. At the time, her imminent mortality was not known, and Scott's account verges on gloating. It was, he says, a 'voluntary degradation. That matter is a fire of straw which has now burnt to the very embers, and those who try to blow it into life again, will only blacken their hands and noses, like mischievous children dabbling in the ashes of a bonfire.' Scott had already broached the topic of a royal visit to Scotland when he first met George in 1815; the Coronation – to his mind – confirmed how such a spectacle could unite and bedazzle disparate classes and political opponents, even in the most infelicitous of circumstances. Both Melville and Scott were convinced that George IV's visit to Scotland would, among other things, be an effective piece of propaganda: it would be a soporific to the 'mechanicals', with bread and circuses distracting them from radical politics, and an intoxicant to the loyal aristocracy, confirming Scotland's trustworthiness. In his account written at the time, *The Gathering of the West*, John Galt explicitly maintained that 'the Radical exploit has clour't the character o' Paisley wi' the King, and a group of weavers form a committee to "gang in to Embro", to behave in a loyal and dutiful manner'.

It was also a matter of tact: in 1821, the new King George had visited Ireland, incorporated into the United Kingdom in 1801. During the celebrations, Dunleary was renamed Kingstown, and George met with Daniel O'Connell, the young lawyer and campaigner for Catholic Emancipation known as 'The Liberator', who presented the King with a laurel wreath. The men loathed each other, yet managed, albeit symbolically, to present a united front. In another iconic gesture, the monarch met with an old man who had participated in the 1798 revolt, who declared that though he had fought against George III he was ready to die for his son. He surveyed the valley of the Boyne, where his ancestor William III had triumphed over James VII and II, ending the Stuart monarchy, and visited Slane Castle there (the lady of the house, the Marchioness Conyngham, was his current mistress). To strengthen his position as a British monarch, ruling a United Kingdom, it was necessary that the Irish visit should be paralleled with a trip to Scotland.

There were, however, certain factions that were more keen for George to travel to Europe before any spree north of the Border. The Ulster-born Castlereagh, who had been Chief Secretary of Ireland during the 1798 rebellion, had developed a diplomatic protocol known as the Congress System. Sometimes seen as a precursor to bodies such as the League of Nations, the United Nations or the European Union, Castlereagh negotiated a series of regular meetings; initially between the Quadruple Alliance of Britain, Russia, Prussia and Austria (in 1812) and quickly expanded to include post-Napoleonic France. Every two years, these powers would meet to decide collectively the direction of European policy and maintain mutual security. Early successes included the resolution of the Polish-Saxon Crisis at the Congress of Vienna in 1814–15 and the approach towards Greek independence at the Congress of Laibach in 1821. Another Congress, in Verona, was scheduled for 1822, in order to deal with the presence of Austrian troops in northern Italy, the ongoing situation between Turkey and Greece, and, most importantly, the proposed French intervention in Spain. This issue would eventually lead to the collapse of the Congress System, as Britain did not support France while Austria, Russia and Prussia did.

The Congress of Verona featured some of the sharpest intellects and most powerful characters of the period. Tsar Alexander I, accompanied by his minister of foreign affairs, Count Nesselrode, came from Russia; Prince Hardenberg and Count von Bernstorff represented Prussia; the French sent Chateaubriand, the dashing, complex poet-diplomat who founded their version of Romanticism and the Duc de Montmorency; and from Austria came Prince Metternich, the brilliant, calculating arch-reactionary and advocate of the strictest state repressions. Wellington – for reasons that will become evident – was the British contingent. The fact that three of the chief diplomats would eventually have dishes named after them – Beef Wellington, the Chateaubriand cut of steak and Nesselrode Pudding (a confection of ice-cream, maraschino cherries and chestnuts, named as a sly retort to English plum pudding) – is one of the weirder curios of diplomatic history.

Princess Dorothea de Lieven, the wife of the Russian ambassador to Britain, was a former mistress of Metternich and his current spy. Metternich was eager – or as eager as that master-strategist could manage – that George IV should attend the Congress of Verona. They had met after George's visit to Ireland, and the Austrian had flattered George that his natural arena should be the international stage, shaping the destinies of whole countries. Through de Lieven, he continually reminded George how European monarchs, on his more authoritarian and arbitrary model, did not worry themselves over parliaments that questioned their expenditure, debated their sexual morality or allowed their public humiliation in the press – his censorship was so stringent that Metternich famously demanded a minimum limit on the word count of any book to be published, reasoning that the lower orders would not embark on a book were it sufficiently daunting in length. Fundamentally, Metternich had realised George IV's overriding characteristic: he could be charming, even brave in the face of illness, and occasionally perceptive – but he wanted, above all, to be liked. A man who could be swayed thus would be easily manipulated at the Congress.

The British Government was well aware that their monarch, among such men, was a liability: the other parties were sending their chess grand masters and hoping Britain sent their top gin-rummy player. The Cabinet needed an alternative, and the King needed to be cajoled in that direction instead. The visit to Ireland demanded a reciprocal arrangement with Scotland; Scotland was riven with potential radicals, both armed and parliamentary; and the King could not be allowed to jeopardise national interest in Verona, given his naivety, silliness, mistresses and gullibility. If there were a nail in the coffin of the Verona trip, it may have been the realisation that the King had once slept with the wife of Prince Hardenberg. The future of Europe should not rest on protracted pique over a youthful moment of slobbering and thrusting. The King would go on a Jaunt to Scotland instead.

Wounds, Old and New

Although lobbying for the King's Jaunt had been going on for years, the actual decision was sudden. In a panic, Edinburgh's City Council of douce councillors that kept their ain coonsil decided to create the role of consultant. Sir Walter Scott had barely two weeks to organise the festivities. Although the specifics of the King's sojourn had to be worked out rapidly, the overall tone and theme were already determined: he would experience nothing that was not 'purely national and characteristic'. The question remained, however, as to what exactly a purely national Scottish characteristic might be.

The actual programme of events was relatively uncontentious. On the King's Birthday, 12 August, before he had actually arrived in Scotland, the Regalia were processed from Edinburgh Castle to Holyrood Palace by dignitaries, the Midlothian Yeomanry and various companies of Highlanders. If Washington Irving's Rip Van Winkle had been rubbing the sleep from his eyes in the crowd, he might have wondered if the Yeomanry were there to march the Highlanders to the scaffold. The King's landing was postponed by inclement weather until the fifteenth, when he disembarked at the Port of Leith (Newhaven – where James IV had ordered the construction of the *Michael*, then the largest warship in Europe – resents the King's choice to this day). The King then travelled up Leith Walk to the City of Edinburgh proper, and was driven to Dalkeith House, home of the 5th Duke of Buccleuch, where he would be based throughout the Jaunt. On Saturday, 17 August, the King held a Levée at Holyrood Palace to meet the Scottish gentry, and at a private function on the following Monday, representatives of the Church of Scotland, the Episcopal Church, the Universities, Burghs and Counties, and the Highland Society were allowed to address the King. The King's Drawing Room, on Tuesday 20 August, was an opportunity for society ladies to receive a 'buss', or kiss on the cheek, from the portly, cherry brandy-quaffing monarch, a chance taken up by 457 ladies, and accomplished in a mere one hour and fifteen minutes. The Grand Procession on Thursday, from Holyrood Palace to Edinburgh Castle, was followed by a review of troops on Portobello Sands the next day, with the Peers' Grand Ball in the evening. The Regalia were returned to the Castle in the King's presence on Saturday, with a Civic Banquet in Parliament House in the evening. Religious observance was a delicate point, and it was agreed that the King should attend a Presbyterian service at St Giles' Cathedral on the Sunday. The text was Colossians 3: 4–5: 'When Christ, who is your life, appears, then you also will appear with him in glory. Put to death, therefore, whatever belongs to your earthly nature: sexual immorality, impurity, lust, evil desires and greed, which is idolatry.' If the King squirmed it was not noted, even when the octogenarian Moderator, David Lamont, inveighed against fornication. A few heads there might have noted the irony: Colossians says, a mere fourteen verses later, 'Husbands, love your wives and do not be harsh with them.'

After a private visit to Holyrood Palace to see Mary, Queen of Scots' chambers, Monday evening was given over to a second ball, the Caledonian Hunt Ball. The King's final public engagement was on the Tuesday, to see a performance of a dramatised version of Scott's *Rob Roy* at the Theatre Royal.

The itinerary is not so very different from the normal round of royal duties. How then did the 'hallucination' of the Jaunt take over Edinburgh so completely? The formal events of the Jaunt excluded all but the highest echelons of society, and yet (as was Scott and Melville's intention) it was to be a display of public loyalty that would inspire the imaginations of the entire populace. After the shock and awe of the Bonnymuir skirmish and the execution of Wilson, Baird and Hardie, this was a chance to win hearts and minds. Scott's masterstroke in the organisation of the King's visit was to have a lasting effect on 'Scottish identity'. Indeed, it precipitated a permanent change in the very idea of Scottishness. In order to accomplish this, Scott had to deal with the legacy of the events of 1745. George IV may have been the first monarch since the Act of

Union to visit Scotland; but he was not the only claimant to the throne to have been rapturously lauded and huzza'd through the streets of Edinburgh in living memory. Scott's genius was to use the emblems of Jacobitism to bolster the Hanoverian rule.

Jacobitism died many times. As a political force, it was effectively spent after the defeat at Culloden. Scott's *Waverley* conjured up the rebellion to dispel it utterly: it was not an alternative, but an impossibility; an anachronism. Bonnie Prince Charlie, who had not been bonnie for many a year, had died in 1788, and ended his life an alcoholic, depressive, overweight wife-beater. His brother, the Cardinal-Prince Henry, never claimed the thrones, nor did the Vatican ever endorse his right to their succession. He died in 1807. By the time of George IV's visit, the Jacobite dream was on the verge of complete evaporation. Charles Stuart's unfortunate wife, the Countess of Albany, was still alive and received a pension of £1600 awarded by George III. Charles's illegitimate daughter, by Clementina Walkinshaw, died in 1789, being officially recognised by her father late in life. She had illegitimate children herself, by the Archbishop of Bourdeaux and Cambrai, and their ecclesiastical parentage rather than any lingering hopes of a Jacobite revival meant they were raised in secrecy: the male heir, 'Count Roehenstart' served in the Austrian and Russian armies, travelled to India, and died without issue after a coach accident near Stirling in 1854. Few people believed his stories about his forebears. Sparse vestiges of Jacobite sympathy endured: the poet Caroline Nairne, who ironically was turfed out of her grace-and-favour apartments in Holyrood Palace for the King's arrival, wrote anonymous Jacobite songs and pointedly did not meet George during the Jaunt.

Scott presented George IV as both the legitimate Hanoverian monarch, and, after the death of Cardinal-Prince Henry, the Jacobite monarch as well. Much was made of George's descent from James VI and I, and Robert the Bruce. The if-we're-being technical Jacobite Pretender, through Charles I's youngest daughter – setting aside Charles Stuart's offspring – was in fact Victor Emmanuel I of Sardinia, an ultra-authoritarian anti-Semite who repealed all the liberties his people had secured under Napoleon: not the kind of ruler Scott would have supported. The loyalist *Observer* newspaper summarised this miraculous double-think:

> We are now all Jacobites, thorough-bred Jacobites, in acknowl-edging George IV. This seems to be one of the feelings that stimulate the people here, at the present time, to make such exertions. Our King is the heir of the Chevalier, in whose service the Scotch suffered so much, shone so much, and he will find many a Flora MacDonald amongst the 'Sisters of the Silver Cross', and many a faithful Highlander attending his Throne with the forester's bugle and bow.

The psychological appeal of the 'return of the king' neatly elided the sentiments of Jacobite song with a Hanoverian holiday. Titles like 'The King shall enjoy his ain again'; 'Hame, hame, hame' and 'The auld Stuarts back again' could be twisted into new meanings. As the 'Jacobite' king, George IV could be honoured with the loyalty of the very Highland clans that had occupied Edinburgh in 1745. He responded to his ersatz-Jacobite lineage with enthusiasm. He had already contributed to Canova's Monument to the Royal Stuarts in St Peter's Basilica on the death of Cardinal-Prince Henry, and had given his current mistress the so-called 'Stuart Sapphire' that had belonged to Henry. While in Scotland, he organised for an annual payment of £50 to be given to the granddaughter of Flora MacDonald, the woman who had saved the life of Bonnie Prince Charlie.

The 'purely national and characteristic' vision that greeted George was a Highland one. Even at the time, Scott's decision provoked scep-ticism and even anger. Under the repealed Dress Act, only military officers in certain regiments could wear the kilt, and gradually, the idea of the 'noble Highlander' began to seep into the public consciousness. The American artist John Singleton Copley portrayed Major Hugh Montgomerie in full Highland dress in 1780, putting down the Mohawks with whom the Highlanders had once been compared. Richard Westmacott's *Monument to Sir Ralph Abercromby* in St Paul's Cathedral, shows the soldier caught, at the moment of death, by an anonymous man in a kilt. Even earlier, in 1749 – a mere four years after the Highlanders occupied Edinburgh – William

Mosman painted John Campbell, cashier of the Royal Bank of Scotland, in Highland dress.

Tartan was encroaching as a loyalist dress, but it still had plenty of opponents. James Stuart of Dunearn wrote: 'Sir Walter had ridiculously made us appear as a nation of Highlanders, and the bagpipe and tartan was the order of the day.' Even Lockhart voiced his discontent.

> Whether all the arrangements which Sir Walter dictated or enforced were conceived in the most accurate taste is a different question. It appeared to be very generally thought, when the first programmes were issued, that kilts and bagpipes were to occupy a great deal too much space. With all respect for the generous qualities with which the Highland clans have often exhibited, it was difficult to forget that they had always consti-tuted a small, and almost always an unimportant part of the Scottish population; and when one reflected how miserably their numbers had of late years been reduced in consequence of the selfish and hard-hearted policy of their landlords, it almost seemed as if there was a cruel mockery in giving so much prominence to their pretentions. But there could be no question that they were not picturesque – and their enthusiasm was too sincere not to be catching; so that by and by even the coolest-headed Sassenach felt his heart . . . 'warm to the tartan'.

Scott was assisted in creating his 'plaided panorama' and 'Celtified pageantry', to use Lockhart's terms, by members of the various, and often mutually antagonistic, societies that had been set up to preserve, promote and discuss the Highland way of life. Principal among these was the Celtic Society – especially Major-General David Stewart of Garth, author of the surprise bestseller, *Sketches of the Character, Manners and Present State of the Highlands of Scotland, with details of the Military Service of the Highland Regiments*. The Celtic Society had an implacable opponent in the 'True Highlanders' of Alasdair Ranaldson MacDonell of Glengarry, described by Scott as 'a kind of Quixote in our age' and who was the target of Robert Burns's ire in the 'Address of Beelzebub'. A deep-seated and acrimonious rivalry existed between Glengarry and Garth (more fuelled by the former than the latter), which, although it has been described as lending a farcical air to some of the proceedings, seemed also to act as a surrogate for more historical antipathies. Among the Committee members was Ranald MacDonald of Staffa – the very man who had overseen the executions of Baird and Hardie. Much of the stage management and set-dressing of the trip was organised by Scott's friend William Murray, the actor-manager of the Theatre Royal. Murray's grandfather was the notorious Secretary Murray, one of Bonnie Prince Charlie's most trusted advisers, who turned King's Evidence in the aftermath of the Rebellion and was thenceforth known as 'Turncoat' Murray. In another small way, the wounds of the past were being bound up.

In *Hints Addressed to the Inhabitants of Edinburgh and Others in Prospect of His Majesty's Visit*, Scott adopted yet another pseudonym – an 'Old Citizen'. This pamphlet dealt with all the intricacies of dress and etiquette required, asserted the King's Scottish lineage and reminded its readers that 'We are the CLAN, and our King is the CHIEF'. Scott specified which dress uniforms were to be worn; gave details of the proper outfit for the middling classes (blue coat, white waistcoat, white nankeen trousers and a Saltire cockade affixed to the hat, with heather) and was most insistent about the Grand Ball in the Assembly Rooms. 'No Gentleman is to be allowed to appear in any thing but the ancient Highland costume.' Scott himself wore trews throughout the proceedings rather than a kilt, and although plenty images of Scott and accounts of his appearance mention a plaid, he seems never to have worn an actual kilt. His excuse during the Jaunt was that on the King's first night (still aboard the *Royal George*), Scott was invited to dinner. The King famously welcomed him with the words, 'Sir Walter Scott! The man in Scotland I most wish to see!' At the end of the evening, Scott asked if he might take, as a gift, the glass from which the King had been drinking his customary cherry brandy. Exhausted back at Castle Street, he flung himself onto the chair, forgetting the glass was in his pocket, and scarred his leg. The whole issue of legs was to be part of the Jaunt's most memorable image.

Part of the whole pageant was to be a Gathering of the Clans. Only five, in fact, attended: the Sutherland Men, the Breadalbane Campbells, the McGregors, Glengarry's Men and the Drummonds. There were no Camerons, MacDonalds, MacLeods, Macphersons, Rosses, Munros, Gordons, Macleans or, to Scott's regret, any of the Atholl Clans. Lockhart's concern that the prominent role played by the Highlanders sat uncomfortably with the reality of life there – 'improvement', eviction and forced emigration – was an explanation for the attendance of some clans. Elizabeth Gordon, the Great Lady of Sutherland, whose factor, Patrick Sellar, had been notoriously murderous in implementing the improving clearances, had been stung by accusations made against her by Stewart of Garth: sending a contingent of men to the festivities was a retort to those who claimed she had depopulated her estates. Glengarry, likewise, was an ardent 'improver'. The irony of many of the Highland Societies was that their genuine and ardent desire to preserve Highland traditions of dress, custom and language was in direct proportion to their own callous disregard for their tenants. John Prebble's study of the 'one and twenty daft days' of the Jaunt makes the point explicitly by prefacing each chapter (à la Scott) with testimonies of the dispossessed.

As the Regalia were being marched along by the Highlanders on the King's Birthday, Castlereagh did the work of the Cato Street Conspirators for them. His mental health had been uncertain for some time, and in his final audience with the King before he left for Scotland, Castlereagh had appeared manic and paranoid, insisting he was being blackmailed for the same crime as the Bishop of Clogher – that is, sodomy. Although his wife had removed all knives and razors from his rooms, he managed to find a letter-opener and cut his carotid artery. Britain would be represented by Wellington at the Congress of Verona.

'Spirit-stirring Spectacle'

When George finally set foot on Scottish soil, he proceeded from Leith to Holyrood Palace with the following entourage arranged by Scott.

Three Trumpeters, Mid-Lothian Yeomanry Cavalry
Squadron, Mid-Lothian Yeomanry
Two Highland Pipers
Captain Campbell, and Tail of Breadalbane
Squadron Scots Greys
Two Highland Pipers
Colonel Stewart of Garth and Celtic Club
Sir Evan M'Gregor, mounted on horseback, and Tail of M'Gregor
Herald mounted
Marischal trumpets mounted
A Marischal groom on foot
Three Marischal grooms abreast
Two Grooms{Six Marischal Esquires mounted three abreast}
Two Grooms
Henchman{Knight Marischal mounted,}*Henchman*
Groom{with his baton of office}Groom
Marischal rear-guard of Highlanders
Sheriff mounted
Sheriff officers
Deputy Lieutenants in green coats, mounted
Two Pipers
General Graham Stirling, and Tail
Barons of Exchequer
Lord Clerk Register
Lords of Judiciary and Session, in carriages

Marquis of Lothian, Lord Lieutenant, mounted
Two Heralds, mounted
Glengarry, mounted, and grooms
Young Glengarry and two supporters – Tail
Four Herald Trumpeters
White Rod, Mounted, and equerries
Lord Lyon Depute, mounted, and grooms
Earl of Errol, Lord High Constable, mounted
Two Heralds, mounted
Squadron Scots Greys
Royal Carriage and Six, in which were the Marquis of Graham,
Vice-Chamberlain;
Lord G. Beresford, Comptroller of the Household;
Lord C. Bentick, Treasurer of the Household;
Sir R. H. Vivian, Equerry to the King;
and two others of His Majesty's suite
Ten Royal Footmen, two and two
Sixteen Yeoman, two and two
Archers 'THE KING' Archers
attended by the Duke of Dorset, Master of the Horse
and the Marquis of Winchester, Groom of the Stole
Sir Thomas Bradford and staff
Squadron Scots Greys
Three Clans of Highlanders and banners
Two Squadrons of Mid-Lothian Yeomanry
Grenadiers of 77th Regiment
Two Squadrons Third dragoon Guards
Band, and Scots Greys

The Archers are worth a small detour. Their position, as bodyguards to the King, was one of the most prestigious in the whole parade. Readers of Scott's novel *Quentin Durward*, published the year after the Jaunt, would learn this tradition dated back to the fifteenth century. Prior to the Jaunt, it had been a private archery club (albeit one with a celebratory poem by Allan Ramsay), frequented by armchair soldiers and young bloods, who had nothing to do with protecting the King. Archery, after all, was hardly part of modern warfare even in the early nineteenth century.

The meticulously planned ceremony did not exactly pass without incident. The King was greeted by Ensign-General Thomas Bruce, 7th Earl of Elgin and Parthenon-plunderer, as a fellow descendant of Robert the Bruce. Then Glengarry, as almost might have been expected, broke ranks, galloped down to the Shore and grandiloquently bawled, 'Your Majesty is Welcome to Scotland!' He had similarly interrupted the procession of the Regalia, and would make a show of himself again at the Levée. But even Glengarry's crass self-promotion was upstaged by an individual of whom history records nothing except that he was called Mr Kent, who did not wait for the King to land but saluted him while 'walking on the water' according to newspapers. Such unforeseen circumstances did not derail the effect of the pageant. To an extent they actually confirmed the solemnity and importance of the events by displaying a surfeit of excitement. Galt's *The Gathering of the West* parodies this by having the Glaswegian Bailie Macfie playing the roles of both Kent and Glengarry.

Most of those thronging the streets, crowding the windows and even teetering on makeshift scaffoldings erected on roofs would strain to catch a glimpse of the King. It is essential to remember that both the King, and Scott himself, lived in a time of rapidly changing media. While newspapers, broadsheets and pamphlets were beginning to circulate likenesses of the great, the good and the infamous, mass media and celebrity images were still in their infancy. The physical, personal presence of a figure such as the monarch (or the most famous living writer) still carried an aura of intangible power. In this context, the first encounter with the King at the Levée was always going to be shocking.

The Long Gallery at Holyrood Palace was lit with numerous candelabra. At the eastern end sat the King, dressed in a bright scarlet belted plaid of 'Royal' Tartan (latterly called Royal Stewart), jacket and diced – or checked – hose. He wore a Glengarry bonnet, with eagle feathers, and a gold badge of emeralds, pearls, rubies and diamonds, valued at £375. His silk and goatskin sporran was fastened with a golden thistle set with Scottish gems. He wore two belts, one holding the kilt around his waist (pulled in as far as possible with a whalebone corset), the other across his shoulder from which his sword hung. Each had a buckle plate in the shape of a Saltire of garnets, with a chased gold figure of St Andrew. Golden rosettes adorned his brogues, and his powder-horn and dirk were equally encrusted in emeralds and gemstones. This entire sartorial extravaganza, ordered from George Hunter & Co., cost £1,354 18s – the modern equivalent of £1,099,407.60. The King weighed nearly twenty stones, and would have been heavily made up with his chestnut-red wig, rouge and face-powder. The famous portrait of the King, by Sir David Wilkie, not only slims several stones from the monarch's portly frame, but airbrushes away the majority of the jewellery. It also omits the most notorious part of the King's outfit. Concerned about the dignity of revealing royal flesh, and no doubt self-conscious that his legs were already grotesquely swollen, the King took the infamous decision to wear the sort of flesh-coloured stockings used by actors on the stage. He was the Chief, and we were the Clan.

'The affectation of Celticism', wrote Henry Cockburn, 'was absurd and nauseous.' Moreover, 'hundreds who had never seen Heather had the folly to arraign themselves in tartan'. Cockburn's pique, though encompassing a majority of the revellers, may well have had a specific referent. The King's friend, Sir William Curtis, was Father of the City of London, an MP and founder of the bank Robarts, Curtis, Were & Co. His wealth had derived from a lucrative line in the manufacture of ships' biscuits. Curtis had chosen to dress as identically as possible to the King. According to Lockhart, 'this portentous apparition cast an air of ridicule and caricature' over the Levée. Curtis was, in Lockhart's phrase both snide and laced with fear, the King's 'heroical *Doppel-ganger*'. Byron also made sport of Curtis in *The Age of Bronze*.

> He caught Sir William Curtis in a kilt –
> While throng'd the chiefs of every Highland clan
> To hail their brother, Vich Ian Alderman

The King more than played his part. At the Civic Banquet, among some forty-seven toasts, the King responded with one of his own: 'All the chieftains and the clans of Scotland, and may God bless the Land of Cakes!' – an epithet used by both Burns in 'On the late Captain Groses's Peregrinations' and Robert Fergusson in 'The King's Birthday in Edinburgh'.

Only a tiny percentage of the suddenly enlarged population of Edinburgh would have the privilege of seeing, face to face, the absurdly attired King or even, the parody of a parody, William Curtis. How did the Jaunt manifest itself to the rest of the city?

It was not just a matter of some bunting and flags. Edinburgh's council had asked Robert Peel, the Home Secretary, to send some of his Bow Street Runners to deal with security on the specious reasoning that they would be more familiar with London pickpockets, who were thought to be decamping en masse to Edinburgh. A large number of opportunistic tradesmen and outright mountebanks had travelled up from London, offering everything from the latest à la mode styles, lace ruffles, Malacca canes and dress-weapons to patent potions, perfumes, perukes and hair oils as used by the Emperor of China and the Tsar of Russia. As in today's Edinburgh Festival, rents on rooms skyrocketed. Cannons were fired from the Castle at regular intervals, and Arthur's Seat was crowned with a bonfire in imitation of the 'fiery cross' that had summoned clans, most recently in *The Lady of the Lake*. The Edinburgh Gas Company lined the route from Holyrood Palace to Dalkeith House with three hundred street-lamps. In the evenings, the city also featured The Illuminations. Each house placed a lamp or candles in the window, and many used transparencies or cut-out silhouettes to display Saltires, thistles, lions rampant, crowns, cherubs and stars. More elaborate exhibitions included The Lady of the Lake herself (in the window of the Provost of Stirling) and a Highlander carrying the King emblazoned in the front of the Crown Hotel. The transparencies also allowed for slogans – 'Vivat Rex!', 'Welcome to Auld Reekie!', 'Welcome to the Land of your Ancestors!' and, in Charlotte Square where the Provost of Glasgow was lodging, 'Let Glasgow Flourish!' During the day, the gardeners had festooned the streets with hollyhocks woven into decorative patterns such as Prince of Wales feathers, trade societies displayed their finest wares, and the glass-blowers had created a vitreous bonnet, coat, sword and shield, worn by one brave member. What happened to these peculiar accoutrements is lost to history. Given the preponderance of besotted enthusiasm for, or curmudgeonly grumbling at, the Highland aspects of the Jaunt, it is easy to overlook other responses. Jane Grant wrote to her mother, Scott's friend Anne Grant of Laggan, gushing, 'My head was full of the *Arabian Nights*. Every spot was light as noon-day, each house illuminated with splendour, but all empty and deserted.' Henry Fox 'walked all over the town to see the beautiful illuminations – quite like fairy-land'. Cockburn thought that the gazing spectators might as well have been watching 'a Chinese Emperor and his gongs, elephants and Mandarins'. Fox, Cockburn and Grant's reaction to the spectacle was to read it as a theatrical fiction.

It was therefore appropriate that the King's final public appearance was at a command performance of Scott's *Rob Roy*, featuring the celebrated actor Charles MacKay, whose rendition of 'Bailie Nicol Jarvie' was so famous that it led to a new phrase in the English language: audiences would thrill if they obtained tickets to 'the real MacKay'. It was an odd choice: a novel which ostensibly praised a Jacobite, anti-Government outlaw and cattle thief was transformed into a 'National Opera' which ended with the cast singing 'Pardon now the bold Outlaw' and 'A' that's past forget – forgie'. Rob Roy was no longer the symbol of an outdated Scotland but the recuperated vision of Highland independence and virtue. Lockhart was at his most acute when he described the whole Jaunt as 'a sort of grand *Terryfication* of the Holyrood chapters in Waverley; – George IV, *anno ætatis* 60, being well contented to enact Prince Charlie, with the Great Unknown himself for Baron Bradwardine'. He marvelled at 'the extent to which the Waverley and Rob Roy *animus* was allowed to pervade the whole of this affair'. The Provost of Glasgow was referred to as 'Bailie Nicol Jarvie' in the streets. In his *Literary Life and Miscellanies*, John Galt recollected that 'although the ceremony in its essence was sacred in the highest degree, yet there were few present that *felt* that it was so. The instant that the performance was finished, the spectators all rose and became as fluent in their talk as the scattering audience after a stage-play.'

But, in a way, the point of the pageant was its similarity to a play. The Jaunt was a spectacle, in the sense that the Situationist writer Guy Debord describes in *The Society of the Spectacle*. This was not just a 'a collection of images', but 'a social relationship between people that is mediated by images', that eroded genuine political engagement by 'the decline of being into having, and having into merely appearing'. One can go one step further. The Jaunt was more than just a mass distraction. By flaunting its fictitious nature, it cunningly short-circuited criticism. It allowed partipants to choose their own level of engagement, to suspend disbelief to a greater or lesser extent. Should anyone point out that the King was not a Highlander, that the Company of Archers was not a historically genuine institution, or that 'garb of old Gaul' was a mere plaid, normally unadorned by diamonds and sapphires, Scott's response would have been 'of course'. Such a criticism would be a *failure to play the game*. To that extent, Glengarry's fulminous denunciations of the Celtic Club in the papers ('I never saw so much tartan *before* in my life, *with so little Highland material* . . . their general appearance is assumed and ficti- tious, and *they have no right to burlesque the national character or dress of the Highlands*') only served to emphasise the Jaunt's integral lack of integrity. The evaluation of a fiction rests on impact not truth.

The neutralising effect of the self-conscious fiction can be seen most clearly in Scott's song, circulated before the King's arrival. 'Carle, now the King's come' is not his finest poetic work, although it neatly draws on Jacobite tropes. A few stanzas will suffice:

> Carle, now the King's come!
> Carle, now the King's come!
> Thou shalt dance, and I will sing
> Carle, now the King's come!
>
> Auld England held him long and fast;
> And Ireland had a joyfu' cast;
> But Scotland's turn is come at last –
> Carle, now the King's come!

> Auld Reekie, in her rokelay gray,
> Thought never to have seen the day;
> He's been a weary time way –
> Carle, now the King's come!

In *The Gathering of the West*, Galt would swiftly produce a satirical version, without diminishing Scott's 'official' song:

> Little wat ye wha's coming
> Little wat ye wha's coming
> Little wat ye wha's coming
> Now the King himsel's coming
>
> There's coaches coming, steam-boats lumming,
> Targets coming, turtles scumming
> Bow-Street and Lochaber's coming
> Wi' pipes to make a braw bumming
> Little ken ye wha's coming
> Clans and Clowns and a's coming . . .
>
> Tartan's coming, Muslin's coming
> Grengarich's coming, Greenock's coming
> Here's the holly-badge o' Drummond
> And there's a CELT, that's but a rum ane
> Little ken ye wha's coming
> Cat and Cammerfae's coming

And Alexander Rodger in Glasgow could produce an outright Republican and Radical version; which for all its bawdy was still dependent on the rules of the game as determined by Scott:

> Sawney, now the King's come,
> Sawney, now the King's come,
> Kneel and kiss his gracious arse
> Sawney, now the King's come!
>
> Tell him he is great and good,
> And come o' Scottish royal blood –
> To your hunkers – lick his fud –
> Sawney, now the king's come . . .

Swear he's sober, chaste and wise,
Praise his portly shape and size,
Roose his whiskers to the skies,
Sawney, now the king's come.

Scott knew exactly what he was doing with the Jaunt. As he wrote to
his son after presiding at the Celtic Society: 'All the members seemed
delighted to escape from the thraldom of their English garments, and
it is certain that very ordinary sorts of folks seemed to catch a spark
of the chivalrous barbarism of the race. The Scotch, more like in that
respect to the French than to the English, are not struck with the
incongruity or even absurdity which must to a certain degree attend
such a scene, but are completely carried along by the feeling which it
is calculated to excite.' Scott was the other heroical '*Doppel-ganger*' of
the Jaunt: despite the fact that extra boats named after Waverley characters (the *Flora McIvor* and the *Jeannie* (sic) *Deans*) were added to the
canals, and the anonymous, though definitely not absent 'Author of
Waverley' was toasted at the Civic Banquet, the Great Unknown
remained Unknown throughout. I would like to think that that
strange fortnight was perhaps the happiest moment of Scott's life.
The clouds had already begun to gather.

The Gathering

John Prebble concluded his study of the King's Jaunt in tones that moved from incomprehension to indignation.

> The Royal Visit could not be dismissed as Atholl set it aside, no more than twenty-one days of daft play-acting. Scotland could not be the same again once it was over. A bogus tartan carica-ture of itself had been drawn and accepted, even by those who mocked it, and it would develop in perspective and colour . . . No other nation has cherished so absurd an image, and none perhaps would accept it while knowing it to be a lie. For that monstrous error, the pageantry of Scott and the euphoria of the King's Jaunt were largely responsible.

Dismissive though he was of Jane Grant's weird metamorphosis of Edinburgh into the Arabian Nights, we would do well to remember that in the *Arabian Nights*, Scheherazade keeps herself alive through her fictions.

In July of 2009, the centrepiece of the Scottish Government's year-long celebrations of the 250th anniversary of the birth of Robert Burns was 'The Gathering'. On Saturday, 25 July, my wife Samantha and I spent the morning attempting to suspend our disbe-lief, defuse any natural propensity towards cynicism or sarcasm and enter into the spirit of things. It lasted about forty-five minutes. Sam is English – or, to be exact, three-quarters English and one-quarter Scottish on her father's father side. In a way, she could allow herself more unself-consciously to appreciate both the exoticism and the eccentricity of the event: she thrilled and giggled while I attempted to suppress a persistent wince. On arriving at Holyrood Park, having queued for a half an hour to use a cash-point and felt sympa-thetic to the person dressed as a dinosaur trying to lure people into

Dynamic Earth, Scotland's museum of geology and earth science, we bumped into a colleague from my work, who was collecting reportage for the next day's newspaper. Sam wisecracked about the number of men with 'roadkill covering the groins'. Entering the actual enclosure in Holyrood Park the throng was impressive. It was also impressively diverse. There were regimented pipe bands, all in perfect full kilt uniforms, marching with military exactness and a look of undeniable seriousness. The neo-pagans and cyber-picts, in combinations of dreadlocks, piercings and swathes of moth-eaten tweed, pummelled away at their bodhràns with equally solemn intensity. Some couples looked as if they were at the wedding of a minor member of the aristocracy; some looked as if they were at a Bay City Rollers revival concert. Lads in rugby shirts and Chinos clustered around the bars, with pints of lager and 80/- in plastic tumblers, while pensioners sat in massed ranks at the various performance areas, eating their picnics. The tartan of their travelling rugs was echoed in the skinny-fit leggings of the girls (and a few boys) swaying at the music venue. Everything matched and clashed.

We had missed the royal visit. The heir to the throne, known here as the Duke of Rothesay rather than the Prince of Wales, had opened the festivities. He had worn the kilt, been introduced to some of the clan chiefs, and formally met with the First Minister. If there were any lingering doubts about the kilt's singular iconography, they were dispelled by the First Minister's decision to wear trews. Not, I should emphasise, because of any vestigial antipathy between the Highlands and Lowlands, or on account of its military overtones, but because the previous incumbent had been mercilessly mocked when he wore a rather inappropriately short kilt for a press call about the New York Tartan Week.

Sam and I wandered round the different displays. In one tent, the Highland Dancing competition was taking place. If one were to strip away the Scottish music and dress, it would appear like any other national dance competition for schoolchildren: hands flung in the air, a lot of flouncing, frozen smiles that edge into grimaces, moments of teeth-clenching emotional tension: and that's just the pushy parents in the audience. Of all the arts, choreography is the one with which I feel least empathy. I could recognise only the simplest of steps – the pas de basques (or paddyba as we called it at school), the preliminary move you learn before they put the swords on the ground for the proper dancing. Whether these pas de basques were good, bad or indifferent I had no idea. The children on stage had numbers pinned to their outfits, reminding me horribly of the markers on cattle at agricultural shows. As they walked off-stage, it was frequently accompanied by the shriek of tugged Velcro. The costumes, of course, are *costumes*.

The Highland Games were more theatrical: cabers were tossed and stones thrown to a soundtrack of grunts, groans and roars. A commentary veered between inexplicable precision over the provenance of the caber, slightly sarcastic asides and biographies of the competitors; most of whom were Scots by descent rather than birth or residence – a Canadian fireman, a Dutch recruitment strategist, an Australian nutritionist. One of the athletes, Harrison Bailey III from Pennsylvania, made me look at the whole event in a different way. Bailey is, he claims, the first African-American to compete in Highland Games. For all the riot of colour on kilts, bonnets, trews, sashes, bustles and stockings, the audience was remarkably mono-chrome. During the Jaunt in 1822, one of Glengarry's more poisonous interventions in the press concerned the 'fact' that he had seen 'a Jew and a Mulatto' wearing the kilt. Things did not seem very much more enlightened or welcoming in 2009. Perhaps not as impressively diverse as on first sight.

The Clan Village, where representatives of hundreds of clans set up stalls depicting their genealogies, their septs, their ancestral lands and their merchandise, only confirmed my unease. 'Every clan,' as Sam said, 'except the Ku Klux.' More than just in its idiosyncratic spelling, the Klan revelled in its Scottish roots, even deriving their notorious burning crosses from the 'Fiery Cross' which raised the clan in Scott's *The Lady of the Lake*; travestied and exaggerated in Thomas Dixon's pro-Ku Klux Klan novel *The Clansman* of 1905 thus: 'The Fiery Cross of old Scotland's hills! In olden times when the Chieftain of our people summoned the clan on an errand of life and death, the Fiery Cross, extinguished in sacrificial blood, was sent by swift courier from village to village.' There is no mention in *The Lady of the Lake* of 'sacrificial blood'. The Clan Village was hardly a hotbed of racist intolerance. A great many of the chiefs had succumbed to the heat, an early whisky and their age, and were having an afternoon nap as we continued, vaguely bemused, around the displays. In some booths, people were welcomed with ebullient bonhomie if their surname corresponded; in others, sour-faced dowagers seemed to dare anyone to cross the threshold.

After waiting for an hour for a plate of over-priced, lukewarm haggis, we decided to catch a few of the bands and then find a place on the Royal Mile to watch the Clan Parade. Having seen so many red-faced and somnolent clan members – Sam confessed the Village reminded her of a cross between an old folk's home and a petting zoo – I was concerned that the ascent towards the Castle might be more stately than the organisers expected. We found a bar (with the affectedly modern Scottish name 'Whiski') and fell into conversation with a couple from Ireland, who had come on holiday to Edinburgh without the slightest awareness of the Gathering. The streets were soon full, with people flouting all sorts of alcohol bye-laws. A few hardy souls who were pedalling tourist rickshaws strained their way up the Mile to mildly mocking, mostly encouraging cheers from the bystanders. Then, to the accompaniment of bagpipes, the clans marched past in alphabetical order. When the Campbells passed by, the crowd jeered and booed. Perhaps the person who started the cat-calling did so in remembrance of the clan's treacherous murder of the MacDonalds at Glencoe; but most of those who were joining in were doing so because the person next to them was booing. The Irish couple were baffled by the whole spectacle: it was, he said, sort of like St Patrick's Day without the spirit of carnival.

We headed back – in a stereotype of Scottish stinginess I thought the cost of a ticket to the finale in Edinburgh Castle would be greater than the amount of pleasure or insight I might derive from it. A pageant, called *Aisling's Children*, written by Raymond Ross, the long-time supporter of devolution and former editor of the influential literary magazine *Cencrastus*, was performed at the Castle. The theatre critic of *The Scotsman*, Joyce McMillan, was unsparing: 'a catalogue of mainly Highland defeat and misery, focusing on the battles of Flodden and Culloden, the Clearances and the butchery of Scottish soldiers in Britain's wars, to the exclusion of almost every other aspect of Scotland's story. It had no geography, no balanced sense of history, and above all no defensible politics, since it utterly failed to leaven this blood-based account of "Scottishness" with any sense of the inclusive concept of citizenship on which modern Scotland is supposed to pride itself.' *Scotland on Sunday*'s critic, Mark Fisher, thought it 'an entertaining spectacle' despite some reservations that it 'plays shamelessly to the partisan ex-pat crowd'. In short, exactly the same criticisms were levelled at the theatrical element of the Gathering as had been raised at the Jaunt.

Perhaps Joyce McMillan should have turned up on the Sunday to hear one of the few literary events of the Gathering. Despite the superficial connection to Burns, literature did not play an especially major role in the proceedings. For the Sunday, however, the organisers had secured an appearance by Diana Gabaldon, author of the *Outlander* series of novels. These books wholly conform to that rare publisher's description, a phenomenon. Her own website, with a beguiling combination of chutzpah and naivety, quotes *Salon*'s review: 'the smartest historical sci-fi adventure-romance ever written by a science Ph.D. with a background in scripting Scrooge McDuck comic books'. The series has sold seventeen million copies and been translated into nineteen languages; it has even spawned a mini-sub-genre – the time-travelling Highland romance, with imitations like Sue-Ellen Welfonder's *Devil in a Kilt* and Karen Marie Moning's *To Tame A Highland Warrior*. Gabaldon's book involves a twentieth-century nurse, Claire Randall, who, via some Celtic standing stones and a pagan ritual, travels back to the eighteenth century, where she falls in love with Jamie Frazer and fights off the unwanted attentions of her twentieth-century ex-husband's great-great-great-great-great-great grandfather. It's a romance trope worthy of consideration by students of feminist theory. Claire and Jamie's relationship is a peculiar exchange of modern expertise with archaic sexual dynamics: she can wear the trousers and be swept off her feet by a man in a skirt at the same time. Gabaldon has an easy rapport with the audience. Men in kilts are, she says knowingly, 'kinda fetching . . . I was still thinking about it the next day (*dramatic pause*) in church! (*rapturous laughter*).' Her inspiration for the series, she publicly confides, was not a great interest in Scotland – 'whichever period I chose I'd have to do the research' – but stems from her love of the BBC television series *Dr Who*. During the 1960s, one of the Doctor's companions was a kilt-wearing Highlander from the eighteenth century called Jamie. Gabaldon is absolute proof that the imaginary space of Scott-land far transcends the geographical borders of Scotland. As she wafted around the lecture theatre, in a striking purple and ultramarine dress, with not a hint of tartan, sprig of heather, or solitary eagle's feather, surrounded by adoring fans, she seemed more of a symbolic descendant of Scott than anyone who had read a Waverley Novel. Maybe that was the 'inclusive concept of citizenship', just there.

Captain Clutterbuck

Can Scott ever become popular again? When Andrew Davies's adaptation of *Pride and Prejudice* set the nation a-swooning at a wet-shirted Mr Darcy, it was followed by an upsurge in lavish nineteenth-century dramas: *Middlemarch, Sense and Sensibility, Emma, Our Mutual Friend, The Tenant of Wildfell Hall, Jane Eyre, Cranford, He Knew He Was Right, The Moonstone, Vanity Fair, Wives and Daughters, The Way We Live Know, Bleak House* . . . under such conditions, the voluminous works of Scott might be considered a treasure chest of potential costume dramas. But instead of *Waverley* or *The Antiquary* or *Heart of Midlothian* or *Bride of Lammermoor*, the BBC commissioned yet another version of *Ivanhoe*: no bustles, no quadrilles, no phaeton coaches, no harpsichord duets. Scott's stock predictably failed to rise. At the time, and ever since, I've been asked which Scott someone should read to *get into* Scott. The answer, probably, is none of them. Each book has its longuers and digressions, its infelicities of style, its purple passages and sepia syntax. Scott's private *Journal*, which he started late in life, has an emotional acuity and is un-self-consciously revealing to the extent that, after reading it, the novels seem even more two-dimensional. In his introduction to the Penguin Classics edition of *Old Mortality*, A N Wilson recommended skipping the first few introductory chapters and plunging straight into the story. I'd take a diametrically opposite view. The way to see Scott anew, to appreciate him at his most congenial, witty and surprising, is to read the prefaces, especially those from *The Monastery* to *Tales of the Crusaders*. They form a loosely connected and playful series of sketches that interrogate ideas of history and fiction, the differing expectations of readers and writers, and the evolving role of the literary marketplace which Scott himself created. They tap into a tradition in English language writing that includes Pope and Swift's satirical *Memoirs of Martinus Scriblerus*, Sterne's *Tristram Shandy* and the *Noctes Ambrosianae* skits in *Blackwood's Magazine*.

The introduction to *The Monastery* introduces Captain Clutterbuck and begins with a delightful shaggy-dog story. Clutterbuck, whose entire ambition has been achieved in becoming a commissioned Scots Fusilier in 'the happy state of half-pay indolence', writes to introduce himself to the Author of Waverley. He has retired to the village of Kennaquhair, and after a few dilatory attempts at angling, shooting, carpentry (where he nearly loses a finger, having already suffered the loss of two at the hands of a French hussar: hence his half-pay retirement) and reading light novels, he has found an agreeable pastime in studying the ruins of the monastery. To prove his independence of mind, he starts his epistle to the Author of Waverley: 'I will not disguise from you,' he says, 'that I have yawned over the last interview of McIvor and his sister, and fell fairly asleep while the schoolmaster was reading the humours of Dandie Dinmont.' He does, however, 'respect . . . the light you have occasionally thrown on national antiquities'. Clutterbuck has become for the Kennaquhair Monastery an equivalent of Johnnie Bower at Melrose Abbey, an unofficial tour-guide to 'those visitors whom the progress of a Scottish tour brought to visit this celebrated spot'. The locals eventually concede that 'the Captain had something in his after a', – there were few folk kend sae muckle about the Abbey'. It is to him, therefore, that they turn when a mysterious man arrives late at night, asking for information about the ruins.

The gentleman in question (of whom the local innkeeper says, 'I haena seen the like o' him since I saw the great Doctor Samuel Johnson on his tower through Scotland') turns out to be a Benedictine monk, whose ancestors fled Kennaquhair during the Reformation and whose order has now fled France since the Revolution. They have been granted lands by a prince of similar conscience (Scott does not specify which, but one contender would be Victor Emanuel I, who hated Protestant schismatics as much as Jews), and the monk is now looking for relics to be relocated to their new home. Far from being in need of assistance as regards the ruins, the monk is far better informed than poor Clutterbuck: 'his indefatigable research into all the national records is like to destroy my trade, and that of all local antiquaries, by substituting truth instead of legend and romance!' he moans to the Author of Waverley, 'all changes around us, past, present, and to come; that which was history yesterday becomes fable to-day, and the truth of to-day is hatched into a lie by to-morrow'. Clutterbuck, having begun as the historian manqué, at odds with the Author of Waverley, is now a novelist *manqué*, another weaver of tales around fragmented historical artefacts. He muses on the idea that the secluded order preserved stories and traditions that had degenerated in the wider culture, and that 'on the Potomac or the Susquehannah, you may find traditions current concerning places in England, which are utterly forgotten in the neighbourhood where they originated' – as indeed, Gaelic culture would be sustained in Canada after the Clearances.

After some joshing with the sexton, who is concerned that the monk takes away only old bones and not treasure – in a typical Scott wink, the sexton confuses pict with pyx – it is agreed that they can excavate Kennaquhair Monastery. This is done at night, and with an even more outrageous nod to the audience, Clutterbuck tells the Author of Waverley that they must have 'personified the search after Michael Scott's lamp and book of magic power'. That scene, of course, occurred in *The Lay of the Last Minstrel*, and the (fictional) Kennaquhair is based on the real town of Melrose, where Michael Scott was suppos-edly buried. Scott apologises for the scene in a later edition, once his masks had been cast aside, saying that the reference was to throw off the scent of those who thought 'there was something very mysterious in the Author of Waverley's reserve concerning Sir Walter Scott'. It throws off the reader in another fashion. Clutterbuck's image hints to the reader that what he and the monk will discover must be the manu-script of the novel we are now holding – another grave, another tome: hence the whole epistle to the Author of Waverley. As it transpires, the casket that they discover contains a 'shrivelled substance which . . . bore now no resemblance to what it might once have been' – in the monk's eyes it is the heart of an ancestor. Bottles of sherries are consumed in celebration of their successful quest, and the parties retire to bed. The reader has been misdirected.

Or has she? The next morning, the anonymous Benedictine gives Clutterbuck a parting gift: 'a large bundle of papers . . . genuine Memoirs of the sixteenth century', which he has had all along in his pocket (in his *pocket*?) and which allowed him to trump the parochial enthusiast's accreted fables with orthodox textual evidence. Moreover, the magnanimous monk is 'induced to believe that their publication will not be unacceptable to the British public; and willingly make over . . . any profit that may accrue from such a transaction'. But Clutterbuck is not so easily persuaded. The hand 'seemed too modern for the date he assigned to the manuscript'. The monk replies that he 'did not mean to say the Memoirs were written in the sixteenth century, but only, that they were compiled from authentic materials of that period'. He continues to explain that they were 'written in the taste and language of the present day. My uncle commenced this book; and I, partly to improve my habit of English composition, partly to divert melancholy thoughts, amused my leisure hours with continuing and concluding it. You will see the period of the story where my uncle leaves off his narrative, and I commence mine. In fact, they relate in a great measure to different persons, as well as to a different period.' The monk insists that there are 'copies of many of the original papers' included in the bundle, so that Clutterbuck can assuage any doubts over this being a work of Catholic propaganda, and is even desirous that putting the book out 'through the hands of a stranger' would take the sting of schism out of the inherent value of the texts. Clutterbuck is self-effacing about his role in this, so much so that the enigmatic friar recommends putting the papers in the hands of 'some veteran of literature' for final approval. After his departure, Clutterbuck reads the papers subject to 'the most inexplicable fits of yawning' and reads them to the local club, who are more enthusiastic. He even allows others to read it out, and finds it more pleasurable himself: 'it is positively like being wafted over a creek in a boat, or wading through it on your feet, with mud up to your knees'. The locals decide it must be published – the schoolmaster is of the opinion that under his hands it could rival the work of Jedediah Cleishbotham – but the end result is to write to the Author of Waverley. He is asked to 'prepare it for the press, by such alterations, additions, and curtailments, as you think necessary', and, gauche and sincere as ever, Clutterbuck even hints that his approach is probably welcome since there are rumours that 'even the deepest well may be exhausted . . . *used up*'. Mirroring the high-mindedness of the monk, Clutterbuck says it would be an honour to have his name on the title-page alongside the 'Author of Waverley'.

Before turning to the Great Unknown's response, let's just retrace this book. In the traditional Gothic framing story, an intact manuscript is literally 'unearthed'. This book, we are led to believe and encouraged to mistrust, is a set of genuine sixteenth-century papers, modernised by a dead monk, expanded by his inscrutable nephew, redacted by the local blatherskite, tweaked and primped by the minister, the schoolteacher, the inn-keeper, the sexton and whoever else was in the 'local club' and eventually given over to the most famous novelist of the day to perform some kind of literary alchemy and transform into a novel? That's not a provenance; it's a conspiracy theory in waiting. But the real conspiracy is even weirder than you might imagine. The Author of Waverley replies, and calls Captain Clutterbuck out on the small problem of him not really being human.

In a tone of both patrician testiness and arch knowingness, the Great Unknown tells Clutterbuck that 'your origin and native country are better known to me than even to yourself' – he is from the '*terra incognita* which is called the province of Utopia', and his fellow countrymen include 'an old Highland gentleman called Ossian, a monk of Bristol called Rowley [a reference to Chatterton's forgeries]', their famous travellers include Sindbad, Robinson Crusoe and Peter Wilkins, and Clutterbuck belongs to 'the Editors of the land of Utopia, the sort of persons for whom I have the highest esteem' alongside Cid Hamet Benengali from *Don Quixote*, Mr Spectator from Addison and Steele's *The Spectator* and Ben Silton from Henry Mackenzie's *The Man of Feeling*. The Great Unknown then deconstructs the whole conceit of the 'found manuscript' – speaking for himself, he has never found anything washed up on the beach shore other than 'a deceased star-fish', and the only waste-paper of bibliographical interest he has encountered was 'a favourite passage from one of my own novels wrapt around an ounce of snuff'. Clutterbuck, he ventures, is embarrassed about being fictional, and to calm his anxieties, the Great Unknown describes a meeting between another fictional editor – his own Jedediah Cleishbotham – and a real person of undoubted reality: the engineer James Watt. Watt was entranced by novels, and the whole anecdote, he says, is 'a wish to encourage you to shake off that modest diffidence which makes you afraid of being supposed connected with the fairy-land of delusive fictions'. If a scientist deigns to be delighted by fantasies, what greater commendation could there be?

That said, Scott's depiction of Watt bears close reading. Watt is praised for having 'discovered the means of multiplying our national resources to a degree perhaps even beyond his own stupendous powers of calculation and combination' – exactly what Scott has done with the 'national resources' of history. The parallel is pressed further: Watt is 'this potent commander of the elements – this abridger of time and space –, this magician, whose cloudy machinery had produced a change on the world'; all terms equally applicable to the Author of Waverley. Throughout the prefaces to *The Fortunes of Nigel, Peveril of the Peak, The Tales of the Crusaders* and culminating in *The Chronicles of the Canongate*, Scott will play with ideas of the unreal nature of fictions, the relationship between history and romance, and industry and sorcery as metaphors for the nature of novel-writing.

The Eidolon

In the next preface, it is the reality of the Author, not his characters that comes into question. Clutterbuck no longer beseeches the Great Unknown, but instead writes to The Reverend Dr Dryasdust, another parody of the antiquarian, whom he claims comes from the same family as he: they are 'all one man's bairns'. Or the product of one man's brains. Clutterbuck has become a literary celebrity and 'no longer stands in the outer shop of our bibliopolists'. Clutterbuck ventures into 'that labyrinth of small dark rooms, or *crypts*, to use our antiquarian language' that form the back of the bookshop, and among the shelves of old volumes and more plentiful unsold stock, concerned that he might be 'intruding on some ecstatic bard giving vent to his poetical fury; or it might be, on the yet more formidable privacy of a band of critics, in the act of worrying the game they had just run down'. This neatly conflates ancient and modern versions of authorship: the antiquarian tomes and the pristine but unread contemporary books; the Romantic inspired *vates* and the critical economy of reviewers. Then, in a 'vaulted room, dedicated to secrecy and silence', he stumbles upon the Author of Waverley himself, correcting proof-sheets. Or rather, he sees 'the Eidolon, or representative Vision' of the author. It is, in fact, only 'filial instinct' that allows him to recognise the famously anonymous 'Author'. Just as modern and ancient jostled in the ante-chambers, the *sanctum sanctorum* confutes all categories and presuppositions. In his own words:

> I sat down with humble obedience, and endeavoured to note the features of him with whom I now found myself so unexpectedly in society. But on this point I can give your reverence no satisfaction; for, besides the obscurity of the apartment, and the fluttered state of my own nerves, I seemed to myself

overwhelmed by a sense of filial awe, which prevented my noting and recording what it is probable the personage before me might most desire to have concealed. Indeed, his figure was so closely veiled and wimpled, wither with a mantle, morning-gown, or some such loose garb, that the verses of Spenser might well have been applied –

> 'Yet, certes, by her face and physnomy,
> Whether she man or woman only were,
> That could not any creature well descry.'

I must, however, go on as I have begun, to apply the masculine gender; for, notwithstanding very ingenious reasons, and indeed something like positive evidence, have been offered to prove the Author of Waverley to be two ladies of talent, I must abide by the general opinion, that he is of the rougher sex.

This peculiar statement relates to two separate magazine reports which had claimed to reveal the true identity of the Author of Waverley. *Blackwood's Magazine* reprinted a comparison made in the *Glasgow Chronicle* between the style of the Waverley novels and the prose of Mrs Anne Grant of Laggan, a friend of Scott's who had acquired some literary fame as the author of some Gaelic translations, the popular description of the Highlands, *Letters from the Mountains* (1806), and an essay on the superstitions of the Highlands (1811). *The Kaleidoscope* and the *London Magazine* both carried reports that the true author was Scott's sister-in-law, Mrs Thomas Scott – wife of the brother whom Scott had first hinted was the real writer. In both cases, Scott was suggested as the editor of the novels. Later in the introduction, Clutterbuck raises the 'letters to the Member for the University of Oxford'; a reference to John Leycester Adolphus's 1821 *Letters to Richard Heber Esq.*, in which the young lawyer marshalled all the available evidence to conclude that Scott was the Author of Waverley. The Author does not dispute it, but instead insists that 'to say who I am not, would be one step towards saying who I am', mock-huffily hoping that Adolphus will find more serious subjects to engage his formidable intellect.

In-jokes aside, the sheer chutzpah of this bathetic non-revelation is majestic. Scott manages to reinscribe a certain mystery to the capitalised AUTHOR, despite the public's wide awareness of his authorship. The Eidolon, the Image is wrapped up and enraptured, oblique and obscure, even hermaphroditic in its multiplicity, whatever the mundane nature of the physical writer. It is the Author as the Great and Mighty Oz.

Clutterbuck is asked about the reception of *The Monastery*, and Scott – despite his voice throwing and mask wearing – cannot quite conceal his pique over its failure. Although parts of his defence, such as his claims to 'harmless amusement' and a 'happy state of indifference', accord with Lockhart's sanitised version of his public image, Clutterbuck neatly needles that the Author protests too much. Scott invokes Shakespeare in defence of the supernatural elements in *The Monastery* and invokes his own self-image in defence of not caring that he can cite Shakespeare as an ally: 'Let fame follow those who have a substantial shape. A shadow – and an impersonal author is nothing better – can cast no shade.'

The Author takes Clutterbuck into his confidence over the 'old plays' which have so often furnished his epigrams, and again, Scott inverts Gothic inventions. Staying with an old Dragoon friend in Worcestershire, he claims ('Then you *have* served, sir?' interjects Clutterbuck. 'I have – or I have not, which signifies the same,' the Eidolon cryptically answers) to have stayed in the haunted bedroom. When a female apparition arises in the watches of the night, he mildly concludes it is his friend's cook-maid, and conducts her to the door. The ghost is put-out and reveals herself to be 'the spirit of Betty Barnes'. Again, the author undercuts the scene, remarking to himself that she 'hanged herself for the love of the coach-man'. But no, she insists that the crime which condemns her to an unearthly existence was nothing less than utter obliteration, as kindling, napkins and trencher wipes, of the lost works of Beaumont and Fletcher, Massinger, Jonson, Webster and even Shakespeare. In expiation for her carelessness, she directs the Author of Waverley towards an old 'coal-hole, not used for many a year' where a 'few greasy and blackened fragments of the elder Drama which were not totally destroyed' remain. Clutterbuck is aghast, and clearly disbelieves the entire yarn – after all, it flatly contradicts his previous assertion about the ruse of the discovered manuscript. The Eidolon's reasons for not publishing such a significant literary discovery are so specious as to be ludicrous: he is worried they might be staged (he himself has been 'Terry-fied into treading the stage, even if I should write a sermon'); that he does not want to compete with Lord Byron's closet dramas; and even that he would perhaps think of writing a play if only he had one of 'Bramah's extra-patent pens'. In effect, the narrative is so pointedly unbelievable – from the genuine ghost to the cocoon of excuses – that it reinforces Scott's previous solemn jests about the 'discovered manuscript' tradition.

Before Clutterbuck has to depart, the Eidolon and he discuss a final aspect with a direct bearing on the nature of contemporary authorship. Clutterbuck is concerned that the 'rapid succession of publication' will lead to the accusation that the Author of Waverley writes only for money. The Eidolon is indignant and accuses Clutterbuck of cant: contrary to the belief of Adam Smith, he says, a successful author is a productive labourer.

> If the capital sum which these volumes put into circulation be a very large one, has it contributed to my indulgences only? or can I not say to hundreds, from honest Duncan the paper-manufacturer, to the most snivelling of the printer's devils 'Didst thou not share? Hadst thou not fifteen pence?' I profess I think our Modern Athens much obliged to me for establishing such an extensive manufacture; and when universal suffrage comes in, I intend to stand for a seat in the House on the interest of all the unwashed artificers connected with literature.

Years after the initial outcry over Scott's advances and earnings, he has formulated a theoretical justification of the financial position of the author. The reference to Smith's economics also explains Scott's sceptical destabilisation of the 'discovered manuscript' trope. Literature, in this particular guise, is something either un-earthed (sometimes literally) or inherited: it is created. Scott is adamant that literature is actively manufactured. Like Watt, he is, by his ingenuity, able to multiply the value of the product. He even refers to 'literary exertion'. There is not a finite amount of literary *stuff* in the system. The language again slips between scientific rationalism and supernatural mystery: the Author describes how novels are 'won by his toil' and a 'degree of industry'; Clutterbuck insists that 'some books will defy all alchemy'.

The Fortunes of Nigel came out at the same time as George IV came to Scotland (bringing full circle the journey begun by James VI in that novel). But the two intertwine in further, stranger ways. The old royalist notion of 'the King's two bodies' had been thrown into satirical relief by the difference between George's bloated legs and his ceremonial function: the Author of Waverley now has two bodies as well; the private rumour of Walter Scott and the public image of the ambivalent Eidolon. The King's extravagance can be factored out into the public benefit accruing to countless tailors, joiners, jewellers, decorators, florists, cooks and coach-men; while Scott's advances too, 'wander, heaven-directed, to the poor'. The Author of Waverley, in many ways, has become the reigning monarch of literature.

Dr Dryasdust, and others

In *Peveril of the Peak*, Dryasdust writes back to Clutterbuck: he too has had a vision of the Author of Waverley. His appearance is pre-empted by the arrival of the manuscript of the new novel, which the antiquarian peruses, through 'strong magnifiers' since 'the hand of our parent is become so small and so crabbed'. His reaction is not heartening: 'here are figments enough to confuse the march of a whole history, anachronisms to overset all Chronology – the old gentleman hath broken all bounds – *abiit – evasit – erupit*'. The shock is so great that he drifts into a dwam, letting his eyes drift over a portrait of his uncle Dr Whiterose (mentioned in *The Heart of Midlothian*) and a pair of pistols that the same uncle had intended to use in support of the Pretender in 1745. He habitually spends an hour in the afternoon 'chew[ing] the cud of sweet and bitter fancy, in a state betwixt sleeping and waking, which I consider as so highly favourable to philosophy, that I have no doubt some of its most distinguished systems have been composed under its influence'. In such a quasi-somnolent state, surrounded by reminders of the Author of Waverley's greatest works and his latest, frustrating endeavour, is, it seems, enough to conjure as if by coincidence the man himself.

This time, the Eidolon appears as a 'visitor of uncommon dignity and importance'.

> a bulky and tall man, in a travelling great-coat, which covered a suit of snuff-brown, cut in imitation of that worn by the great Rambler [Samuel Johnson]. His flapped hat, for he disdained the modern frivolities of a travelling-cap, was bound over his head with a large silk handkerchief, so as to protect his ears from the cold at once, and from the babble of his pleasant companions in the public coach from which he had just

alighted. There was something of sarcastic shrewdness and sense, which sate on the heavy penthouse of his shaggy grey eyebrow – his features were in other respects largely shaped, and rather heavy, promising wit or genius; but he had a notable projection of the nose . . . his age seemed to be considerably above fifty, but could not amount to threescore [Scott was 52 at the time], which I observed with pleasure, trusting that there would be a good deal of work out of him yet; especially as a general haleness of appearance – the compass and strength of his voice – the steadiness of his step – the rotundity of his calf – the depth of his hem, and the sonorous emphasis of his sneeze, were all signs of a constitution built for permanence.

In another literary in-joke, Dryasdust suggests that, had it not been for his eminent civility towards the landlady, he would have thought that the Author of Waverley was exactly the same as the Stout Gentleman No. II, who appears in *The Sketch-book of Geoffrey Crayon*. It might even mean that Crayon had met the Great Unknown and modelled the Stout Gentleman on him – and, of course, Crayon's creator had indeed met the Author of Waverley.

Dryasdust upbraids the Author on the 'aberrations, which it is so often your pleasure to make from the path of true history' – *Peveril of the Peak*, as he says, features the Countess of Derby alive and well twenty years after her death. The Author's immediate retort is to labour a distinction. His work is not history, but 'a romance or fictitious narrative founded upon history'. Dryasdust responds that this is precisely the cause of the complaint, 'the inconsistent nature of the superstructure', which he compares to 'a Turkish kiosk rising on the ruins of an ancient temple'. 'But since we cannot rebuild the temple,' replies the Author, 'a kiosk may be a pretty thing, may it not? Not quite correct in architecture, strictly and classically criticized, but presenting something uncommon to the eye, and something fantastic to the imagination.' There are two important themes here. Firstly, the Author makes a clear demarcation between the forms of history and romance – later he adds, 'Odzooks, must one swear to the truth of a song?' and suggests that the Countess of Derby can sue him as in the case of Dido *versus* Virgil. Any attempt to use historical accuracy against literary composition is as futile as 'a discharge of artillery against a wreath of morning mist'. This is a crucial distinction in Scott's thinking: the inherently fictitious nature of fictions. Secondly, he rebukes Dryasdust for his classicism. The old rules, as set out in Aristotle, Horace and neoclassical commentators, are no longer valid as aesthetic yardsticks. As with his discussion with Clutterbuck, the Author presents 'history' as 'boundless' and 'no more exhausted or impoverished by the hints thus borrowed, than the fountain is drained by the water we subtract for domestic purposes'.

Dryasdust and Clutterbuck both appear, along with a host of other Scott pseudo-authors (Jonathan Oldbuck from *The Antiquary*, a son of *Guy Mannering*'s Dandie Dinmont, Laurence Templeton from *Ivanhoe*, the Reverend Josiah Cargill from *Saint Ronan's Well* and presumably others) for the preface to *Tales of the Crusaders* in 1825. It is announced as a form of found document – a clandestine newspaper report of the 'Minutes of Sederunt of a General Meeting of the Shareholders' of the Waverley Novels. The Author is now The Preses – an old Scots word meaning President or Presiding Officer – and again, his actual appearance is unknown, as the journalist is hidden beneath the table in the Waterloo Tavern on Regent's Bridge in Edinburgh. The Preses announces his intention of forming 'a joint-stock company for the purpose of writing and publishing the class of works called the Waverley Novels'. There is a tone of conspiratorial gloating as he exclaims

> while the public have been idly engaged in ascribing to one individual or another the immense mass of various matter, which the labours of many had accumulated, you, gentlemen, well know, that every person in this numerous assembly has had his share in the honours and profits of our common success. It is, indeed, to me a mystery, how the sharp-sighted could suppose so huge a mass of sense and nonsense, jest and earnest, serious and pathetic, good, bad, and indifferent, amounting to scores of volumes, could be the work of one

hand, when we know the doctrine so well laid down by the
immortal Adam Smith, concerning the division of labour.

The Preses' plan is that they become 'a corporate body'. This is not
the author as inspired prophet, or patronised minstrel, or bardic
retainer, or eldritch sorcerer. The author, now, is a brand, a
company, a legal fiction determined on maximising profit. The
Preses even compares the idea of a joint-stock company to Watt's
'ingenious hydraulic machine, which, by its very waste, raises its
own supply of water'.

The fictitious authors are less than impressed with the Preses' idea,
and their insubordination – a striking first example of characters
disagreeing with their creator, that will reverberate down through a
host of post-modernist comedies by such authors as Luigi Pirandello,
Flann O'Brien and Gilbert Sorrentino – is such that he reveals his true
intention in forming the company was to reign in their autonomy. In
a fit of fury he rages, 'I will discard you – I will unbeget you . . . I will
leave you and your whole hacked stock in trade – your caverns and
your castles – your modern antiques, and your antiquated moderns –
your confusion of times, manners, and circumstances . . . I will vindi-
cate my own fame with my own right hand, without appealing to
such halting assistants, *Whom I have used for sport rather than need.* He
will, instead, write HISTORY – much to the harrumphing of his
alibis, who jest that he is the 'greatest liar since Sir John Mandeville'.
But perhaps it would take a great fabricator to succeed in this particular project. In it, 'every incident shall be incredible, yet strictly true':
it is, in short, the *Life of Napoleon Bonaparte* by the *Author of Waverley.*
The triumphant cultural conqueror of Europe will write about the
vanquished military conqueror of Europe.

This is a moment rich in awful irony. Were Scott's life a Greek
tragedy, this might well be the moment of hubris and peripeteia, or
pride and reversal of fortune. The *Tales of the Crusaders* was published
on 22 June 1825, and the first tale, *The Betrothed*, was a form of gift
to Scott's son, Walter Jnr, on his marriage. *The Talisman* showed
a slight return to form and is especially noteworthy in being the
first instance of a device that would become cliché. The villain

Montserrat is apprehended by a medieval sniffer-dog; not in itself enough to convict him. But when he is asked to 'deny the charge', he implicates himself by revealing that he knows more about the crime in question than has been made publicly available. The depiction of Saladin as the noble enemy is particularly deft, and the scene where he and Richard the Lionheart compete in strength is astute. Richard smashes an iron bar to smithereens with his broadsword. Saladin replies by just drawing his scimitar across a cushion, splitting it in half. Whether strength lies in brute force or assiduous application would soon be tested on Scott's life.

By 18 December that year, Scott would learn that the real companies he was embroiled with, as principal debtor and chief source of income, could not cover their bills.

Apex and Fakes

But we have slipped a little, from the glory days of the Jaunt to the beginning of the decline. The early years of the 1820s were Scott's apex. In the annus mirabilis of 1822 alone he published three novels – *The Pirate, The Fortunes of Nigel* and *Peveril of the Peak*. They were all transformed into chapbooks, operas and dramas – as *The Witch of the Winds, George Heriot* and *The Singular History of Julian Peveril and Alice Bridgenorth* – and all three appeared simultaneously in Berlin, Leipzig, Boston, Philadelphia and New York. In addition, he also wrote a closet drama, *Halidon Hill* – hence, perhaps, Captain Clutterbuck's queries about a possible volume of plays – and edited *Chronological Notes of Scottish Affairs from 1680 to 1701; being Chiefly Taken from the Diary of Lord Fountainhall* and the *Military Memoirs of John Gwynne*. He circulated 'Carle, now the King's come' and *Hints Addressed to the Inhabitants of Edinburgh* as part of his role in staging the King's Jaunt, contributed a pamphlet obituary of his old friend William Erskine, Lord Kinedder, and wrote a new poem, 'The Death of Don Pedro' which was included in an edition of the works of Cervantes. Abbotsford was completed, his work in establishing clubs to reprint medieval Scottish classics was well underway, and he was a newly minted baronet.

Imitation may be the sincerest form of flattery, but Scott suffered from a more deceitful kind of awe-struck admiration during these years. In 1818, the first of a crop of shadowy publications appeared in London: *Tales of my Landlady*, purportedly by 'Peregrine Puzzlebrain', the assistant to Jedediah Cleishbotham. Scott's name – or more exactly the lack thereof on the world's bestselling novels – tempted expedient publishers to produce 'fake' Waverley Novels. A vitriolic exchange took place in the pages of *Blackwood's Magazine* and the *Athenaeum* between a small-time London publisher called William Fearman and John Ballantyne in 1819. An advert had appeared announcing the imminent publication of *Tales of my Landlord, Fourth Series, containing Pontefract Castle*. Ballantyne immediately took out rival adverts, warning the public that *Pontefract Castle* was not by the Author of Waverley. Fearman retorted, saying 'The name of Jedediah Cleishbotham is notoriously a fictitious name, and belongs to no one – to say, that there is any one of that name having property in any thing, is a *fraudulent* assertion; it is open to any body to assume it, as it is to write a continuation of "Tales of my Landlord".' In a letter to the Kelso-born critic and editor of the *Literary Gazette*, William Jerdan, 'W. Kerbey', who describes himself as 'Mr. Fearman's man' angrily refuted claims that Longmans had refused to stock it. If anything, spat whetted the public's interest. *Pontefract Castle* was translated into French and a copy even ended up in the University Library of Christiana in Norway.

Although Lady Abercorn referred to *Pontefract Castle* in a letter to Scott as the 'mere catchpenny of some hack author' – and despite the fact it is sloppily written, tedious and sententious – it is nevertheless a curious barometer to Scott's fame and public perception. Firstly, it is set in England. *Ivanhoe* had been published the year before, and there was an evident desire for non-Scottish Waverley Novels. It is also tragic rather than comic. Set during the Civil War, it is politically ultra-Tory. Milton is accused of forgery, domestic abuse and secretly being a Royalist; Hobbes is 'the Paine of that day' and Cromwell is compared to Satan. An authorial 'proem' deals with the change of publisher. There are 'some rumours of the various motives attributed to the present shape in which he appears', primarily 'amor numi [love of money]', whereas the actual reason is 'to please himself'. Fearman, in a publisher's preface, denounces Ballantyne again, insisting that 'the only cause of complaint which is likely to rise against it [i.e. *Pontefract Castle*] will spring from the Scotch Booksellers, whose monopoly it will break. The London Booksellers have felt this galling yoke upon their necks . . . too long.' That monopoly was real, and it would have serious consequences for Scott in the future.

The fake *Tales of my Landlord* explains another joke in the Author of Waverley's first epistle to Captain Clutterbuck. He laments that 'my old acquaintance Jedediah Cleishbotham has misbehaved himself so far as to desert his original patron, and set up for himself. I am afraid the poor pedagogue will make little by his new allies, unless the pleasure of entertaining the public, and for aught I know, the gentlemen of the long robe [i.e. judges], with disputes about his identity'. A footnote corrects this, claiming that the real Jedediah died recently, and ends, 'Hard that the speculators in print and paper will not allow a good man to rest quiet in his grave.' The powers of resurrection are the Author of Waverley's alone.

Nevertheless, Fearman issued another fake Waverley Novel in 1821, *The Fair Witch of Glas Llyn*, set in Wales during the conflict of Richard II and Henry Bolingbroke. Up-to-the-minute, this novel has a Clutterbuck style preface, with characters called Mark Plethora and Tom Adage discussing the reputation of the novelist. 'The Author' approvingly quotes Horace Walpole: 'If the God of eloquence were to write a book, no one would read the first line, unless the name of some favourite author were written on the title-page,' and adds, 'name, I repeat, does everything; it is, in fact, the old magical Tetragrammaton.' Joining in with Scott's own game, *Pontefract Castle* is almost admitted as a forgery, and the publisher requests that it be 'delivered into the hands of its lawful father Martinus Scriblerus'. There is, however, another layer of mystery about the book. Fearman, in his preface, states 'the rank he claims for *Pontefract Castle* is that of a political warning . . . What has the author demonstrated in *Pontefract Castle*? . . . A striking, fearful, spirit-stirring analogy' between 1649 and 1820. Radicals, Scottish Publishers, Freemasons and Cato Street Conspirators, Fearman claims, are implicated in a plot to overthrow or even assassinate George III and the Prince Regent. After publishing a novel called *Tales of my Aunt Martha* in 1822, Fearman disappears. Scott, bizarrely, would write a story called *My Aunt Margaret's Mirror* in 1828.

Eager for Scotch novels, publishers would continue falsely to attribute work to Scott as late as 1842, when Pierre Auguste Callet and Javelin Pagnon published *Aymé Verd*, the sequel to *Allan Cameron*, complete with a preface in which Clutterbuck reveals that he was real all along and Dryasdust denounces *Aymé Verd* as a forgery. Often, work by other Scottish authors, most notably James Hogg and John Galt, would appear in French or German translation under the rubric 'by the Author of Waverley'. Poor Alice in *Scotch Novel Reading* was mortified that the 'Ettrick Shepherd' was not another Scott pseudonym and in fact another author, worst of all one called Hogg, and goes around pining, 'What's in a name? That which we call a rose / By any other name would smell as sweet; / And so would *Hogg*, if he were not *Hogg* call'd!'

The year 1825 was something of an anomaly, in that Scott did not publish a single novel. That did not stop publishers redressing the problem, with both a parodic pair of volumes called *New Landlord's Tales, or Jedediah in the South* and a book described by its author cum translator as 'the most complete hoax that can ever have been perpetrated'. The previous year Scott had written two novels, *Saint Ronan's Well* and *Redgauntlet*. Both novels show Scott trying to avoid 'the character of a mannerist', despite both works returning to a Scottish setting. *Saint Ronan's Well* is his only contemporary fiction, a valiant if flawed effort to fashion a romance among satirically observed fashionable society. Compared to Jane Austen's Bath, Scott's spa town is second-rate and down-at-heel but gilded over, full of nouveau-riche nabobs, corrupt officials and louche gentry. Famously, Constable and Ballantyne persuaded Scott to change the ending. Clara Mowbray, the heroine, was originally intended to have been seduced by the vile Etherington: instead we get a 'mock-marriage' aborted at the altar, before the bed, and her madness and guilt are consequently disjointed from the plot. It also produced one of the first spin-off titles. Christian Isobel Johnstone, the pioneering journalist, wrote a book entitled *The Cook and Housewife's Manual, containing the most approved modern receipts for making soups, gravies, sauces, ragouts and made-dishes; and for pies, puddings, pastry, pickles and preserves; also for baking, brewing, making home-made wines, cordials &c.* The author, however, was given as 'Mrs Margaret Dods, of the Cleikum Inn, St. Ronan's'. Meg Dods is the Mowbray's old retainer and proprietor of the Cleikum in the novel. Johnstone's book attained the same popularity as Mrs Beeton's in England, and *Saint Ronan's Well* was described as 'literary suicide' by the critics.

Redgauntlet was far more enthusiastically received but is equally unusual in Scott's oeuvre. It begins in a form new to Scott, the epistolary novel, but after the letters between Darsie Latimer and Alan Fairford stretch to over twenty pages and include short stories, Scott dropped the conceit in favour of third-person narrative. *Redgauntlet* is widely accepted as Scott's most autobiographical novel, with both Darsie and Alan reflecting aspects of his character, and the relationship between Alan and the enigmatic 'Greenmantle' recasting Scott's wooing of Williamina Belsches, albeit with a happier ending. The most astonishing aspect of the book is that it is a form of science fiction: a counter-factual historical novel, or *uchronie*. Darsie, whose father was executed in 1745, is abducted by the uncle he never knew, Redgauntlet, as part of the preliminary preparations for a third Jacobite uprising. Based on a misty 'urban myth' that Charles Edward Stuart had returned to Scotland in 1753, Scott depicts the now ageing Young Pretender launching a final attempt on the British throne in 1765. Scott effectively says in the novel: 'Imagine that a third rebellion happened in 1765. It would have to be completely imaginary.' It's like the old joke that if Elvis hadn't died in 1977, then he wouldn't be alive today. The old feudal structure that supported the 1745 campaign has vanished, and instead of dying with their masters on the gallows, as Evan Dhu did in *Waverley*, it is the former feudal retainer Cristal Nixon who betrays the cause. Even more damning and elegiac is that there are no gallows in *Redgauntlet*. When the Hanoverian General Campbell discovers the plotters, his reaction is one of crippling moderation: 'I have come here, of course,' he says to them, 'sufficiently supported both with cavalry and infantry, to do whatever might be necessary; but my commands are – and I am sure they agree with my inclination – to make no arrests, nay, to make no further inquiries of any kind, if this good assembly will consider their own interest so far as to give up their immediate purpose, and return quietly home to their own houses.' It is the kind of benevolence made only possible by absolute victory. 'Is this real?' asks Redgauntlet, a line to my mind more rending than his more famous cry of 'The cause is lost for ever'. Dr Dryasdust tidies up the remaining plot elements and suggests that Redgauntlet died as a Catholic monk and a candidate for sainthood.

Given that his previous two novels had been so far removed from the typical formula of a 'Waverley Novel', it is no surprise that the 'perfect hoax' of 1825 is such an intriguing text. The initial and deliberate fraud was written in German by George Wilhelm Heinrich Häring, who had written derivative novels under the name Willibald Alexis. Johann Bohte, a German bookseller resident in London, saw the novel, *Walladmor*, at the Leipzig Book Fair in 1824 and brought the German original, posing as a translation from English, back to Britain. Bohte's then lodger was Thomas De Quincey, the author of *Confessions of an English Opium-Eater*, who saw the novel and wrote to James Hessey, owner of the *London Magazine*, saying, 'We must have *Walladmor* . . . if Heaven or Earth can get it.' In his later essay on *Walladmor* he sketched out the background: 'the demand for Waverley Novels came to be felt as a periodical craving all over Europe; just as, in the case of Napoleon, some bloody battle by land or by sea was indispensable, after each few months' interval, to pacify the public taste for blood, long irritated by copious irritation'. Hessey agreed to publish *Walladmor*, 'freely translated' by De Quincey.

De Quincey turned a hoax into a prank. He changed many parts of the narrative, corrected errors, renamed characters and gave a more tragic cast to the whole. *Walladmor* is supposedly set in Wales in the present day, and De Quincey draws on the now established cast of Scott-style characters: Bertram is the dilatory and Quixotic hero; Mother Gillie is the astrological, prophetic, crazed woman; Dulberry, the radical reformer, is analogous to Triptolemus Yellowley or Dominie Sampson; and Harnois, the roguish sea-captain, is indebted to Nanty Ewart in *Redgauntlet* and Dirk Hatteraick in *Guy Mannering*. But the register keeps slipping into knowing comedy. Bertram sketches places with names like Cape Sugarcandy and Buttermilk Bay. While in prison he is allowed a pile of books, and a footnote mentions that 'Amongst which we are happy to say (on the authority of a Welch friend) was the *first* volume of Walladmor, a novel, in 2 vols. post 8vo.; the second being not then finished.' It is difficult to take De Quincey's claim of the hoax's 'perfection' seriously. The 1824 review that appeared in the *London*

Magazine prior to De Quincey's translation is even more problematic. It advertises the book as appearing in three volumes, and although parts quoted in the review are identical to De Quincey's version others are completely different. Moreover, it singles out for criticism an occurrence which never happens in the two-volume *Walladmor*. Bertram supposedly meets 'Mr Thomas Malbourne', a character who is described as 'inert', and who reveals himself to be 'the Author of Waverley, and also of Guy Mannering, The Antiquary, Tales of my Landlord'. 'Author of Guy Mannering!' says Bertram 'Do I hear you right?' 'Yes, Sir, and likewise of Kenilworth, The Abbot, the Pirate. . .'

Scott, his publishers and Lockhart were discomfited by the appearance of *Walladmor*, especially since Scott's work-in-progress (*The Betrothed*) was also set in Wales, and the German imposture might indicate that someone in the print shop was passing on confidential details to rival publishers. By the time he came to write the preface to *The Betrothed*, Scott was detached enough and amused enough to work in the *Walladmor* hoax. The ostensible impetus behind the proposal for creating a joint-stock company is the revelation that Dousterswivel, the German villain from *The Antiquary*, may be about to patent 'a little mechanism' by which 'some part of the labour of composing these novels might be saved by the use of steam . . . It is to be premised, that this mechanical operation can only apply to those parts of the narrative which are at present composed out of commonplaces, such as the love-speeches of the hero, the description of the heroine's person, the moral observations of all sorts, and the distribution of happiness at the conclusion of the piece. Mr Dousterswivel has sent me some drawings, which go far to show, that by placing phrases technically employed on these subjects, in a sort of framework . . . and changing them by such a mechanical process as that by which the weavers of damask alter their patterns, many new and happy combinations cannot fail to occur, while the author, tired of pumping his own brains, may have an agreeable relaxation in the use of his fingers.' Scott is to all extents and purposes describing computer-generated texts. The assorted surrogate authors are aghast, and Lawrence Templeton suggests that *Walladmor* has been created using the very machine. Like General Campbell at the end of *Redgauntlet*, Scott is magisterially dismissive.

This form of piracy of literary works, of which *Pontefract Castle*, *Aymé Verd* and *Walladmor* are examples, is relatively unusual – most forgeries are uncovered swiftly and indignantly. Ireland's fake Shakespeare plays, such as *Vortigern and Rowena*, staged in 1796, or *Henry II*, were contemptuously exposed. What sets the Scott forgeries apart is that they managed decent sales (*Walladmor* was praised, in couched terms, in *The Eclectic Review*) and even those who were fully aware of their spurious status were nevertheless sufficiently curious to purchase a copy. The only modern equivalent is the spate of Chinese 'Ha li po te' books. The success of J K Rowling's Harry Potter series led a number of Chinese publishers to produce 'new' works, with titles like *Harry Potter and the Leopard-Walk-Up-To-Dragon*, *Harry Potter and the Waterproof Pearl*, *Harry Potter and the Chinese Porcelain Doll*, *Harry Potter and the Golden Turtle* and *Harry Potter and the Chinese Overseas Students at the Hogwarts School of Witchcraft and Wizardry*. It is a phenomenon not solely associated with China: the boy wizard took on Bengali myths in *Harry Potter in Calcutta*; a Russian author called Dmitri Yemets offered 'cultural competition' with *Tanya Grotter and the Magic Double Bass* and a Belarus version, *Porri Gatter and the Stone Philosopher*, made the wizard into a grenade launcher-toting partisan of the White Russian wars.

The 'novel engine' is Scott's most drastic re-imagining of the traditional images of authorship. While the 'high' Romantic poets used metaphors of nightingales, Aeolian harps, opium dreams, boats scudding on perfectly reflective lakes and Attic vases to represent the creative, poetic mind itself, Scott offers the image of a machine. It is at once more radical and more conservative. Given how he would end his life, the playful take on hoaxes and imitations seems almost foreboding.

Crash

Who was to blame for the most spectacular financial disaster of the age? The very nature of the crisis involved a web of transactions and indebtedness, reckless optimism and poisonous cynicism, and a precarious nexus of trust and deceit. The crash involved individual lack of responsibility, corporate mismanagement and governmental chaos. At one extreme, one can place the onus of guilt on Scott himself – his earliest biographer, George Allan, wrote 'the *pus* had been accumulating for years, and Scott *could not* but have been perfectly aware of it'. At the other, one could look at the overall economic collapse. Facing a dangerously inflated bubble of specula-tion, the Bank of England restrained credit; its gold reserves fell by two-thirds; and six London and sixty regional banks failed over the course of the year.

The crash became a reality for Scott in a manner so mundane as to be nearly comical. J O Robinson, of Hurst, Robinson & Co., Constable's London agents, had invested in £40,000 worth of hops. It was not a wise venture. The market was already sated, and he was forced to sell at a massive loss – having borrowed £30,000 from the publishing company. The bills of Hurst, Robinson & Co. were backed by Constable & Co.; the printing company James Ballantyne & Co. was guaranteeing the bills of Constable. Scott was in effect the sole owner of Ballantyne & Co. and was currently under contract with Constable (who had pioneered payment in advance for as-yet-unwritten works) for a total of nine new works. In the preface to *The Betrothed*, the Revd Josiah Cargill, from *Saint Ronan's Well*, is irked that 'his' book, *The Seige of Ptolemais*, is deferred again: Scott had joked that he would write the book the minister is toiling over in the novel, and Constable had taken that as a verbal contract and adver-tised it. Unbeknown to Ballantyne or Constable, Scott had entailed

Abbotsford to his son, with the provision that he enjoyed life possession of the house: Ballantyne and Constable believed that Abbotsford was an asset of the company and could be used as security for their liabilities. The domino that fell might have been Robinson's stock of hops, but it toppled into an interconnected, mutually self-supporting and self-deluding house of cards. It is testament to the absurdity of the time that Scott was seriously thinking about drawing £30,000 from his companies in the summer of 1825 to add Faldonside to his estate, and by January 1826 was musing over his butler Dalgleish's offer to work for free and the proposal that his daughters' music teacher, Mr Poole, would gift him his life savings.

When the Crash came, it was exacerbated by Scott's reliance on 'bills of accommodation'. In a situation where confidence was high but liquidity was low, they were an easy way to raise cash quickly. Scott (via Ballantyne) would make out a credit note for a sum to be repaid at a fixed future date, endorsed by Constable, and Constable would make-out a counter-bill endorsed by Ballantyne. The first such bill would be cashed at the bank (for less than its face value), and in some instances the second would as well. All three men would use bills of accommodation, and not always for company expenses: Scott's, Constable's and Ballantyne's homes were all financed in part by such bills. The fundamental flaw in the use of bills of accommodation was that, in the event of either of the participants failing to repay the debt, the full amount of both bill and counter-bill fell on one signatory. Scott, in essence, had to pay back more than double (taking discount and interest into consideration) what he had borrowed. The total debt stood at £116, 838.11s.3d. By far the greatest part of it – over £75,000 – was in the form of 'bills discounted and in the hands of third parties'; half of it in bills and half of it in counter-bills.

The Crash severed relations between Constable and Scott completely. It is an ignominious story, with Scott, encouraged by Lockhart and Cadell who had their own agendas, pouring the whole of the blame on Constable. 'He paid well and promptly, but, devil take him, it was all spectral together,' Scott told a friend: an interesting choice of word. Constable filed for bankruptcy, repaying two shillings and nine pence in the pound, lost his house, and died within a year.

Scott did not attend the funeral. Although it would have been easier for Scott to file for bankruptcy as well, it would also reveal the extent to which the Laird of Abbotsford was no more than a common tradesman. Bankruptcy would also mean the loss of Abbotsford, and his library, and might mean he would have to live abroad. Nor was bankruptcy in the interests of the creditors: Scott was still the most profitable living author, and any resolution which maximised their return could be seen as shrewd as well as generous. Eric Quayle, the author of *The Ruin of Sir Walter Scott* and a descendant of the Ballantynes, wrote, not without rancour, that 'it is doubtful if any other debtor in Britain would have been let off the hook in quite so generous a fashion as Scott was by the bankers and moneylenders of London and Edinburgh'. By comparison, the 'career' of Thomas De Quincey, whose later life involved midnight flits, pawning clothes and books, and frequent imprisonment is telling. In 1832 De Quincey was sought after for such sums as £37.16s.6d due to an Edinburgh book-seller, £10 to his landlord, and £180 defaulted on a mortgage. Thanks to the entail to Walter Jnr, Scott continued to live in Abbotsford, rent-free, with his own furniture and library, his legal salary, and the profits from any work he undertook in his 'spare time'. His Edinburgh home, 39 Castle Street, however, was sold; although he was allowed to transfer 350 dozen bottles of wine and 36 dozen bottles of spirits to the cellars of Abbotsford.

Disgrace, exile and separation from the very materials on which his future earnings rested: bankruptcy was not an option for Scott or his creditors. What is remarkable, however, is how Scott created a psychological carapace for his situation. *Not* accepting bankruptcy became, in Scott's mind, an act of heroism. 'My own right hand shall pay my debt' was his famous rallying-cry. The settee-soldier streak in his character now had a real and pressing opportunity to demonstrate courage in the face of adversity. Scott had recently started his *Journal*, a work which, in the words of John Buchan, 'gives us that very thing in which Hazlitt declared him lacking, "what the heart whispers to itself in secret". The greatest figure he ever drew is in the *Journal*, and it is the man Walter Scott.' The language of the *Journal* figures his dilemma in constantly martial terms. 'I will not yield without a fight for it.' Had Ballantyne been deprived of work by Constable's shenanigans, he claimed he would 'put a knife to my throat'. In terms of bankruptcy, he wrote that, as a lawyer, it was 'the course I would have advised a client to take . . . but for this I would in a court of Honour deserve to lose my spurs'. During the negotiations, and concerned that his creditors might force a bankruptcy, he confided in his diary that 'if they take the sword of the law, I must lay hold of the shield'. It was not a legal and financial obligation, but a 'debt of honour'. 'I will be their vassal for life,' he wrote, 'and dig in the mine of my imagination to find diamonds (or what they sell as such).' Even at this pitch of play chivalry, in creeps an allusion to pretence and forgery.

Later biographers, starting with Lockhart, use the crash as the polarising glass that revealed Scott's intrinsic heroism and decency. 'He paid the penalty of health and life, but he saved his honour and his self-respect: "The glory dies not, and the grief is gone",' wrote Lockhart, and in the closing cadenza on his father-in-law he plays brilliantly to the gallery.

> How well he kept his vow, and what price it cost him to do so – all this the reader, I doubt not, appreciates fully. It seems to me that strength of character was never put to a severer test than when, for labours of love, such as his had hitherto almost always been – the pleasant exertion of genius for the attainment of ends that owed all their dignity and beauty to a poetical fancy – there came to be substituted the iron pertinacity of daily and nightly toil, in the discharge of a duty which there was nothing but the sense of chivalrous honour to make stringent. It is the fond indulgence of gay fancy in all the previous story that gives its true value and dignity to the voluntary agony of the sequel.

Scott is not just a hero, but a tragic hero. His flaw is the twin source of his apex and nadir.

> We should ask ourselves whether, filling and discharging so soberly and gracefully as he did the common functions of the social man, it was not, nevertheless, impossible but that he

must have passed most of his life in other worlds than ours; and we ought hardly to think it a grievous circumstance that their bright visitors should have left a dazzle sometimes on the eyes which he so gently reopened on our prosaic realities. He had, on the whole, a command over the powers of his mind – I mean that he could control and divert his thoughts and reflections with a readiness, firmness and easy security of sway – beyond what I find it possible to trace in any other artist's recorded character and history; but he could not habitually fling them into the region of dreams throughout a long series of years, and yet be expected to find a corresponding satisfaction in bending them to the less agreeable considerations which the circumstances of any human being's practical lot in this world must present in abundance.

This is a myth more invasive and adaptive than any of the Romantic self-presentations of Wordsworth, Byron or Shelley; the myth of the author as inherently unworldly. The history of literature is littered with casualties of this idea that a great poet should not be expected to understand finance: Dylan Thomas, Barry McSweeney, Alex Trocchi. It is a legacy that would have raised Scott's notoriously shaggy eyebrow.

Lockhart's portrayal is carried on by Buchan, Grierson, Hesketh Pearson and A N Wilson – indeed, Pearson is even more dewy-eyed: 'He fought without yielding to his last breath, and won the battle, though he did not live to taste the triumph.' But there is a counter-tradition, in which the idea of the old warrior, strapping on his rusty armour for a final, suicidal battle and the notion of a distracted, unmindful dreamer, are equally fake. William Weir and George Allan's biography raised the idea that greed, not fey lack of concentration, was at the root of the crash, and both Quayle and Sutherland take a more sceptical and aggressive attitude towards Scott. As soon as Lockhart's *Life of Sir Walter Scott* was published, the Ballantyne family issued a *Refutation of the Mistatements and Calumnies contained in Mr Lockart's Life of Sir Walter Scott, Bart*. Lockhart – now that his father-in-law was dead, he slipped back into the more waspish and vicious elements of his youth – replied with *The Ballantyne Humbug Handled*. The family reiterated their accusations, and it came to nothing until Eric Quayle, to borrow a Lockhart-like phrase, took up the broken lances of his forebears. Throughout the initial dispute, one faction was suspiciously quiet. The *Life of Sir Walter Scott* certainly criticised the Ballantynes as inept, ungrateful and pretentious, but the real villain of the piece was left in little doubt: Archibald Constable. The Ballantyne brothers could be dismissed with silly names by Lockhart – Rigdumfunnidos and Aldiborontiphoscophornia, both derived from *Chrononhotonthologos* by Henry Cary in 1734; one is blunt, the other baroque in speech – but Constable was 'the *Czar*', 'Napoleon' and Lockhart described viciously his 'tyrannical temper', how he 'gesticulated like some hoary despot' and pronounced 'haughty ravings of scorn and wrath'. This was the Constable who, Lockhart claimed, asserted he was 'half the Author of Waverley myself'. Why did the family of Constable not respond? Well, the son was driven mad by his father's financial collapse, and the business now resided in the hands of son-in-law and successor Robert Cadell and the publisher of Lockhart's *Life*. Cadell also persuaded the Lockharts, after Scott's death, to sign over the copyrights to the Waverley Novels, for a nugatory fee. He later wrote: 'I am left alone of those behind the curtain. I came here as a raw young man and have cuckooed all those men out of their nests.' Systematic dissimulation is not too strong a phrase to describe Lockhart's and Cadell's game of pass-the-blame: two sons-in-law, of more powerful fathers, hampered and liberated by their association. Cadell allowed Lockhart to slander Constable and canonise Scott, and in return, he cheated Lockhart and Scott Jnr out of the copyrights. Of all the principal players, only Cadell ended up richer and more powerful. In truth, both portraits are true. Scott was generous and mean-spirited, noble and venal, cautious and feckless; in a word, antisyzygical; in a phrase, all too human. However one apportions the blame, the emotional impact on Scott was clear and devastating. As he confided in the *Journal*:

> What a life mine has been! – half educated, almost wholly
> neglected, or left to myself; stuffing my head with most

nonsensical trash, and undervalued by most of my companions for a time; getting forward, and held a bold and clever fellow, contrary to the opinion of all who thought me a mere dreamer; broken-hearted for two years; my heart handsomely pieced again; but the crack will remain till my dying day. Rich and poor four or five times; once on the verge of ruin, yet opened a new source of wealth almost overflowing. Now to be broken in my pitch of pride, and nearly winged (unless good news should come); because London chooses to be in an uproar, and in the tumult of bulls and bears, a poor inoffensive lion like myself is pushed to the wall. But what is to be the end of it? God knows; and so ends the catechism.

Bang

The spectacular nature of Scott's fall can blind us to its more typical aspects. He was susceptible to a degree of self-dramatisation at times – as when he met an old friend, Skene, and said, 'My friend, give me a shake of your hand – mine is that of a beggar.' (A beggar, let us recall, with a castle, one of the finest private libraries in Britain, a salary and at least 432 bottles of whisky in his cellar.) Countless individuals suffered worse privations and perhaps an even a greater sense of disgrace, but two in particular exemplify the craziness of the 1825–6 crash. It was not 'Scott's crash'; it was a national crisis.

John Murray II was the other half of the 'Scotch Monopoly'. He was the publisher of Byron, Austen, the *Quarterly Review* and Thomas Moore. In late 1825, a cocky young man turned up at his offices at 50 Albermarle Street and suggested they start a Tory newspaper to rival *The Times*. Since the young man in question was the son of one of Murray's friends and authors, he went ahead with the scheme, despite the fact that part of the finance supposedly came from lucrative shares in a South American silver mine. It ended in catastrophe. The newspaper, *The Representative*, lasted only six months, failed dismally, and Murray lost over £26,000 in the debacle. Murray bitterly rued his '"entanglement" with a newspaper, which absorbed my money and distracted and depressed my mind'. In later years, when he was impressed upon to start another newspaper, Murray would look gloomy, point at the bookshelves where the entire run was kept, and grumble 'twenty thousand pounds are buried there'. What makes the whole fiasco even more surprising is that the young man was Benjamin Disraeli, the future Prime Minister.

Murray had dispatched Disraeli to the Scottish Borders, to secure Scott and Lockhart's involvement. It would appeal to their politics, and their vanity might be swelled by the offer to Lockhart of editorship. Lockhart had other plans: editor of a *newspaper* was socially less distinguished than editor of a *Review*, especially since he thought he ought to get a seat in Parliament as well. Disraeli wrote back reports in breakable code (Scott is 'The Chevalier' and he himself was the 'Political Puck') and failed in every assignment. He did, however, express a penchant for Scottish breakfasts, particularly grouse with marmalade. Despite lacking the high-profile support of Scott and Lockhart, *The Representative* went ahead with a frankly inexplicable combination of amateurism and grandiosity – Disraeli was intent on hiring a cousin to design new offices for the newspaper, while failing to secure the necessary government contacts to provide the actual news for the newspaper. He did manage to get William Maginn the job of Parisian correspondent, with a salary of £700 a year and a grace-and-favour house. 'The result was,' writes Murray's biographer Samuel Smiles, 'a number of clever *jeux d'esprit* . . . but these were intermingled with some biting articles, which gave considerable offense.' Maginn apparently 'drank much and wrote little'. The leaders were 'tedious to a degree and intolerably long' and Scott wrote to his daughter that 'its jokes put me in mind of the child's question whether a pound of feathers or a pound of lead is the heaviest'. Despite Disraeli and Murray's high hopes for its political influence, not even a General Election led to any increase of sales; and its nickname, 'The Rip', soon became 'The Demi-Rip' when advertising revenue started to haemorrhage.

The whole sorry story had a sorrier sequel. *The Representative* soured and nearly extirpated relations between Murray and his friend and author Isaac D'Israeli, particularly because Benjamin Disraeli used the whole affair as the basis of his first novel, *Vivian Grey* (1826). The attempt to start a newspaper is transformed in the fiction into the foundation of a new political party. The novel appeared anonymously, with the rather exaggerated claim that the author was 'a man of fashion' who moved in high society, which encouraged readers to speculate about its roman-à-clef qualities. Murray is lampooned as the ineffectual 'Marquess of Carabas', and Disraeli even insinuated that Murray had an alcohol problem (an accusation strikingly uncorroborated by any other letter, memoir or

article of the period). Disraeli's conscience over the vengeful caricature must have needled him to the extent that the novel was heavily
revised and altered for the 1853 version, omitting the slurs on
Murray. Oddest of all, one of the characters in the novel is given the
name 'Lord Beaconsfield', fifty years before Disraeli would choose
that as his title.

Disraeli's audacity and insensitivity pales in comparison with that
of 'General' Gregorio McGregor. Born in Edinburgh in 1786, he
joined the Navy in 1803 and saw action taking San Ferdinanda, an
island off the coast of Florida, from the Spanish. The feat was accomplished with only a minimal complement of men, and Gregorio then
sold the entire place to a pirate. Nevertheless, he was singled out by
Simon Bolivar, during a period of Romantic independence movements (Greece; Hungary later on, and all of the South American
revolutions), as a capable and intrepid friend to South America. He
returned to London in 1820 claiming to be the cazique, or de facto
ruler, of an independent nation on the Bay of Honduras called
Poyais. Poyais – all 32,400 km² of it – was abundantly fertile and now
had an army, a democracy, a capital city called St Joseph, friendly
locals who hated the Spanish and loved Protestant Christianity, and
untapped silver and gold mines. McGregor – who claimed descent
from Rob Roy McGregor and one of the sole survivors of Scotland's
abortive attempt at a colony in Darien, prior to the Union of the
Parliaments – was fêted by the Lord Mayor of London and hosted
dinner parties with foreign ambassadors keen to establish diplomatic
ties to Poyais. A book, entitled *Sketch of the Mosquito Shore, including
the Territory of Poyais* – most likely by McGregor but attributed to
Captain Thomas Strangeways – described the country in glowing
terms. By 1822 the first settlers were headed there, blissfully unaware
that the country was a fiction. Most of the first settlers were Scottish,
their pockets full of worthless 'Poyais Dollars'.

Fewer than fifty returned to Britain, but not because Poyais was the
earthly Paradise the prospectus had conjured. Its Edenic qualities
probably began and ended with the presence of snakes. When his
ruse was discovered, McGregor fled to France and started exactly the
same scheme, with the slight alteration that Poyais was a Republic,

not a monarchy whose king had made him the chief executive. Despite legal action taken against him, McGregor eluded prison and was back in London by 1826. In London – even with the previous failed scheme and French trial – he was still able to raise £800,000 in twenty-year bonds in order to promote emigration to 'Lesser Poyais'. At the last minute, the scheme was rumbled, not because McGregor's fantasies had been disproven, but because other con men were trying the same trick. The *Edinburgh Annual Register* described the situation precisely: 'We assure you there is no Poyais sea or city of Poyais in existence, nor any appearance in any part of the country to warrant such an assertion; and indeed, to sum up the whole, we cannot better exemplify it than by declaring that the whole scheme of the estab-lishment has been built "upon the baseless fabric of a vision".' The *Quarterly Review* was equally vociferous. 'After all, we have, perhaps, been contending with shadows, and the "lands" and the "loan" and the "Macgregor" (notwithstanding the fierce portrait as a fron-tispiece) are non-entities, and the whole affair merely, what is vulgarly called, a hoax – if, however, they are realities, we think the proper authorities would do well not only to disavow all sanction of such pernicious fooleries, but to put an instant stop to them.' McGregor eventually lived out the rest of his life in Venezuela.

Poyais, *The Representative* and Scott are bound together in oblique ways. Disraeli's fictitious South American mines are akin to the Poyais natural resources. In more jocular fashion, just before his own financial collapse, Scott had wagered 'all Abbotsford to an acre of Poyais' when congratulating a friend on her son's marriage. McGregor put into practice what Scott had done: he sold an imagi-nary country. It is telling to compare the fraud and the fiction. McGregor sold 'Poyais' for three shillings and thruppence an acre, and found two ships full of Scots eager to pay the money. Lord Dudley wrote to Scott's friend Morritt saying, 'Let every man to whom he has given months of delight give him a sixpence and he will rise to-morrow richer than Rothschild.'

These three interconnected narratives also bring to mind a feature of money itself that, in the months after the Crash, would become important to Scott: that it is, intrinsically, a form of fiction.

A banknote is not 'ten pounds': it is a promise, from the bank, to pay the bearer on demand that sum in sterling. In the first issue of the *Edinburgh Review*, Francis Horner defended the concept of paper currency, appealing to the readership to show their trust in their fellow countrymen by accepting the note as promise. The Poyais scheme, the funding of *The Representative* and the crash of Constable and Scott show how precarious that concept of trust still was.

Wallop

Early in 1826, Scott's business affairs were put into a trust. With what must have been an uncomfortably ironic twist, the trust was chaired by Sir William Forbes, the man who had married Scott's first love, Williamina Belsches. Forbes communicated Scott's 'earnest desire to use every exertion in his power on behalf of his creditors, and by a diligent employment of his talents and the adoption of a strictly economical mode of life to secure as speedily as possible full payment to all concerned'. Only one person – a London moneylender called Mr Abud – did not agree to the terms. This led to some unpleasant anti-Semitic sniping from Lockhart and Scott himself. Scott even wrote to his son, saying, 'If London should ever be plundered by the soldiery, I recommend his shop to your particular attention, which as he deals in gold bars cannot but repay it.' Forbes, with customary generosity and self-effacement, paid off Abud from his own pocket.

On 15 May, Lady Scott died. She is, like most of Scott's female characters, at some level inscrutable. Scott hinted that she had not been as supportive as he had expected when news of the crash came through, but his absolute grief on her death cannot be underestimated. The passage from his *Journal* is worth quoting in full:

> For myself, I scarce know how I feel, sometimes as firm as the Bass Rock, sometimes as weak as the water that breaks on it. I am as alert at thinking and deciding as I ever was in my life. Yet, when I contrast what this place now is, with what it has been not long since, I think my heart will break. Lonely, aged, deprived of my family—all but poor Anne; an impoverished, an embarrassed man, deprived of the sharer of my thoughts and counsels, who could always talk down my sense of the

calamitous apprehensions which break the heart that must bear them alone. – Even her foibles were of service to me, by giving me things to think of beyond my weary self-reflections.

I have seen her. The figure I beheld is, and is not my Charlotte – my thirty years' companion. There is the same symmetry of form, though those limbs are rigid which were once so gracefully elastic – but that yellow masque, with pinched features, which seems to mock life rather than emulate it, can it be the face that was once so full of lively expression? I will not look on it again. Anne thinks her little changed, because the latest idea she had formed of her mother is as she appeared under circumstances of extreme pain. Mine go back to a period of comparative ease. If I write long in this way, I shall write down my resolution, which I should rather write up, if I could. I wonder how I shall do with the large portion of thoughts which were hers for thirty years. I suspect they will be hers yet for a long time at least. But I will not blaze cambric and crape in the public eye, like a disconsolate widower, that most affected of all characters.

May 18. – Another day, and a bright one to the external world, again opens on us; the air soft, and the flowers smiling, and the leaves glittering. They cannot refresh her to whom mild weather was a natural enjoyment. Cerements of lead and of wood already hold her; cold earth must have her soon. But it is not my Charlotte, it is not the bride of my youth, the mother of my children, that will be laid among the ruins of Dryburgh, which we have so often visited in gaiety and pastime. No, no. She is sentient and conscious of my emotions somewhere – somehow; *where* we cannot tell; *how* we cannot tell; yet would I not at this moment renounce the mysterious yet certain hope that I shall see her in a better world, for all that this world can give me. The necessity of this separation, that necessity which rendered it even a relief, that and patience must be my comfort. I do not experience those paroxysms of grief which others do on the same occasion. I can exert myself, and speak even cheerfully with the poor girls. But alone, or if any thing touches me, the choking sensation. I have been to her room; there was no voice in it – no stirring; the pressure of the coffin was visible on the bed, but it had been removed else-where; all was neat, as she loved it, but all was calm – calm as death. I remembered the last sight of her; she raised herself in bed, and tried to turn her eyes after me, and said, with a sort of smile, 'You all have such melancholy faces.' These were the last words I ever heard her utter, and I hurried away, for she did not seem quite conscious of what she said – when I returned, immediately departing, she was in a deep sleep. It is deeper now. This was but seven days since.

They are arranging the chamber of death; that which was long the apartment of connubial happiness, and of whose arrangements (better than in richer houses) she was so proud. They are treading fast and thick. For weeks you could have heard a foot-fall. Oh my God!

If that were not grief enough, Sir John Sinclair came up with the single worst plan to solve Scott's financial woes. Given his wife had died, what would prevent him from marrying the Dowager Duchess of Roxburgh? In the *Journal*, Scott is 'struck dumb' by the 'absurdity' that the 'wretch' is proposing; in his letter to Sinclair he politely mentions that he is 'disinclined again to enter the matrimonial estate'.

The domestic crisis was paralleled with a national crisis. In the wake of the Crash, the Government attempted to overhaul the banking system. The key proposal was to ban private banks from issuing notes for sums less than five pounds. Indeed, it had been the inability of English banks to honour small denomination notes that had precipitated the wave of bank failures in 1825 and 1826. Scott, and many other Scots, were absolutely opposed to the idea, and saw in it a pernicious and surreptitious attempt to impose uniformity across the British banking system. Scott retaliated with three pamphlets, entitled *The Letters of Malachi Malagrowther*, with the conceit that Malachi is a descendant of Sir Mungo Malagrowther, the loyal but cantankerous courtier in *The Fortunes of Nigel*.

'Whimsical enough,' he wrote in his *Journal*, 'that when I was trying to animate Scotland against the currency bill, John Gibson brought me the Deed of Trust, assigning my whole estate, to be subscribed by me; so that I am turning patriot, and taking charge of the affairs of the country, on the very day I was proclaiming myself incapable of managing my own.'

Scott's argument was pragmatic. No Scottish banks had actually collapsed during the 1825–6 panic, proving that the use of low-denomination notes was not in itself a problem north of the Border. It was, moreover, essential to the stable running of the economy since Scotland had relatively less gold and silver, so small notes made up the vast bulk of circulating currency. The effects of the proposed reforms would be more punitive in Scotland, where there was less need for any intervention. Scott called for a legislative strike by Scottish and Irish MPs as a means of derailing the proposals. The *Malachi Malagrowther* pamphlets managed to infuriate both Scott's Tory allies and his Whig opponents, but they succeeded in their aim. Scott's portrait remains on Bank of Scotland notes in tribute to his campaign.

There was a peculiar sense of *déjà vu* in 2008 when the Government, panicked by a run on the Northern Rock bank, attempted to restrict the Scottish banks' right to print and distribute their own banknotes. Alex Salmond, the leader of the Scottish Government, described the scheme as a 'dagger at the heart' of Scottish banking, revealing the extent to which such a technical economic issue can incite genuine patriotic fervour: when the Treasury dropped the idea, his rhetoric was triumphalist: 'This is great news. It's a victory for Scotland and its financial sector. I'm delighted the Treasury have dropped their ludicrous proposals that threatened the very existence of Scottish bank notes. Let's hope they've finally learnt their lesson and never jeopardise our bank notes again.' In all the column inches, nobody remembered Scott's contribution.

The Letters of Malachi Malagrowther still generate contention, because of the insight they provide on the vexed issue of Scott's 'nationalism'. The *Letters* and Scott's private letters and *Journal* can be quoted in and out of context to uphold diametrically opposed positions: Scott as arch-Tory defender of the Union, Scott as crypto-nationalist. 'We had better remain in union with England, even at the risk of becoming a subordinate species of Northumberland, as far as national consequence is concerned, than remedy ourselves by even hinting at the possibility of a rupture' is the public statement. In private, he wrote to Croker saying, 'Scotland, completely liber-alised, as she is in a fair way of being, will be the most dangerous enemy to England that she has had since 1639. There is yet time to make a stand, for there is yet a great deal of good and genuine feeling left in the country. But if you *unscotch* us you will find us damned mischievous Englishmen.' No individual has fixed opinions throughout their life. In 1806 Scott rebuked Jeffrey, saying, ' 'tis no laughing matter; little by little, whatever your wishes may be, you will destroy and undermine, until nothing of what makes Scotland Scotland shall remain'. In 1822 he was a model of 'British' loyalty.

In part, the problem arises from the imposition of anachronistic modern conceptions of 'nationalism' and 'Unionism' on a period when such ideas did not exist. The 'National Party of Scotland' was formed in 1928, amalgamating a group of nationalist-inflected move-ments and associations. Even at its outset, Scott was a problematic precursor. Sir Compton Mackenzie, the eccentric author of *Whisky Galore*, attributed his nationalism to Scott. In his acceptance speech on becoming Rector of Glasgow University (the first electoral victory by a self-proclaimed nationalist) he said, 'The vision of Scotland which as a boy I beheld in *Tales of a Grandfather* [Scott's 1828–31 history of Scotland for children] was no longer a dream that faded when the book was closed: it was ever-present in the daily round of life.' Hugh MacDiarmid, another early member of the National Party, penned a four-line squib on Scott's centenary in 1932, which raged

> No poet did you honour, Scott,
> No master of your craft, and you
> Are welcome to the royalty and rubbish
> Who saw your dud centenary through.

The Letters of Malachi Malagrowther have provided fuel for those who wish to co-opt Scott as a prototype nationalist in their insistence on Scotland's right to (economic) self-determination. But a closer analysis is more revealing. Scott does invoke the Act of Union, claiming that the currency proposals would damage Scotland's creditworthiness. The Act, however, had specific provisions that no laws would be introduced that were not to Scotland's benefit. Scott's anger was focused on the fact that the Westminster Government was breaking the Union by attempting to create a law in clear opposition to the terms of the Act of Union. To use an analogy, Scott behaves like a marriage guidance counsellor, not a divorce lawyer. Scott was – and this is not a paradox – a Unionist nationalist.

Having lost his fortune and wife, and saved his country, Scott's mild recurrent strokes started to become not so mild.

Unmasking the Author of Waverley

Speculating about the identity of the Author of Waverley was an industry in itself. In 1822, Robert Chambers – who would, in later life, write the most successful exposition of pre-Darwinian ideas of natural selection, *Vestiges of the Natural History of Creation* – published *Illustrations of the Author of Waverley*. Unlike Adolphus's *Letters to Richard Heber*, Chambers was not intent on unmasking the author, but rather unmasking the fictions. He catalogued the real-life counterparts of characters and incidents – Helen Walker is the original of Jeanie Deans; David Ritchie is the Black Dwarf; Janet Dalrymple's story mirrors Lucy Ashton's. No reader, browsing through Chambers' research, would be in any doubt about the only other person to have such a voluminous knowledge of the more recondite episodes in Scottish history. To emphasise the point, the book had a portrait of the Author of Waverley: an engraving of Scott from his poetry, but with his entire face concealed by a drape. The curtain would soon be drawn away.

Woodstock was to be the last Waverley Novel by the Author of Waverley. It was begun before the crash and concluded after it, and the shadow falls over it. Sir Henry Lee, a noble Cavalier, is languishing under Cromwell's republic and facing eviction from his Oxfordshire lodge. He is a widower, and although Scott began it as a married man, he too was a widower when it was published. *Woodstock* is also notable in that it is set in roughly the same period as one of the Waverley forgeries, *Pontefract Castle*. There are uncanny similarities: haunted houses with secret passages were not typical of Scott, but appear in both novels, and the characterisation of the Parliamentary radicals is similar. Cromwell appears in both novels, and the opposition of Shakespeare readers and Milton readers also coincides.

The next work, *Chronicles of the Canongate*, is marbled through with Scott's own situation. It appeared in two volumes, rather than three, for fear that any three-volume work might be considered part of the outstanding agreement with Constable and therefore jeopardise the settlement with the creditors. The book has often been filleted: the 'stories' – *The Highland Widow, The Two Drovers* and *The Surgeon's Daughter* – have often been cut from their frame and presented as independent, self-standing works. The framing story is Scott's most elaborate. The narrator, Chrystal Croftangry, is another avatar of Scott: after the half-pay soldier Clutterbuck, the antiquarian Dryasdust, the enigmatic Eidolon, the eccentric Cleishbotham and the swindler Dousterswivel, Croftangry is the broken and resilient Scott. He is 'a Scottish gentleman of the old school, with a fortune, temper, and person rather the worse for wear'. He has 'known the world . . . and does not think it is much mended'. He was a lawyer, and 'emulated to the utmost the expenses of men of large fortune'. His ruin – partly his own fault, partly the fault of the 'fat man of business' he allowed to run his affairs, a nasty dig at Constable – means that he now lives in the debtors' quarter of the Canongate. The sanctuary of the Canongate is beautifully evoked, as is Croftangry's bemused fury: 'all Elysium seemed opening on the other side of the kennel, and I envied the little blackguards, who, stopping the current with their little damdikes of mud, had a right to stand on either side of the nasty puddle which best pleased them'. Having wasted then sold his estate, he returns to it while posing as a prospective buyer, but a bruising encounter with an old family retainer disabuses him of any romantic notions of returning in triumph. Nevertheless, he pays a significant sum to his veteran accuser, along with a sarcastic poem. If Croftangry resembles any part of Scott, it is the part that is so ashamed and livid at his situation that his only catharsis can be fictional.

Having been forced to sell 39 Castle Street, Scott took lodgings in Edinburgh when he was conducting business there. There is an element of self-dramatisation in his refusal to stay with rich friends and pay cash for a bedbug-ridden mattress instead. In an awful way, he liked his distress. It is as if love during success is merely flattery, but love in calamity is proof. The Croftangry prefaces show a dim awareness of diminishing returns. At first, Chrystal has the aged society lady Mrs Martha Bethune Balliol as a source for stories, but even then only after her death. The second story is snaffled from his landlady, while the publisher's boy is standing at the door waiting for copy. The third is from the lawyer who is dealing with his bankruptcy (and is the worst story, although it does involve an elephant stamping the villain to death). The second series of the *Chronicles* features Chrystal wholly reliant on his own invention, although it begins with a witty description of a Cockney visitor to Holyrood Palace trying to remove Rizzio's bloodstains with Detergent Elixir Scouring Pills. Chrystal describes the murder to Mrs Balliol: 'You surely mean to novelize, or to dramatize if you will, this most singular of all tragedies?' she asks. 'Worse – that is, less interesting periods of history have been, indeed, shown up, for furnishing amusement to the peaceable ages which have succeeded; but, dear lady, the events are too well known in Mary's days, to be used as vehicles of romantic fiction.' Scott seems dimly aware of his own waning powers. Periods which once easily furnished him with the material for romances now seem exhausted and too well known.

The Chronicles of the Canongate still claims to be by 'The Author of Waverley &c' on the title page, but its prefatory preface is the grand unveiling. Scott finally confessed to being the Author of Waverley on 23 February 1827, at a dinner for the Edinburgh Theatrical Fund. He began his speech with a haunting comparison. He opens by discussing Arlecchino, or Harlequin, the *commedia dell'arte* clown with a black mask and diamond motley. 'The mask,' he says, 'was essential to the performance of the character.' But the character is worth staying with: subconsciously, Scott reveals a huge amount about himself by choosing this particular avatar during his most public speech. Arlecchino started as Hellequin in French passion plays and was a demon who scoured the country with a troop of monsters, seeking souls to drag to Hell. He was, in the Italian pantomime version, physically agile and mentally clumsy. Harlequin was in love with Columbine, but his venal nature and stupidity usually prevented any happy ending. He was also, crucially, a servant. Scott had spent a lifetime indulging in his self-image of a demonic sorcerer; he now downplayed his role in public as a mere functionary. Scott was not physically agile – his lameness had been the source of many of his fantasies – and finally revealing himself as a clown, albeit a nimble clown, is psychologically acute. It is as easy to imagine the laughter of the audience, who all understand that Scott was no kind of Harlequin, as it is to imagine his sadness, unveiled as the clumsy, pitiable dependant he had become.

The extended discussion of Harlequin is a preamble to an anecdote about the actor who

> played Harlequin barefaced, but was considered on all hands as having made a total failure. He had lost the audacity which a sense of incognito bestowed, and with it all the reckless play of raillery which gave vivacity to his original acting. He cursed his advisers, and resumed his grotesque vizard; but, it is said, without ever being able to regain the careless and successful levity which the consciousness of the disguise had formerly bestowed. Perhaps the Author of Waverley is now about to incur a risk of the same kind, and endanger his popularity by having laid aside his incognito. It is certainly not a voluntary experiment, like that of Harlequin; for it was my original intention never to have avowed these works during my lifetime, and the original manuscripts were carefully preserved, (though by the care of others rather than mine), with the purpose of supplying the necessary evidence of the truth when the period of announcing it should arrive. But the affairs of my publishers having unfortunately passed into a management different from their own, I had no right any longer to rely upon secrecy in that quarter; and thus my mask . . . having begun to wax a little threadbare about the chin, it became time to lay it aside with a good grace, unless I desired it should fall in pieces from my face, which was now become likely.

Scott's speech continues in a manner reminiscent of Chambers' *Illustrations*, as he describes the genesis of some of the most famous novels – the 'real life' Old Mortality, the locations he transformed, the family friends who might have inadvertently exposed him when they realised they appeared, thinly disguised, in the novels. It would seem to be the success of this speech that led to the structure of the *Magnum Opus*. Finally, he addresses the question of *why*. As mentioned earlier, Scott would later cite Shylock. At this time, however, he quotes Corporal Nym's refrain in *Henry V* – 'that is the humour of 't'. Nym was in his mind a great deal during these months. The quote 'Things must be as they may' was his constant bulwark when thoughts of his crash, bereavement and illness got too much.

Realia

On the fifth floor of the University of Edinburgh Library in George Square – overlooking the house where Walter Scott grew up as a boy – is a collection in an air-conditioned, windowless, temperature-controlled strong room. I had been allowed to visit and examine one part of this collection in particular; a unique and slightly surreal sub-category called the Realia. The collection was assembled by Dr James Corson, a former librarian at Abbotsford. He lived in Lilliesleaf, the same village where I grew up, and on his death I was asked by the lawyer who acted as executor to his will to assist in identifying the items to be sent to the University of Edinburgh. I was sixteen at the time, and had only known Dr Corson to wince away from in church. It was a task out of Dickens: not only did every book, every index card and every scrap of paper in his study have to be checked; but an entire, disused church next door housed his library, which had to be sifted as well. Corson was something of a monomaniac. Scott had been his life, and he had clipped from newspapers and magazines each and every reference to Scott. He had worked all his life on a bibliography so fanatically precise as to be almost unusable. Throughout, he had engaged in the kind of intense, slow-burning academic rivalries that characterise keepers of the flame, and had not only denounced slacker rivals but published an entire edition to 'correct' the work of one of the only people who maintained cordial relations with him. On the sixth floor of the University of Edinburgh Library I was about to reacquaint myself with a man I had only really known after his death.

The bulk of the Corson collection is his own notebooks, his copious scrapbooks of ephemeral references (I remembered a recipe from the *Radio Times* for Abbotsford Buns), his impressively complete sets of different editions of Scott's work and thousands of picture postcards with some overt or abstruse connection to Scott. There are also paintings and etchings and file after file of correspondence. The boxes moved up from the strong room to the Special Collections reading room were the Realia. In the company of Paul Barnaby, the Senior Library Assistant for the Walter Scott Digital Archive, I re-enacted a parodic version of the reopening of the Regalia.

'Realia' means 'real things'. In the case of literary studies, it refers specifically to objects, rather than manuscript papers, printed books or images, with a connection to the author. At one extreme there are *unica*, the one-and-only, personal artefacts (the very pen with which he wrote, the shoes he wore, the snipped) lock of hair: the literary equivalent of relics. The Corson collection is not made up of *unica*. Quite the contrary, it is an assortment of mass-produced articles, most of them made many years after Scott's death. It is an eerie miscellany of knick-knacks and trinkets and bibelots and doodads. It is, as another librarian ruefully said, 'some boxes of old tat we'd probably not take nowadays'.

One by one we unwrapped: miniature bed-warmers, ashtrays, bells, egg timers, door-knockers, thermometers in the shape of the Scott Monument, bottle openers, shoehorns, miniature coal-buckets, ornamental kettles, napkin holders, coal scuttles, a piggy bank, various plaster and bronze busts, of varying qualities of verisimilitude to the man himself, a porcelain replica of his favourite chair, tea sets, dishes, cups, a calendar with Scott tartan, a picture of Abbotsford and the legend 'Frae Bonny Scotland', a calling card case made of elm from the Rhymer's Glen, a stick of lettered rock, its box, a box with nothing in it ('a gift from Abbotsford'), packets of pencils, a bronze plaque, framed cameos, an 1871 pewter square profile of Scott, a bar of Scott Monument soap, medals from anniversaries, a cruet set, porcelain knights, a set of toy Templars, the backing card for an MGM-endorsed *Ivanhoe* action figure, a wooden case of postcard photographs, tea towels, a photograph framed in a circular wooden device, a jigsaw, whisky glasses, a printing block of Scott's face, a blue vase (chipped), a cigarette tin (Lambert & Butler's Waverley Mixture, coarse cut), cigarette cards depicting scenes from the novels, a tea tray, table mats, coasters, complete sets of china, and several shortbread tins. One of them had something in it, and we opened it (McVitie & Price Ltd. Shortbread) to find a stamp box, a set of combs, some crayons and a piece of paper in Corson's handwriting attached to some stone from Kaeside quarry used in the building of Abbotsford, and two hand-made nails from its roof. I must have breathed in some musty oxygen from the time, twenty years ago, when I sealed the box.

By far the greater part of this historical jetsam was items deliberately constructed to be smaller than practically useful: the bedwarmers, all of two inches across, could never have warmed a bed. Lacking a function, they were decorative clutter. They were little bits of individuality from a production line to be hung by the gas fire or displayed on the windowsill. Scott, the first modern literary celebrity, started to become branded goods very soon after his death. The Library also has an 1840s pop-up theatre for children to re-enact their favourite Waverley scenes, and such curiosities as a stereoscopic portrait (looked at from the left it's Byron; from the right, it's Scott) were produced in the same period. Most of Corson's collection was twentieth-century, and a good deal of that post-World War II. Memory misled me into thinking it had been a larger, more *antique* set of objects I had once wrapped up. For an awful moment I wondered if this was actually decades' worth of presents from his wife: what *do* you get the man who's only interested in one thing?

Mr Chainmail

Scott was satirised at the beginning of his career as an upstart, unknown novelty. Towards the end of his life, he was satirised as a predictable, conventional, all-too-well-known author. In 1831, the year before his death, Scott appeared in Thomas Love Peacock's novel *Crotchet Castle*, twice; first as Mr Chainmail, the medievalist, and then as 'the Northern Enchanter' whose novels are discussed over dinner. Mr Chainmail is described as

> a good-looking young gentleman ... with very antiquated tastes. He is very fond of old poetry, and is something of a poet himself. He is deep in monkish literature, and holds that the best state of society was that of the twelfth century, when nothing was going forward but fighting, feasting, and praying, which he says are the three best purposes for which man was made. He laments bitterly the inventions of gunpowder, steam, and gas, which he says have ruined the world. He lives within two or three miles, and has a large hall, adorned with rusty pikes, shields, helmets, swords, and tattered banners, and furnished with yew-tree chairs, and two long, old, worm-eaten oak tables.

The sample of Chainmail's poetry is clearly an attack on Scott's early poetics – one sample, about a philosopher called Gwenwynwyn who discovers the Philosopher's Stone, reads:

> He took castles and towns; he cut short limbs and lives;
> He made orphans and widows of children and wives:
> This course many years he triumphantly ran,
> And did enough mischief to be called a great man.

This caricature of Scott highlights the same elements of his personality as in Mark Twain's philippic, and harks back to William Hazlitt's scintillating essay on Scott in *The Spirit of the Age* (1825). In that elegant and incisive sketch, Hazlitt begins by calling Scott 'just half of what the human intellect is capable of being: if you take the universe and divide it into two parts, he knows all that *has been*; all that it *is to be* is nothing to him . . . he is a *"prophesier* of things past" '. Hazlitt's essay also hints at the darker aspects of Scott's archaeophilia: 'The cells of his memory are vast, various, full even to bursting with life and motion; his speculative understanding is empty, flaccid, poor, and dead.' When he pithily summarises Scott's condition – 'the old world is to him a crowded map; the new one a dull, hateful blank' – we can catch the first notes of the theme that would swell into Edwin Muir's apocalyptic attack on the 'vacuum' of Scottish culture; in love with the past and alienated from the future.

Hazlitt's critique of the novels – about which, despite his outright political antipathy, he is generous and enthusiastic – finds a sympathetic echo in a more minor key in Peacock's rather more caustic appraisal of the Waverley Novels. At dinner, the classicist Dr Folliott, who hates contemporary culture as much as Chainmail, discusses the similarity between modern novels and pantomimes.

> There is the same variety of character, the same diversity of story, the same copiousness of incident, the same research into costume, the same display of heraldry, falconry, minstrelsy, scenery, monkery, witchery, devilry, robbery, poachery, piracy, fishery, gipsy-astrology, demonology, architecture, fortification, castramentation, navigation; the same running base of love and battle. The main difference is, that the one set of amusing fictions is told in music and action; the other in the worst dialects of the English language. As to any sentence worth remembering, any moral or political truth, any thing having a tendency, however remote, to make men wise or better, to make them even think of thinking, they are both precisely alike: *nuspiam, nequaquam, nullibi, nullimodis.*

Hazlitt and Peacock were the real futurologists here – Hazlitt posed the question 'Must we look to Scotland for a supply of whatever is original and striking in this kind?' and answered 'Yes! . . . We have no room left for violent catastrophes, for grotesque quaintness, for wizard spells.' Victoria would ascend the throne, and the literature of her reign would be more moralistic, more realistic, less of wizard spells and more of social ills. The great Victorian novelists – Dickens, Eliot, Thackeray, the Brontës, Trollope, Meredith, Gaskell – are descended from Scott in the same way he pretended George IV was the Jacobite heir.

William Maginn, despite, or because of, his intemperance, violence and reactionary politics, was one of the most unpredictable, outrageous and occasionally astonishing miscellaneous writers of the period. Although he lived well into Victoria's reign, he was a product of the Regency era. Educated at Trinity College Dublin (he was born in Cork) and a contributor to *Blackwood's Magazine, Fraser's Magazine* and, in its first issue, *Punch*, he was, in his own way, a serious scholar, and his posthumous *Shakespeare Papers* offer intelligently contrarian positions on many characters. Maginn was a reader who eschewed the obvious. His Falstaff is melancholic; his Lady Macbeth is 'not meant to be an embodiment of the Furies'; his Iago has no 'motiveless malignity' but displays what a series of exponential slights might do to a brittle egomania.

None of this deep reading can be found in his 1827 novel, *Whitehall, or the Days of George IV*. Although Maginn would probably have thought Scott's most reactionary political views a touch too liberal, Scott is collateral damage and sometimes prime target in this rag-bag burlesque. Maginn claims that he is only editing a volume, from 'Teyoninhakawaranenopolis, capital of the great empire of Yankeedoodoolia', which dates from the year 2227. It is 'useless to divulge' how it came into his hands. The plot, about a Jamaican planter called Smithers who comes back to England to meet the woman with whom he is in love, having seen but once, is a featherlight pretext for satirical onslaughts by both stiletto and trebuchet. Let it stand as an example for the rest of the 'novel' that the climax is an ultra-politically incorrect battle, where ungrateful Jews, Irish, Germans and poets attempt to besiege the Duke of Wellington. I hate to admit how much I laughed, when, during the battle,

Coleridge is struck a mortal blow, and delivers a fantastically convoluted death-speech about swans, ending with the immortal line 'Therefore, as I shall explain hereafter – but for God's sake a glass of brandy and water – therefore when we consider the ramifications of the idea, that idiosyn–'

Scott is mocked in many ways. The late Angus Calder, who co-wrote an excellent introduction to Scott, once told me that he would never write a novel because he was 'insufficiently interested in clothes'. The following extract from *Whitehall* shows exactly how ludicrous Scott's obsessions and precisions could become:

> There was a patch, neither short nor narrow, on the left knee of his grey pantaloons; his boots had obviously been *foxed** and a very shabby surtout or cassock of blue cloth exhibited no epaulettes whatever to denote the regimental rank of the wearer. A button having given way, the back flap of an unembroidered cocked hat or *chapeau-bras*** dangled loose upon the collar, and the folds of a huge neckcloth, which had once probably been white, appeared arranged in a manner that would have caused the bosom of a Nichol† to thrill with indignation. But the compact and rigid massiveness of the countenance – the bronzed cheeks, aquiline nose, and eyes of more than aquiline brilliancy – the picturesque simplicity of the short curling hair and whiskers, both of which were as white as wool – and the extraordinary quickness with which, while the left hand rested on the pummel of a beltless sabre, the right played a basket-handled rattan about the knuckles, elbows, and skins of the more awkward soldiery – these were circumstances which could not but arrest the close observation of so shrewd a spectator as Smithers.

---

* *Foxed Boots.* See Vie privée des Anglais, tom. IV, p 551. ** *Chapeau-bras.* Ibid, tom. 1, pp 50, 371, 403. † *Nichol* of Jermyn Street, the first neckclothier of the period. See *Vie privée*, tom. 1, p 70.

The footnotes throughout Maginn's book lampoon Scott's scholarly trappings and spiral into further antiquarian comedy as Maginn keeps on quibbling with 'the Revd Dr Toddy', who, like de Selby in Flann O'Brien's *The Third Policeman* almost becomes a character in himself. The greatest dig at Scott, however, comes in the form of a 'Recipe' for a historical novel. It demonstrates how awfully *easy* Scott had come to seem.

> He went to the private desk, and took out a greasy, well thumbed MS., like a house-wife's hereditary cookery-book, and began to read sonorously, the following – 'RECIPE FOR A HISTORICAL NOVEL'.
>
> 'Take Pinnock and Maunder's History of England, and there find a time when there was a war or a plot. Take an ass, and bray him in a mortar until you make him a hero. Saddle your ass with panniers, full of the adventures of the time, and let him work. This is the principal ingredient. For a heroine, take a young lady of mild manners, who is expected to go mad in the course of the book, and, during her paroxysms, to quote scraps of verses. To balance her, have a gay lady, who can talk French, and fall in love with the hero, who, however, is always to take the tame one, to the great despair of the other. This will make some pretty *hors-d'oeuvres* and side-dishes, to be served up with love-apple sauce. The disappointed lady will do for a devil.
>
> 'The other ingredients are a fool, an old woman, and a bore. For your fool, take Touchstone, and pluck out all his wit, stuffing him instead with scraps of sentences, which are more consistent with the meaning of the word fool, at present, they being sheer folly. Your old woman must be picked out of the filthiest classes of society, and endowed with the gift of prophecy. She is to make the plot thick. Your bore must be a punster, or a fellow with a catchword – or something of the same kind. Have him perpetually in the dish.
>
> 'For style, please your honour,' he continued, 'take a book of scandal, or chit-chat of the day, and steal entire pages from it without mercy, the more the merrier. To make the conver-

sations consistent, stuff in all the words of the time, without any regard as to who is to say them. Make no distinction between the language of a duchess and a coal-heaver. If you introduce an Irishman, be his rank however high, or his talents however great, he must talk redolent of Munster – if a Scotchman, let him be ever so noble, he must talk the patois of the gutter-bloods of Edinburgh. A Welchman, of course, can utter nothing but the gibberish of Leekland.

'Regard not historical facts, for that will only annoy. Make a man, for instance, see the towers upon Westminster Abbey a hundred years before they were built. So with persons. Describe a good-humoured and good-natured gentleman as a ferocious executioner – degrade a gallant and soldier-like figure into that of a bandy-legged drummer – and so on. Mix up the hero well with every thing. Make him run *by accident* into the very room where Milton is writing his *Paradise Lost*; and when you want to empty the contents of your scrapbook, make him fall in, *by accident*, with a man who, *by accident*, knows every body of the time.

'If you copy the works of a great man in your line, carefully preserve, with Chinese accuracy, every defect. It is much easier than to copy his beauties; and as you want to make yourself one of the *servum pecus*, the easiest way is best. At first you might think it impossible to copy so closely the works of that great man, and yet weed out the beauty, the grace, the honour, the poetry, the gush of genius and of gentlemanlike feeling – that flows over every page, and leave nothing but the dry bones; but, "patience, perseverance, &c."– Ah! God bless your honour,' said he, looking up from the book, 'them there are the things for us poor operatives – never fear, Sir, they will carry a hard working man over any obstacle.'

Reuben paused for a moment, and resumed reading in a lower note – in fact, a whisper – 'Serve up, hot and hot, with puff's; them you manufacture yourself, or you hire a regular baker. Apropos of that,' said he, ringing a bell, 'the puff-manufacturer has not been here to-day.

'And finally,' continued Reuben – addressing our hero from the book – 'and finally, Sir, get yourself connected with a magazine, which you supply with light goods – and in return it will set off your work in its front window; and – but, hang me, I should not be telling you every thing. You may also gratify yourself by using it for the purpose of saying every thing spiteful against the works of the great man whose model you have purloined. "Here one of the operatives came up, and with a reverent air addressed the foreman: 'Musha, then, agra, God be wid you, but would not yee be after tellin a body whether I oft for to spell 'of' wid an f or a v ?' 'With a *wee*,' said the foreman – 'no – stop – with a *hef*, I believe. Let me see, don't be in a hurry – but, Sir, do you expect me to be doing *your* business? Go look out for it in Johnson. Do you think I am bound to answer questions?'

Maginn skewered not just Scott, but the future of the historical novel with this glittering piece of vitriol. It shows just how ephemeral, exciting and excrescent Maginn's reputation was, compared to Scott's perpetual, purpureal, putrescent afterlife. Scott may have been the embarrassing uncle in the attic to the Victorians, but he had his unironic, unashamed acolytes. There was Harrison Ainsworth, author of *Sir John Chiverton, Rookwood, Crichton, Jack Shephard, The Tower of London, Guy Fawkes, Old Saint Paul's, The Miser's Daughter, Windsor Castle, Saint James's, James the Second, The Lancashire Witches, Auriol, The Flitch of Bacon, The Star Chamber, The Spendthrift, The Life and Adventures of Mervyn Clitheroe, Ovingdean Grange, The Constable of the Tower, The Lord Mayor of London, Cardinal Pole, The Projector, The Spanish Match, The Constable de Bourbon, Old Court, Myddleton Pomfret, Hilary St Ives, Talbot Harland, The South Sea Bubble, Tower Hill, Boscobel, The Good Old Times, Merry England, The Goldsmith's Wife, Preston Flight, Chetwynd Calverley, The Leaguer of Lathon, The Fall of Somerset, Beatrice Tyldesley, Beau Nash* and *Stanley Brereton*. There was Edward Bulwer-Lytton, famous now for inventing the word 'Vril' in his science-fiction novel *The Coming Race*, which was neologised into 'Bovril' for a meat drink beloved of invalids and Scottish football supporters, and for having written the line 'It was a dark and stormy night' in his 1830 novel *Paul Clifford*. But he was also responsible for *Pelham, The Disowned, Devereux, Eugene Aram, Godolphin, Falkland, The Last Days of Pompeii, Rienzi, The Student, Ernest Maltravers, Alice, Night and Morning, Zanoni, The Last of the Barons, Lucretia, Harold, or The Last of the Saxon Kings, The Caxtons, My Novel, What Will He Do With It?, A Strange Story* and *Kennelm Chillingly*. At the same time he managed to be Secretary of State for the Colonies. Mrs Margaret Oliphant Oliphant, who got her tic of a name through the expedience of marrying a cousin, churned out *Adam Graeme, Magdalen Hepburn, Lilliesleaf, The Laird of Norlaw, Salem Chapel, The Rector, Doctor's Family, The Perpetual Curate, Miss Marjoribanks, Phoebe Junior, Madonna Mary, Squire Arden, He that will not when he may, Hester, Kirsteen, The Marriage of Elinor, The Ways of Life, The Beleaguered City* and *A Little Pilgrim in the Unseen*. There is a haunting sound poetry in the titles of books you will never read, and it would be a melancholy whim to fill Wikipedia with non-existent writers with cubit-length stretches of titles that seem, almost onomatopoeically, to tell you all you need to know.

The Vestiarium Scoticum

Although they were born John Carter Allen and Charles Manning Allen, their gravestones in Eskadale churchyard, Inverness-shire, name them as John Sobieski Stuart and Charles Edward Stuart. Their father, Thomas, was practically disinherited, as the bulk of his father's fortune was settled on his younger brother. Thomas married the daughter of the Revd Owen Manning, the author of a *History of Surrey*. About their early life, date of birth, place of birth and education, almost nothing is known. Although John later denied being in Edinburgh for the King's Jaunt, it was reported in the newspapers that two men named 'Allan' (just a single vowel, but already they appear to be undergoing some kind of metamorphosis) were presented to the King by the Earl of Strathmore and the Earl of Leven. In the same year, 1822, John Hay Allan published a volume of poetry, called *The Bridal of Caölchairn*, which included, as well as a piece of Ossiana in rhyme, 'Stanzas for the King's Landing'. It attracted a few reviews, none particularly flattering, and most of them concerned with upbraiding the author for his servile imitation of Scott. *The Literary Gazette* wrote that he was 'apparently touched with the enthusiasm of national sentiment' and ended that he would do well to 'look on the beauty of his own romantic land, and forget Sir Walter Scott if possible'. That Scotland was not his native land, by birth or parentage, went unmentioned. His persistent habit of spelling 'lady' 'ladye' was frequently cited.

The reviewers also overlooked a peculiar variant edition of *The Bridal of Caölchairn*. As well as the version published by Thomas Hookham in London and William Tait in Edinburgh, another proclaimed itself the fifth edition, published in London by Hurst, Robinson & Co. and in Edinburgh by Archibald Constable, with the author's name being given as 'Sir Walter Scott, Bart'. The brothers' career in dissimulation had begun wholeheartedly.

The change to 'Hay Allan' was a further step towards the outright fantasy of their later years. John published a *Genealogical Table of the Hays* in 1840, expanding on their claim to be descended from the Earl of Erroll. But even in 1822, one of the poems in *The Bridal of Caölchairn* purported to be a translation from a set of Gaelic verses he had discovered 'in an old MS history of the Hays'. The lines are certainly worth quoting:

> The Hay! the Hay! the Hay! the Hay!
> MacGaradh is coming! Give way! give way!
> The Hay! the Hay! the Hay! the Hay!
> MacGaradh is coming, give way!
> MacGaradh is coming, clear the way!
> MacGaradh is coming, hurra! hurra!
> MacGaradh is coming, clear the way!
> MacGaradh is coming, hurra!

Sir Walter Scott recollected seeing John wearing the badge of the High Constable of Scotland – one of the hereditary offices of the Earl of Erroll – and remarked of it that 'he could have no more right to wear than the Crown'. There is an element of unwitting prescience in his put-down.

Whatever else one might say about the brothers Allen, they must have been singularly charming individuals. They were befriended by Robert Chambers; the irascible Glengarry; Sir Thomas Dick Lauder, the 7th Baronet of Fountainhall and the author of two sub-Waverley novels, *Lochandhu* and *The Wolf of Badenoch*; the Earl of Moray (who granted them permission to hunt on his lands); and the Earl of Lovat, who built them a hunting lodge on Eilean Aigas on the River Beauly (later inhabited by Compton Mackenzie). On Eilean Aigas they finally changed their surname to 'Stuart', and in another romance, *Tales of the Century* (1837), revealed their true lineage.

According to the book, their father is in fact the legitimate son of Bonnie Prince Charlie and his wife, the Countess of Albany. Fearful of the infant's murder or abduction by Hanoverian agents, he is given over to the Allen family and brought up in secret. John and Charles are therefore the true Jacobite heirs to the British throne.

On Eilean Aigas they surrounded themselves with the trappings and paraphernalia of monarchy and 'held court' amidst stags' heads and tartan curtains. To complete the transformation, they converted to Roman Catholicism. Elizabeth Grant of Rothiemurchus described how 'they actually "reigned" in the north country', and mentioned that Charles's wife would play the harp in the garden next to an artificial waterfall, 'like Flora McIvor'. Although John died in 1872 and Charles in 1880, their lives were dramatically compromised in 1847. That year, the *Quarterly Review* carried a long article, 'The Heirs of the Stuarts', which lambasted their claims. The discredited brothers went into voluntary exile on the Continent, giving their address variously as 'Versailles, France' and 'The Hradshin, Bohemia'. Their European life is as vague and mysterious as their upbringing – the Austrian court tolerated, though it did not promote, their assertions of blue blood – and they returned to London by 1868, where they lived in moderately genteel poverty.

What lifts the Allens/Sobieski Stuarts out of being a mere curio footnote is that despite their 'exaggerating imagination', as Scott called it, they for ever changed the face of Scottish life. In 1829 they wrote to Sir Thomas Dick Lauder to inform him they had a copy of an invaluable Scottish manuscript. It had once belonged to John Leslie, the Bishop of Ross and Mary, Queen of Scots' ambassador to Elizabeth's court, had been sequestered in the Scots College at Douay, where it was gifted to Bonnie Prince Charlie, who then passed it into Thomas Allen's possession. The manuscript was called the *Vestiarium Scoticum, or The Garde-rope of Scotlonde* – their addiction to the fake antiquarian suffix -e was undiminished – and it gave details of the original clan tartans of some seventy-five separate clans.

Early accounts of the plaid tended to mention that its dun colour-scheme was more appropriate for moorland camouflage than ceremonial procession, although it was known that particular areas – rather than families or clans – had distinctive patterns. The kilt as it is now known was 'invented' by a Lancastrian Quaker called Thomas Rawlinson in the 1730s as an outfit 'handy and convenient for his workmen'. It quickly became adopted and was proscribed after the 1745 Rebellion, with exceptions made for the

Highland regiments, especially the Black Watch. The disjunction between the modern kilt and the ancient plaid is clearly seen in the various paintings and engravings based on the Ossianic works of Macpherson, such as those by Runciman, Ingres, Gérard and Girodet, where the principal characters wear a combination of classical toga and homespun plaid. After the repeal of the Act, the association of kilts with the military zeal and heroism of the Highland regiments eased its passage into polite society. The defining redemption of the kilt was, of course, the pageantry of the Jaunt.

Even then there was no unanimously agreed-upon idea of 'setts', or definitive clan tartans. William Wilson & Sons of Bannockburn, the principal tartan weavers and salesmen, kept accurate enough records for us to know that the Macpherson tartan, worn by Cluny Macpherson for the Jaunt, was originally called Kidd (after several bails of it were bought by a Mr Kidd) and prior to that was known as 'No. 155'. They even advertised exclusive 'new patterns' – hardly a time-honoured ancestral tradition dating back to misty Ossian.

The Sobieski Stuarts created the missing link between contemporary fashion and invented historical precedent. Garth of Stewart and Glengarry might have insisted on the longevity of their tartans, but it was two English fraudsters who completed the picture. The *Vestiarium Scoticum* did more than just create distinctive patterns for other clans; it extended the whole idea of clan tartans into Lowland families, who never had a clan system. It is these patterns that persist to this day along the Royal Mile and beyond. Royal Stewart is now defined as 'G4 R60 B8 R8 Bk12 Y2 Bk2 W2 Bk2 G20 R8 Bk2 R2 W2', based on the pattern drawn by the brothers Allen.

Sir Thomas Dick Lauder was so excited by the discovery that he wrote to Scott, asking for his expert opinion. From the very title, which he realised was incorrect Latin, it was evident to Scott that this was not a genuine fifteenth-century manuscript. Thomas had hoped that the *Vestiarium* would staunch the 'uncouth, spurious, modern tartans which are every day invented, manufactured, christened after particular names, and worn as genuine'. Instead Scott suggested that 'I had rather supposed the author had been some tartan-weaver zealous for his craft, who wished to extend the use of tartan over the whole kingdom.' Scott was adamant that 'the general proposition that the Lowlanders ever wore plaids is difficult to swallow'. The Sobieski Stuarts had their revenge with 'G8 R6 Bk2 R56 G28 R8 G8 W6 G8 R8' – the Scott family tartan. When pressed for the original manuscript, the brothers forged a letter from their father (now apparently calling himself J T Stuart Hay) stating that his secret possession of the book should never have been revealed, as 'private memorandums' were written on the blank pages. 'As to the opinion of Sir Walter Scott,' they wrote, 'inasmuch as I never heard it respected among antiquaries as of the least value, it is quite indifferent to me.'

After Scott's death, the *Vestiarium* was eventually published in 1842 and in a more costly edition as *The Costume of the Clans* in 1844. Despite the *Quarterly Review* reiterating the grounds for suspicion which Scott set out in a wide-ranging attack on 'the Jacobite heirs', and noting several more errors in terms of internal self-contradiction, it remains the most influential, if controversial, work of 'Scottish design' in three hundred years.

Given his fame, the fact that the Allens fixated on Scott is hardly surprising. But the seeds of their fury and fascination may have been sown long before *The Bridal of Caölchairn*. Although we know very little about their childhood – and one rumour puts their birth in Wales – it does not seem improbable that their maternal grandfather, the Revd Owen Manning, had a significant influence. It is a tantalising coincidence that Manning was an antiquary, given his grandsons' predilections. It is even more of a niggle in the brain that he lived in Godalming – only a few miles down the road from Waverley.

Balmorality, Tartanry and Scotlandshire

Just as the Sobieski Stuarts were being exposed by the *Quarterly Review*, Queen Victoria and Prince Albert were signing a lease for a Highland estate. Over the next eight years Balmoral would be transformed into Victoria's principal Scottish residence, and its version of Scottishness would crystallise across Scotland. Albert designed Balmoral in its entirety; from the mock-medieval, fairyland Scots Baronial architecture, to the interior design, to the lifestyle they adopted while staying there. It thrilled Victoria: 'the house is charming, the rooms delightful, the furniture, papers, everything, perfection'. It looked uncannily like the lodge on Eilean Aigas. It was a tartan fantasia, and the walls were bedecked with the antlers of the stags Albert ineptly shot. Their life there was a curious mixture of frugality and excess, plain porridge and scores of slaughtered animals. In his passion for field sports, Albert was the equal to the Sobieski Stuarts, who had also written the *Lay of the Deer Forest; with Sketches of Olden and Modern Deer-Hunting*. Scott's *Lady of the Lake* had established the stereotype of the hunting monarch, and in the later nineteenth century Highland estates were cleared, not for sheep, but as aristocratic playgrounds. Victoria enthusiastically patronised Highland games with their pageants of loyal, be-kilted rustics, and the royal pair were depicted in full Highland dress. Her inspiration in all of this was Scott. *The Bride of Lammermoor* was the first novel she ever read. *Peveril of the Peak* was the last novel Albert read; with the page he expired on bordered in black in the Windsor Library copy. It is not a particularly interesting page.

The word 'Balmorality' – meaning a superficial enthusiasm for Scottish culture, coupled with a douce, staid conservatism – does not appear in the *Oxford English Dictionary*; nor do its associated terms 'Balmoralisation' and 'Balmoralism'. In *Scotland and the Union*

(1977), David Daiches mentioned 'the whole process of what might be called Balmoralisation, with the associated burgeoning of the tourist trade in tartanry . . . represented an extraordinary distortion of the history of Scottish culture'. Terms like 'tartanry' and 'Balmorality' are of surprisingly modern origin. The *OED*, again, first cites 'tartanry' in 1976, 'fake Scottishry' in 1979, and the neologism 'Scotlandshire' – used by Alasdair Gray in *Old Men in Love* in 2007 – dates back to 1981. It does not seem coincidental that this outbreak of anxiety about Scotland's identity is approximately contemporary with the debate around the 1979 devolution referendum. In Scott's day, the term his own son-in-law used to denote a particular kind of phony Scottishness was 'celtified'.

One of the keenest ironies of Scott's posthumous success is the manner in which his literary formation of national identity was used to cement the Union and the Empire at home, yet inspired nationalist movements abroad. Elias Lönnrot's *Kalevala* (1835) was instrumental in promoting Finnish independence. Other examples include the Estonian *Kalevipoeg* (1853), the Polish *Pan Tadeusz* (1834), the Latvian *Lāplčēsis* (1872), the Armenian *Sasuntzi Davit* (1873), the Hungarian *Death of King Buda* (1864), the work of Vuk Stefanović Karadžić (1787–1864) in Serbian, the Argentine *Martín Fierro* (1872), let alone the novelistic versions of Dumas, Manzoni, Galdós, Tolstoy and Fenimore Cooper, the ethnographic fairytales of Charles Perrault and the Brothers Grimm, or Wagner's Ring Cycle. Scott inspired cultural and political nationalism everywhere except Scotland.

The Scottish Renaissance of the early twentieth century had different detested icons of twee, kitsch Scottishness – Harry Lauder, for example – and the playwright James Bridie memorably denounced 'Wallacethebruceism, Charlieoverthewaterism, Puirrabbieburnsism, Bonniebonniebanksism, Myainfolkism and Laymedoonandeeism' in 1948. The avowed aim of the Scottish Renaissance was to restore Scotland's indigenous culture and wrest it away from Imperial caricatures; but such an ambition could seem parochial in the face of poverty, global war and the possibility of a pan-nationalist Communist Utopia. Nationalism itself could be seen as an archaic, counter-revolutionary sentiment. Lewis Grassic Gibbon, a fellow traveller of the Scottish National Party, wrote:

> I cannot play with these fantasies when I think of the hundred and fifty thousand in Glasgow. They are something that stills the parlour chatter. I find I am by way of being an intellectual myself. I meet and talk with many people whose interests are art and letters and music. Enthusiasm for this or that aspect of craft and architecture, men and women who have very warm and sincere beliefs regarding the ancient culture of Scotland, people to whom Glasgow is the Hunterian Museum with its fine array of Roman coins, or the Galleries with their equally fine array of pictures. 'Culture' is the motif-word of the conversation: ancient Scots culture, future Scots culture, culture ad lib and ad nauseam . . . The patter is as intimate on my tongue as on theirs. And relevant to the fate and being of those hundred and fifty thousand it is no more than the chatter and scratch of a band of apes seated in a pit on a midden of corpses . . . There is nothing in culture and art that is worth the life and elementary happiness of one of those thousands who rot in the Glasgow slums. There is nothing in science or religion. If it came (as it may come) to some fantastic choice between a free and independent Scotland, a centre of culture, a bright flame of artistic and scientific achievement, and providing elementary decencies of food and shelter to the submerged proletariat of Glasgow and Scotland, I at least would have no doubt as to which side of the battle I would range myself. For the cleansing of that horror, if cleanse it they could, I would welcome the English in sovereignty over Scotland till the end of time. I would welcome the end of Braid Scots and Gaelic, our culture, our history, our nationhood under the heels of a Chinese army of occupation if it could cleanse the Glasgow slums.

From Scott's death onwards, there has been a cacophony of competing versions of Scottishness: Red Clydeside and Tartan Tories, Silicon Glen and Glenbogle, a nation of Calvinists who disapprove of sex standing up in case it leads to dancing and a nation of dipsomaniac knife-wielding neds. Scotland was Kipling's McAndrew, the restrained, religious ship's engineer who did not want to be captain, since he knew captaincy was only possible through his silent duty. Scotland was Para Handy, the independent, irreverent, trickster-skipper of the *Vital Spark*. What Scotland could be and what Scotland was seem locked in a perpetual stranglehold. Scott-land is the double-sign of this not-only-ness, like the optical illusion that switches between rabbit and duck, duck and rabbit. Scott's symbols of Scottishness, so often reviled as backward and nostalgic, still work against this backdrop of contradiction. Even Hugh MacDiarmid, a clever man and an iconoclast to the core, was happy to wear a kilt.

The Late Works

In the most perceptive of his critical notices, that of Mary Shelley's *Frankenstein; or, The Modern Prometheus*, Scott employs yet another financial metaphor to explain the nature of speculative fiction.

> In the class of fictitious narrations to which we allude, the author opens a sort of account-current with the reader; drawing upon him, in the first place, for credit to that degree of the marvellous which he proposes to employ; and becoming virtually bound, in consequence of this indulgence, that his personages shall conduct themselves, in the extraordinary circumstances in which they are placed, according to the rules of probability, and the nature of the human heart.

By the end of the 1820s and the early 1830s, Scott's readers might well have felt their author was bouncing the cheques. Not that his late novels particularly break the rules of probability; although an orang-utan does solve the crime in *Count Robert of Paris* – mind you, an orang-utan also stands for Parliament in Peacock's *Melincourt* and one would famously commit the crime in Poe's *Murders in the Rue Morgue*. No, Scott has become indulgent on the level of the sentence. Increasingly ill and constantly under pressure, there is an uncomfortable element of accuracy in George Gilfillan's 1831 parody of Scott's imitators in the style of Scott's 'Blue Bonnets Over The Border':

> WRITE, write, tourist and traveller,
> Fill up your pages and write in good order;
> Write, write, scribb'ler and driveller,
> Why leave such margins? – come nearer the border.
> Many a laurel dead flutters around your head,

> Many a tome is your *memento mori*
> Come from your garrets, then, sons of the quill and pen,
> Write for snuff-shops, if you write not for glory.

The opening sentence of *Castle Dangerous* in *Tales of my Landlord, Fourth Series*, shows how ponderous, slack and verbose his prose had become.

> It was at the close of an early spring day, when nature, in a cold province of Scotland, was reviving from her winter's sleep, and the air at least, though not the vegetation, gave promise of an abatement of the rigour of the season, that two travellers, whose appearance at that early period sufficiently announced their wandering character, which, in general, secured a free passage even through a dangerous country, were seen coming from the southwestward, within a few miles of the Castle of Douglas, and seemed to be holding their course in the direction of the river of that name, whose dale afforded a species of approach to that memorable feudal fortress.

You can almost hear the effort of dragging the quill across the page, churning out sub-clauses and eking out the details. That is not to say that there are not good things in Scott's late novels. *The Chronicles of the Canongate* was universally melancholy in tone, from the engineered filicide of 'The Highland Widow' and the self-immolating honour of 'The Two Drovers' to the suicidal cowardice and reckless intemperance of Conachar and Henry Gow in *The Fair Maid of Perth*. Scott's final reconciliation with his disgraced brother is his transformation into Conachar, the divided, charming, disgraced, honourable failure. The first of the 'late' works proper, *Anne of Geierstein, or The Maiden of the Mist*, was originally intended as a sequel to *Quentin Durward*. During its writing Scott complained that 'most weary, stale and unprofitable have been my labours', a rare confession of the strains under which he now composed; but what seems more remarkable is that he would envisage a sequel at all. It shows how far he had declined from the time when he started *Ivanhoe* precisely to avoid the imputation of repetition. In the end, *Anne of Geierstein* was a thematic sequel; with Charles the Bold on-stage and Louis XI off-stage. Most notable is Scott's depiction of the Vehmic Tribunal, a secret society for the punishment of criminals. The *Vehmgericht*, hooded, arbitrary and immensely powerful, are precursors for many modern fictional variations of such conspiratorial bodies: having used the Freemasons, Templars and Illuminati already, I'd place a bet on the Vehmic Tribunal appearing in the next Dan Brown thriller.

In the final *Tales of my Landlord* Scott's mock-modesty is transformed into actual apologies. As regards *Count Robert of Paris*, his Byzantine-set tale, he tells the reader that 'a dangerous disorder, incident to the time of life which he has reached' has hampered its production, and the unauthorised early appearance of a section in the *Philadelphia National Gazette and Literary Register* means he feels committed to publishing it in Britain, with the strong imputation that had it not been leaked abroad, he would not have published at all. These circumstances are expanded at the end of *Castle Dangerous* into a final Cleishbotham plot, in which Peter Pattieson's long-lost younger brother Paul steals the manuscripts which Jedediah had withheld from the public on account of their fragmentary and incomplete nature. In the few pages, Jedediah mentions Jeanie Deans, Old Mortality and the Bride of Lammermoor, as if seeking in past glories the inspiration necessary to continue. It ends with him hoping that he does not resemble the character in Dr Johnson's 'Vanity of Human Wishes': 'superfluous lags the veteran on the stage'.

Scott was increasingly reliant on James Ballantyne and John Lockhart to help with the novels. Ballantyne had expressed extreme unease about the opening of *Anne of Geierstein*, and had wondered if it was wholly wise for Scott to set books in places he had never visited. 'If I have not seen the Alps I have seen Salvatore Rosa's pictures of the Apennines which will do as well' was his snappish reply. By *Count Robert of Paris*, Ballantyne and Lockhart were simply circumventing Scott. The manuscript of the novel shows that Scott intended to end, not with a chivalric contest between the eponymous Count and Hereward, a Saxon member of the Emperor's retinue, but with a mock-heroic battle between Count Robert's wife, Brenhilda, and the Emperor's daughter, the historian Anna

Comnena. The version which went to press was not just subtly but substantively altered. *Castle Dangerous* shows the flagging of inspiration in a different manner: James Hogg was infuriated by *Castle Dangerous*, since its plot had been part of his own *Three Perils of Man*, a work Scott attempted to dissuade Hogg from publishing, and which contains a version of the Michael Scott story as well as a less than flattering, identically named forebear of Walter Scott. On top of Hogg's older perceived slight from Scott – Hogg maintained Scott had pre-empted the market with his Covenanter book *The Tale of Old Mortality* when he knew Hogg was working on a Covenanting tale himself, *The Brownie of Bodsbeck* – this rankled to the extent that it led to an irredeemable breach in their friendship at the end of Scott's life. Immediately after Scott's death, Hogg wrote to Lockhart with the gauche suggestion that Lockhart write his *Life of Scott* under the pseudonym 'James Hogg'. Lockhart was furious, and wrote 'the man is no more qualified to delineate the intellectual character of the illustrious giant of modern literature than he is able to build a bridge of goats across the Hellespont'. Hogg wrote his version anyway. Lockhart was incandescent. 'It had been better for his fame had his end been of earlier date, for he did not follow his best benefactor until he had insulted his dust.'

Sir Walter Scott's Theory of Fiction

The idea that Sir Walter Scott even had a 'theory' of fiction can seem anathematic to the portrait he presents of himself, and which is expanded and confirmed in Lockhart's *Life*. He repeatedly stresses his whim, his amateurism (despite being a professional author) and his desire only to please himself. At the end of *Count Robert of Paris* he clings to this extempory aesthetic, 'nor is it pleasant to feel one's self discharging, with pain and toil, a task which, upon other occasions, has proved as light to himself, as it might be fairly held trifling by the public'. The most explicit statement of his anti-theory theory comes in the preface to *The Fortunes of Nigel*, where the Eidolon expounds thus:

> Believe me, I have not been fool enough to neglect ordinary precautions. I have repeatedly laid down my future work to scale, divided it into volumes and chapters, and endeavoured to construct a story which I meant should evolve itself gradually and strikingly, maintain suspense, and stimulate curiosity; and which, finally, should terminate in a striking catastrophe. But I think there is a demon who seats himself on the feather of my pen when I begin to write, and leads it astray from the purpose. Characters expand under my hand; incidents are multiplied; the story lingers, while the materials increase; my regular mansion turns out a Gothic anomaly, and the work is closed long before I have attained the point I proposed.

In the Magnum Opus preface to *The Monastery* – Scott was *still* evidently brooding over its failure – he set out in detail the defining characteristics of different forms of fictitious prose compositions. On one hand, there is the form that we would call the picaresque, 'where the hero is conducted through a variety of detached scenes, in which various agents appear and disappear, without, perhaps, having any permanent influence on the progress of the story' and where the plot elements 'are only connected with each other by having happened to be witnessed by the same individual, whose identity unites them together, as the string of a necklace links the beads, which are otherwise detached'. Crucially Scott claims that this form of composition is 'what most frequently occurs in nature', and equally crucially, insists that 'the province of the romance writer being artificial, there is more required from him than a mere compliance with the simplicity of reality, – just as we demand from the scientific gardener, that he shall arrange, in curious knots and artificial parterres, the flowers which "nature boon" distributes freely on hill and dale'. This comparison derives from a book called *The History of Fiction* written by John Dunlop in 1814. It opens: 'The art of fictitious narrative appears to have its origin in the same principles of selection by which the fine arts in general are created and perfected. Among the vast variety of trees and shrubs which are presented to his view, a savage finds, in his wanderings, some which peculiarly attract his notice by their beauty and fragrance, and these he at length selects, and plants them round his dwelling.' For Scott, the word 'inartificial' is always a term of disapprobation, and 'artificial' has a positive meaning. The word has slipped between the early decades and the present, and to capture some of Scott's sense we should perhaps mentally superscribe the word 'inartificial' with the phrase 'done without art'. The ending of *The Monastery*, Scott says, 'was objected to as inartificial'; his first attempt at prose (the completion of Strutt's *Queenhoo Hall*) had a 'hasty and inartificial conclusion'; Dryden's *Cymon and Iphigenia* 'must be confessed, is otherwise inartificial'; and the 'History of Leonora, is equally unnecessarily and inartificially, into that of *Joseph Andrews*'.

To summarise: in the best books, things happen in a manner unlike reality. At the end of *Peveril of the Peak* Scott introduces a self-conscious, metatextual version of this theory. Charles II says, 'Here is a plot without a drop of blood; and all the elements of a romance, without its conclusion. Here we have a wandering island princess, (I pray my Lady of Derby's pardon) a dwarf, a Moorish sorceress, an impenitent rogue, and a repentant man of rank, and yet all ends without either hanging or marriage.' 'Not altogether without the latter,' said the Countess, and announces the happy ending.

It is difficult to underestimate how significant this seemingly simple realisation is: books and reality are different. It is a fissure in the theory of the novel itself. Is it a mirror or a mirage? Does it make up or lay out? It underlies the dispute between Henry James and Robert Louis Stevenson, where Stevenson takes Scott's approach. In *A Humble Remonstrance*, Stevenson is even more incisive than Scott on the utter chasm between the written and the real.

> The novel, which is a work of art, exists, not by its resemblance to life, which is forced and material, as a shoe must consist of leather, but by its immeasurable difference from life, which is designed and significant, and is both the method and the meaning of the work . . . Life is monstrous, infinite, illogical, abrupt and poignant; a work of art, in comparison, is neat, finite, self-contained, rational, flowing and emasculate.

The same dichotomy becomes more grandiose in the face-off between naturalism and symbolism, when Oscar Wilde could write, 'I love acting. It is so much more real than life,' while Emile Zola was scientifically anatomising the lives of prostitutes, train drivers, department store employees and miners. It is the epiphany of Oedipa Maas in Thomas Pynchon's *The Crying of Lot 49*.

> Or you are hallucinating it. Or a plot has been mounted against you, so expensive and elaborate, involving items like the forging of stamps and ancient books, constant surveillance of your movements, planting of post horn images all over San Francisco, bribing of librarians, hiring of professional actors and Pierce Inverarity only knows what-all besides, all financed out of the estate in a way either too secret or too involved for your non-legal mind to know about even though you are co-executor, so labyrinthine that it must have meaning beyond just a practical joke. Or you are fantasying some such plot, in which case you are a nut, Oedipa, out of your skull.

It is the contemporary issue of contention between the lovely James Wood, the Professor of the Practice of Literary Criticism at Harvard and the lovely Zadie Smith, author of *White Teeth, The Autograph Man* and *On Beauty*. Wood has advocated 'lifelikeness' as the novel's supreme quality; Smith has maintained that real life is too surreal to be real. Wood wants Scott's narrative perfection without his artificiality; Smith wants Scott's artificiality without his narrative perfection. Every time someone thrills that 'it was just like in a novel' – when they witness a terrorist atrocity, when they lean out of a train carriage to hold out a wedding ring, when they think the phone is about to ring and then it rings, when they console themselves that a grandparent's death was pre-empted by a grandchild's birth – they silently affirm Scott's greatest idea. Scott knew that books and reality were different. For one thing, you could always change reality.

The Last Works

Crippled by strokes, conscious of his debts, debilitation and dwindling talent, Walter was prevailed upon to forgo his beloved, misty, phlegmish Scotland for the healthy, sunny Mediterranean. 'I am perhaps setting,' he wrote, on the advent of his trip to Europe. While abstaining from writing might have been the most efficacious method of stabilising his health, it was never a possibility. He arrived in Malta on 22 November 1831 and was already planning a story set there, *The Siege of Malta*, as well as a short story *Il Bizarro* and a final poem on Rhodes and the Templars to complete the Magnum Opus. In *The Tale of a Tub* by Swift, which Scott had edited at the start of his career, there is a famous point where Swift indulges in a macabre speculation: 'I am now trying an experiment very frequent among modern authors, which is to write upon nothing, when the subject is utterly exhausted to let the pen still move on; by some called the ghost of wit, delighting to walk after the death of its body.' This is very close to what had happened to Scott by this stage. Reading *The Siege of Malta* and *Il Bizarro* – of which Buchan had said 'It may be hoped that no literary resurrectionist will ever be guilty of the crime of giving them to the world' – is heart-breaking. Scott cannot remember what he has written the day before; the works lack any narrative cohesion, trapped in a perpetual present. There are flashes of the old Scott, and in happier times his idea of introducing Miguel de Cervantes as a character would have been carried off with both charm and wit. Even more sadly, Scott thought the pages he had written were as good as *Ivanhoe*. They were duly mailed back to Cadell and Lockhart, both of whom drew a discreet veil over the works but kept the manuscripts. Later, pages would be sold to autograph hunters or gifted to friends, and later still, the whole would be reassembled and published. Seeing it in a bookshop, I wish they'd stickered it 'For Academic Use Only'.

The whole voyage – taking in Malta, Italy and Germany – was marbled with mortality. He learned that his beloved grandson, Johnny Lockhart, whom he had transformed into Hugh Littlejohn for *Tales of a Grandfather*, had died. He had intended to visit Goethe, who had first inspired him to become a writer, but Goethe passed away on 22 March 1832. He visited Pompeii, the 'City of the Dead' as he called it, and saw the tombs of the Stuarts in Rome. During his travels he was accompanied by the archaeologist Sir William Gell, who kept a diary of their time together. One striking incident occurred when Gell sketched a chapel in Rhodes which had the skeleton of the dragon killed by St George on the ceiling. Scott thought it was more likely to be some 'tremendous lizzard'. He was falling away from the realm of the imaginary.

When it became obvious that sunshine and travel were not improving his condition, Scott returned home. He was in a coma in London for three weeks. The newspapers carried daily reports about his condition, and everyone from the Royal Family to gangs of labourers made enquiries about his prospects. John Henry Newman – not yet Cardinal or even a Catholic – led prayers for him. But Scott did live to see Abbotsford again, proclaiming, 'I have seen much, but nothing like my ain house.' Lockhart's death-bed scene is a pious fiction; the ending of a novel, not the end of a life. In Lockhart's version, Scott's final words are, 'Lockhart, I have but a minute to speak to you. My dear, be a good man – be virtuous – be religious – be a good man. Nothing else will give you any comfort when you come to lie here.' Given that Scott had been trepanned by one Dr Watson, who later would treat Dickens, and was holding the pain in check with copious amounts of laudanum (as much as De Quincey, the famous Opium-Eater, would be ingesting at the height of his addiction) such clarity seems unlikely. According to another report, he screamed for twenty-seven hours at the end.

In his story, 'P's Correspondence', Nathaniel Hawthorne imagines Scott's last days. 'For my part, I can hardly regret that Sir Walter Scott had lost his consciousness of outward things before his works went out of vogue. It was good that he should forget his fame rather than that fame should first have forgotten him.' On 21 September

1832, Scott expired. Thomas Carlyle commented on the strangely appropriate nature of an autumn death, compared to Goethe's death the previous spring. For Carlyle, Goethe was reinvigoration, future and promise, while Scott was atrophy, the past and ending. Scott was buried in Dryburgh Abbey, with a copy of the *Lay of the Last Minstrel* in his coffin. Lockhart would later be laid at his feet.

Almost immediately, biographies were produced. The very first biography actually appeared before Scott's death. In 1831, Henry Dilworth Gilpin published with Carey & Lea of Chestnut Street, Philadelphia, the *Autobiography of Sir Walter Scott*. It is, in fact, the various prefaces of the Magnum Opus and the speech revealing himself as the Author of Waverley which opened *Chronicles of the Canongate*. Scott, perhaps, would have been delighted that his elaborate self-constructions were taken as gospel truth. A more substantial *Life of Sir Walter Scott* appeared in 1834, written by William Weir, who died during the project, and was completed by George Allan. Although they obviously lacked access to the *Journal* and the majority of the correspondence, Weir and Allan made a fairly passable job at constructing their biography. It is not uncritical, in terms of Scott's financial affairs, but has one eulogy clearly influenced by Scott's own position on the productivity of literature:

> It is therefore, we repeat, what we reckon one of the highest points of excellence in Scott's character, moral as well as intellectual, that, unstimulated by necessity, and even afterwards when he had fondly believed himself in the possession of a magnificent fortune and a fame that had no parallel (or only one) in the annals of literature, his pen was as busy as if the mouths he fed depended upon its activity for the supply of their wants. Let us think for a moment, – 'what if Scott, satisfied with his happy independence, and still happier prospects, had settled himself down in easy indolence, discharging perhaps all the duties of a good member of society, in the conventional meaning of the phrase, but distinguished for nothing else, perhaps, than the goodness of his dinners, or,

at best, the faithful fulfilment of his office as a country magistrate?' This is the true way of putting the position to the test. The loss to the cause of literature is the least considera- tion in this supposition; and we leave to the philanthropist to calculate the amount of human enjoyment, and that of the highest kind, which would thereby have been lost. But the question assumes a more substantial form, when we reflect upon the impulse which industry and the fine arts have received by the exuberant genius of this one man. How many thousands of individuals, from the printer to the bookbinder, have derived, are deriving, and will continue to derive subsis- tence from the labours of his single pen? This is a point in the economy of society which seems to have been hitherto entirely overlooked in judging of the comparative merits of literary men among their fellows. People never seem to consider that a voluminous author, if he does nothing else, confers the greatest of all possible benefits on an immense portion of those who are somewhat too exclusively termed the 'working classes', by giving them the means of honest employment. And too often, alas! the man who is effecting all this may himself be the while pining in obscurity and starvation! – his only reward, perhaps, for all the good he has done to his fellow-creatures, abuse or ridicule. It is so far well that such was not the fate with the subject of our narrative.

It was the 'working classes', according to Hogg, that did for Sir Walter. In his *Familiar Anecdotes of Sir Walter Scott*, which Lockhart desperately wanted to suppress, Hogg claims that

the Whig ascendancy in the British cabinet killed Sir Walter. Yes I say and aver [*sic*] it was that which broke his heart and deranged his whole constitution and murdered him. As I have shown before a dread of revolution had long preyed on his mind; he withstood it to the last; he fled from it but it affected his brain and killed him. From the moment he perceived the veto of a democracy prevailing he lost all hope of the prosperity and ascendancy of the British Empire.

Hogg is referring to the Reform Bill of 1832, which enlarged the electoral franchise, a development that Scott regarded with utter horror and dismay. The Empire, of course, was strengthened by the Reform Bill, but Scott by this stage was insanely paranoid. Hogg recounts that he claimed if the Bill were passed, he would turn terrorist and blow up the Earl of Buchan's awful statue of William Wallace at Dryburgh. (It still stands: the singer Jessie Rae led a campaign to restore it, and organised for a comments book in a box to be placed there. I have never laughed so much as when, after the release of *Braveheart*, some kid wrote in it, 'You can take oor burds, oor booze and oor blaw, but ye cannae take oor freedom.') Scott joked to friends that the only way to save the country was to make Wellington Regent, force William IV to abdicate, and kidnap Princess Victoria so that she could be immured in Glamis Castle until such time as she was ready to reign.

At the end of his life, Scott witnessed the horror of *history still happening*. The most productive and inspiring years of his creativity had rested on the idea that history was in some way over: the great dialectic clashes had all been resolved; the final foe of Napoleon defeated. His absolute incomprehension at mill workers turning out to jostle his carriage and shout 'Burke Sir Walter' haunted his last days – those when he didn't think he was King Lear, who divided a kingdom to tragic results. Hogg's version of Scott's last days reveals just how queasy and protective Lockhart was.

> He was then reduced to the very lowest state of degradation to which poor prostrate humanity could be subjected. He was described to me by one who saw him often as exactly in the same state with a man mortally drunk who could in nowise own or assist himself the pressure of the abcess on the brain having apparently the same effect as the fumes of drunkenness.

Lockhart's *Life* was essentially the conclusion of the Magnum Opus. Instead of the embarrassing *Siege of Malta*, it would finish with the greatest Waverley Novel: *The Life of Sir Walter Scott, Bart*. Published in the same format as the forty-eight volumes of the Magnum, the twelve volumes of the *Collected Poems* and the *Miscellaneous Prose*

Works in thirty volumes, the seven-volume biography turned Scott's life into a final fiction, an arc of triumph over adversity. Lockhart makes Scott's literary talent into a tragic flaw. The financial disaster was not caused by avarice or ignorance, but was rather the unfortunate necessary consequence of Scott's own aesthetic sensibilities. It was not a mortal failing, but an immortal failing. In Lockhart's words, 'he must pay the penalty, as well as reap the glory of this lifelong abstraction of reverie, this self-abandonment of Fairyland'. In Lord Cockburn's rather more sarcastic estimation, 'poets may be excused for being bad political economists'. Lockhart recasts Scott as the Waverley hero par excellence: a man who moderates between national pride and political pragmatism; between amateurism and professionalism; between being a man of the world and being otherworldly.

The Second Death

Thomas Carlyle reviewed Lockhart's *Life of Scott* for the *London and Westminster Review*, issue 12, and set out many of the criticisms that would become more commonplace as the century progressed. At the time, however, it was mildly shocking. Carlyle begins by questioning 'whether Sir Walter Scott was a great man'. He was, Carlyle admits, 'distinguished', 'considerable' and 'in this generation there was no literary man with such a popularity in any country; there have only been a few with such, taking-in all generations and all countries'. But mere popularity is a 'falsifying *nimbus*', and Carlyle rightly points out that Lope de Vega and August Kotzebue were in their day popular authors. 'We will,' he writes, 'omit this of popularity altogether; and account it as making simply nothing towards Scott's greatness or non-greatness, as an accident, not a quality.' Popularity would become a sign of Scott's ephemerality, and Carlyle's main critique – that Scott's genius was one *in extenso* not *in intenso* – abides to this day. He is not *deep*. In Carlyle's most grandiloquent prose, 'the great Mystery of Existence was not great to him; did not drive him into rocky solitudes to wrestle with it for an answer'. Taken with Lockhart's intrinsic respectability, the Scott that emerges from the biography has 'no features' and is 'white, stainless, an impersonal ghost-hero'. He even reiterates the point: this is a 'vague ghost of a biography, white, stainless; without feature or substance; *vacuum,* as we say, and wind and shadow'. It is striking that this sense of vacuum is exactly what Edwin Muir would identify as Scott and Scotland's chief characteristic.

Scott's potential greatness, for Carlyle, is seriously compromised by his worldiness. 'There is nothing spiritual in him; all is economical, material, of the earth earthy,' he wrote. Scott becomes very nearly the incarnation of all that Carlyle found detestable in the modern world: his only conquests were against 'good metallic coin of the realm'; he was, by the end, a 'Novel-manufactory, with its 15,000*l*. a-year'. The cash nexus and the triumph of the machine rob Scott of any vestige of heroism. The best that Carlyle can manage is to praise Scott's robust 'healthiness'. This is not as condescending as it sounds. Scott's healthiness was vital in an era when 'British Literature lay all puking and sprawling in Werterism, Byronism, and other Sentimentalism tearful or spasmodic'. Scott's healthiness also masked a secret sickness, and it is here that Carlyle delivers the killing blow. Yes, he says, Scott was ambitious, but that ambition was small-minded. 'So poor a passion can lead so strong a man into such mad extremes' that the end of all his labours was 'to cover the walls of a stone house in Selkirkshire with nicknacks, ancient armour and genealogical shields, what can we name it but a being bit with delirium of a kind?' Scott, in the final assessment, is 'a shabby small type edition of your vulgar Napoleons'.

Turning to the novels rather than the man, Carlyle's prognostication is gloomy. 'Are they to amuse one generation only? One or more! As many generations as they can; but not all generations: ah no.' They lack a purpose more serious than 'harmlessly amusing indolent, languid men', and therefore 'the stuffed Dandy, only give him time, will become one of the wonderfulest mummies'. Carlyle inverts here Scott's image of necromancy: his novels once brought the dead to life; now they merely preserve the corpse. 'Shakespeare fashions his characters from the heart outwards; your Scott fashions them from the skin inwards, never getting near the heart of them!' he writes. This is probably the most incisive and influential attack on Scott: that he lacks a certain interiority. Even when praising Scott's ability to show that the past was filled with 'living men' rather than 'state papers', Carlyle returns to this sense of externality. Scott showed men 'in buff or other coats and breeches, with colour in their cheeks'. When Virginia Woolf claimed that Scott was the last novelist to have Shakespeare's gift of revealing character purely through dialogue, it is a double-edged compliment. Scott gives us speech, not thought; costume, not psychology; the glittering surface of life, not its wellsprings and sources.

Walter Bagehot, in an essay of 1858 on the Waverley Novels, continues Carlyle's sense of the Waverley Novels being 'of their times' – already they are 'papa's books' – and extends Carlyle's exasperation at Scott's lack of a 'spiritual' dimension. For Bagehot, Scott 'omits to give us a delineation of the soul'. This flaw manifests itself in two ways. First, Scott cannot describe romantic love. His heroines are all comely pasteboard, nothing more. 'The hero and heroine walk among the trees of the forest according to rule, but we are expected to take an interest in the forest as well as in them.' Second, his characters have no metaphysical aspect, except, perhaps, in moments of grief. Bagehot admits that these two spheres – the romantic and the theological – have become more important to novelists than they were in Scott's day. Literature is evolving: 'a third generation has now risen into at least the commencement of literary life, which is quite removed from the unbounded enthusiasm with which the Scotch novels were originally received, and does not always share the still more eager partiality of those who, in the opening of their minds, first received the tradition of their excellence. New books have arisen to compete with these; new inter-ests distract us from them.' The same awareness of Scott passing out of the contemporary can be seen in George Eliot's *Middlemarch*. In chapter 32, the pompous Borthrop Trumbull eulogises Scott: 'I have bought one of his works myself – a very nice thing, a very superior publication, entitled "Ivanhoe". You will not get any writer to beat him in a hurry, I think – he will not, in my opinion, be speedily surpassed. I have just been reading a portion at the commencement of "Anne of Jeersteen". It commences well.' – which Eliot immedi-ately undercuts with the parenthesis '(Things never began with Mr. Borthrop Trumbull: they always commenced, both in private life and on his handbills)', as well as inviting us to slyly mock Trumbull's mispronunciation. Similarly, in chapter 27 Lydgate confesses that he 'read[s] no literature now . . . I read so much when I was a lad, that I suppose it will last me all my life. I used to know Scott's poems by heart.' That *used to* is prophetic. Dickens barely mentions Scott – his correspondence includes a note on visiting Abbotsford, his reading of the *Journal* and an abortive attempt to dramatise *The Bride of*

Lammermoor, as well as the peculiar assertion that he suspects Scott never dreams of his own characters. In *A Child's History of England*, while discussing Elizabeth I and Amy Robsart, Dickens writes that 'Upon this story, the great writer, SIR WALTER SCOTT, has founded one of his best romances' and in *Sketches by Boz* he draws a comparison with a moment in Scott's *Letters on Demonology and Witchcraft*. Dickens' silence on Scott needs to be explained. He certainly read Scott, and *Bleak House* has many points of connection with *Heart of Midlothian*. It may be that for Dickens, Scott became an *eminence grise*. Having grown up in poverty, and become rich through writing, Dickens' only comparison for an authorial career was one that ended in financial ruin. The shadow of Scott's life, not his work, falls across Dickens.

Despite the conspicuous ebbing of his reputation, Scott was still a kind of common currency among the literate. Popular magazines like *Punch, Figaro, Funny Folks, Fun* and *The Weekly Echo* regularly relied on Scott for parodic comedy. A selection includes:

> THE Tide was low, the wind was cold,
> Upon the sands the minstrel strolled;
> His burnt-cork cheek and croaking lay
> Seemed to have known a better day;
> His banjo, sole remaining joy,
> Was thrummed by an obstreperous boy;

The last of all the band was he
Who sang of nigger minstrelsy.

> THE sun was hot, the clay was bright,
> The statesman found his collars tight;
> He threw the starchy things aside,
> And round his neck no choker tied;
> In summer suit he quickly dressed
> True Paisley cloth, and of the best,
> Presented by admiring Scots
> Who gave him presents, lots on lots.

(*The Weekly Echo*, on the occasion of Gladstone not wearing a tie.)

THE LAY OF THE LAST MINISTRY.

THE way was long, the voters cold,
The Minister was weak not old;
His wither'd hopes and messes gay
Seem'd to have known a better day;
The lyre, his sole remaining joy,
Was carried by the Office Boy;
The last of the stop-gaps was he,
And which his name was Salisbury.

The *Warreniana* collection had used the conceit of poets advertising boot-blacking; but by the mid-nineteenth century it was commonplace to co-opt the styles and cadences of poets such as Scott for advertising purposes, as in these examples:

BREATHES there a man with soul so dead
Who never to himself hath said,
'To have moustaches would be grand'
Whose heart hath ne'er within him burned
As o'er the paper he hath turned
And Wright's advertisement hath scanned?
If such there be, go, mark him well,
And in his ears the good news tell:
Pilpsagine has gained a name,
All who have tried it own its fame:
While thousands prove its great renown
By the moustaches they have grown;
Whiskers and beards on many a face
Their origin likewise to it trace,
It contains no oil, is free from grease,
And now forsooth our rhyme must cease.
But what, you ask, is the expense?
'Tis sent post free for eighteenpence.

LIVES there a man with soul so dead,
Who never to his wife has said,
'I love a bit of home-made bread!'

Or can a man of aught be prouder,
Than to have cried in tones still louder,
'I like it made with Berwick's Powder!'

BREATHES there a man with taste so dead,
Who never to himself hath said,
'This is the spirit of my choice,'
As he his steaming glass hath stirred?
Who hath not slightly raised his voice,
So that his words might all be heard
O soothing Whiskey, strong yet mild,
Sweet spirit, pure and undefiled;
From thee, as doctors oft have proved,
The fusil oil has been removed;
Unlike the other spirits, thou
Bring'st not an aching to the brow.
Of thee no biliousness is born,
No coppers hot the following morn;
Men drink of thee at noon, at night,
And rise quite fresh at morning light;
Men drink of thee, and drink again,
To guard 'gainst rheumatism's pain

Books by Sir Walter Scott were a staple of school prize givings; and by 1873, Harriet Barton published the first edition aimed at children: *Tales from the Waverley Novels for Children*. By the end of the century, Zola could dismiss Scott as a 'boarding school writer'. The most successful of these products was S R Crockett's *Red Cap Tales, Stolen from the Treasure Chest of the Wizard of the North* (1904). Crockett, himself a fine novelist, explained in the introduction his thinking:

It struck me that there must be many oldsters in the world who, for the sake of their own youth, would like the various Sweethearts who now inhabit their nurseries, to read Sir Walter with the same breathless eagerness as they used to do – how many years agone? . . . I claim no merit in the telling of the tales, save that, like medicines well sugar-coated, the patients mistook them for candies and – asked for more. The books are open. Any one can tell Scott's stories over again in his own way. This is mine.

However honourable his intention, it is the complaints of the children that stand out. 'Scott writes such a lot before you get at the story,' says one girl. 'Why couldn't he just have begun right away?' 'But – I can't read the novels – indeed I can't,' says another. 'I have tried *Waverley* at least twenty times. And as for *Rob Roy* . . .' only to be interrupted by her brother, who says, 'It is true about *Rob Roy*. She read us one whole volume, and there wasn't no Rob Roy, nor any fighting in it. So we pelted her with fir-cones to make her stop and read over *Treasure Island* to us instead!' Their preference for Stevenson is telling. Despite the high regard in which he held Scott, Stevenson himself was not blind to the flaws of the novels. Reading Scott often, for him, meant 'wading forward with an ungrammatical and undramatic rigmarole of words' and resenting being 'fob[bed] off with languid, inarticulate twaddle'. In one respect, Scott would assuredly have agreed with Stevenson: 'He was a great day-dreamer, but hardly a great artist; hardly, in the manful sense, an artist at all.' The Scott that died throughout the nineteenth century is more Victorian than the twentieth-century stereotype of a Victorian. He was bluff, venal, prolix, plain, profligate, unimaginative, healthy, ailing and out of date.

Scott's Selkirk

The mist coagulated into drizzle, the drizzle intensified into rain, the rain abated back to mist. I was in Selkirk, in the Scottish Borders, where Sir Walter Scott had sat as 'Shirra' for twenty-nine years. It was early December, and the grey statue of Scott was almost camouflaged against the sky. For the last ten years, Selkirk has hosted a little winter festival, part town pageant, part Christmas Fayre, part historical re-enactment, part desperate rejuvenation – and it's called Scott's Selkirk. On the way in, the bus snailed past a melancholy strip of old factories turned into modern facilities and modern factories turned into strange, post-industrial wildernesses. Scott's Selkirk seems smaller this year than in any of the previous years. There are stalls in the marketplace, but fewer down the High Street than before. The butcher's shop, usually bedecked with game birds, hasn't opened. They've stopped having horse-drawn carriage rides and chestnut-roasters, and the absence of the sound of hooves and the smell of braziers contributes to the lack of atmosphere. There are plenty of old women in bonnets and shawls, usually with a mobile phone clamped to an ear; and groups of French soldiers and plaided shepherds are having a fly cigarette behind the music tent.

'Meg Dod's Kitchen' is selling mulled wine and plates of corned-beef stovies, and I chatted to one of the fairground operators – an Edwardian ring of merry-go-round horses, like those from the film of *Mary Poppins*, undulates in the background to an electronic version of 'Santa Claus is Coming to Town'. The others aren't coming, he says, as they hardly made enough to cover their costs last year. He's not wearing period dress (and in fact, it's difficult to tell what period the dress is: generic mock-Victoriana, perhaps). The stalls are selling cashmere and merino pashminas, tartan swatches, home-made soaps, local whisky, cheeses and pickles, Celtic silver jewellery. One stand specialises in reindeer made from logs – one for the body, one for the head, and seven sticks for legs, neck and antlers, a daub of red paint across the front and an axe-split for the mouth. There's a lot of New Age mysticism: statuettes of Arthur Rackham-style fairies; dragons hatching out of porcelain eggs, crystals with healing properties, luxury essential oils. One stand has scores of golden Buddhas. A man in ministerial black robes is parading around with a bear on a leash, or rather a person in a bear costume on a leash. The bear looks worryingly like Bungle from *Rainbow*. The music is the queerest combination of Scottish folk, silver bands, Eastern European accordions and pagan bodhráns. In one vacant shop lot, there's a dummy of Sir Walter Scott you can have your picture taken with; across the boarded-up windows of another are poems by Scott, Hogg and local worthies like J B Selkirk.

In previous years, there was a town play – *The False Alarm* – which toured around; but it seems to have fallen into abeyance. There's a torch-lit procession instead, and a local actor is re-enacting a couple of Scott's more famous trials in the courtroom. They're well-chosen pieces of pawkiness, featuring Scott's more likeable sympathy for the renegade. There are plenty of trials they could have dramatised showing his more irascible and draconian side, the side that thought it would be no bad thing if one local rogue killed another, effectively ridding the shire of two problems. The whole affair is a valiant attempt, and is almost more affecting in its struggle than its success. At the beginning of the year, the unemployment statistics showed a 111 per cent rise on last year's figures. The median weekly wage – £370.20 – is only 80 per cent of the Scottish average. In the last census, the population aged between 15 and 29 fell by 22.3 per cent and the population aged over 75 rose by 32.4 per cent. For the week after Scott's Selkirk, the local newspaper's court pages carried the following stories: 'a drunken man who assaulted his 15-year-old sister was fined £400'; 'a babysitter dialled 999 after a drunken man began punching his wife following a night out'; 'a 24-year-old man denied sending a voicemail message to a man, threatening to cut his face off'; 'a drunken man who refused to leave his sister's home was jailed for two months . . . he threatened to hit police officers with a coffee table'; and in a double-Scott-reference story, a pensioner from *Talisman* Avenue, found drunk on *Abbotsford* Road, assaulted ambulance staff. I wonder what the Shirra would have done.

Such problems are not unique to the Borders, or Scotland as a whole. But they show that for all the rhetoric of Scott's 'unification' of Scotland's fissiparous sections, it remains a divided country, blighted by exclusion and poverty.

In a sense, Selkirk is unrecognisable as the Selkirk of Scott's day and is perpetually Scott's Selkirk. The tweed mills and electronic factories may have come and gone, but Scott's influence is seen everywhere. There's a statue to the dead of Flodden, looking more Victorian than late medieval, and as well as Scott there are commemorations to the explorer Mungo Park, to J B Selkirk, to Montrose and to Robert Burns. Selkirk keeps on having to remember that it is Selkirk, and Sir Walter Scott demonstrated how culture and history, rather than politics, industry or religious affiliation are the keys to sustaining that sense of self.

Scott's Scott-land

In Glasgow's George Square, the public statuary announces its identity as the Second City of Empire, at once British and Scottish, military and political, artistic and scientific. Named after George III, it
features Queen Victoria and Prince Consort Albert; prime ministers
Peel and Gladstone; James Oswald MP; Sir John Moore and Lord
Clyde, respectively commanders in the Peninsular and Indian
campaigns; chemist Thomas Graham; engineer James Watt; poets
Thomas Campbell and Robert Burns; and the cenotaph. But there
is no statue of George III, or George IV, and on the central pillar,
instead of or in lieu of, as substitute for or representative of the
monarch, stands Sir Walter Scott, towering above them all. Glasgow
beat Edinburgh to having a public commemoration of Scott – theirs,
designed by John Greenshields and carved by Handyside Ritchie,
appeared in 1837, before the completion of Lockhart's *Life* and
thirteen years before the Edinburgh Monument – despite Scott's
tangential links to the city. His prominence is a stark reminder that
Scott changed the whole of Scotland.

In his *History of England from the Accession of James II* (1848),
the politician Thomas Babington Macaulay wrote perceptively
about Scott's immense impact on the idea of Scotland. His literary
works were

> executed with such admirable art that, like the historical plays
> of Shakespeare, they superseded history. The visions of the
> poet were realities to his readers. The places which he
> described became holy ground, and were visited by thousands
> of pilgrims. Soon the vulgar imagination was so completely
> occupied by plaids, targets, and claymores, that, by most
> Englishmen, Scotchman and Highlander were regarded as

synonymous words. Few people seemed to be aware that, at
no remote period, a Macdonald or a Macgregor in his tartan
was to a citizen of Edinburgh or Glasgow what an Indian
hunter in his war paint is to an inhabitant of Philadelphia or
Boston. Artists and actors represented Bruce and Douglas
in striped petticoats. They might as well have represented
Washington brandishing a tomahawk, and girt with a string of
scalps. At length this fashion reached a point beyond which it
was not easy to proceed. The last British King who held a court
in Holyrood thought that he could not give a more striking
proof of his respect for the usages which had prevailed in
Scotland before the Union, than by disguising himself in what,
before the Union, was considered by nine Scotchmen out of
ten as the dress of a thief. Thus it has chanced that the old
Gaelic institutions and manners have never been exhibited in
the simple light of truth. Up to the middle of the last century,
they were seen through one false medium: they have since
been seen through another. Once they loomed dimly through
an obscuring and distorting haze of prejudice; and no sooner
had that fog dispersed than they appeared bright with all the
richest tints of poetry. The time when a perfectly fair picture
could have been painted has now passed away. The original has
long disappeared: no authentic effigy exists; and all that is
possible is to produce an imperfect likeness by the help of two
portraits, of which one is a coarse caricature and the other a
masterpiece of flattery.

The felicitous homonymy between the author and the country did
not go unnoticed. The *Letters* of David Gray, published in 1836,
already made the connection: 'I call that his "land" in which his
bones are laid, but, sooth to say, the whole of Scotland is Scott-land.'
The American traveller Bayard Taylor used the word in his 1846
Views A-Foot: 'It was all *Scott*-land.' Exactly the same formula
appears in Alexander Smith's *A Summer in Skye* in 1856: 'Scotland is
Scott-land. He is the light in which it is seen. He has proclaimed over
all the world Scottish story, Scottish humor, Scottish feeling,

Scottish virtue; and he has put money into the pockets of Scottish hotelkeepers, Scottish tailors, Scottish boatmen, and the drivers of the Highland mails.' There is no greater indicator of the extent to which Scott's reputation plummeted in the twentieth century than that the same coining becomes a term of despair. In a Saltire Society pamphlet of 1945, J M Reid wrote that

Nineteenth-century Scotland was one of the chief centres of the industrial world. Its society was complex and curious enough to feed and excite any keen observer of human nature. Yet there is no Scottish Balzac or Dickens, not even any Scottish Thackeray or Trollope. Scottish writers and their readers both inside the country and elsewhere preferred Scott-land to Scotland.

The connection between Scott and Scottishness goes beyond Macaulay's awareness of the 'Highland transposition', and Reid's irritation at the ubiquitous romantic patina. In contemporary historical debates about Scotland's 'national' status, the 'holy trinity' of Scottish Courts, Kirks and Schools has often been invoked to account for the endurance of 'Scottishness' from the pre-Union to the devolutionary periods. It is not a watertight argument – as Neil Davidson has shown, few of Scotland's population had ongoing access to the legal or educational systems, and there was no homogeneity of religion across the country; moreover, education was never part of the legislation that accomplished the Union. The prevalence of the myth of the 'holy trinity' can in no small part be traced back to the Waverley Novels. The most 'Scottish' of the middle-class characters are the lawyers, the dominies and the ministers that populate the novels. Scott circumscribes the debate about Scottishness to such an extent that a critic like the Ayrshire-born Andrew O'Hagan, while lamenting the grip of outdated sensibilities, is forced to make his point by twisting around Scott: 'In place of "Heartless Midlothian" and "Young Mortality" – as yet unwritten accounts of the country's vast self-pity, arrested development and the way out of that – we are served with another "Portrait of the Artist as a Reluctant Patriot".'

Scott's impact is, in fact, more than just a Scottish affair. Yes, Edinburgh has the only football team in the world named after a novel (Heart of Midlothian); yes, Glasgow's Westerton area has such street-names as Crusader Avenue, Wamba Place, Rowena Avenue and Waldemar Road (all after *Ivanhoe*). But his legacy is more surreal and global than that. In Crockett's *Red Cap Tales*, one of the children asks if the Waverley was named after the Waverley pen. Of course, it's vice-versa, and this infiltration of reality extends to ships called the 'Monkbarns', pubs called the 'Kenilworth', Australian wines called 'Ravenswood', strawberries called the 'Redgauntlet', a Cornish breed of rose (R. Eglanteria) called 'Anne of Geierstein', a compound express train engine called *Jeanie Deans,* and the Waverley Camisole modelled by Sienna Miller.

Scott changed world culture. His most lasting alteration is the move from the classical to the romantic, from the epic poem to the novel. Macaulay, again, wrote a brilliant satire in 1824 for *Knight's Magazine*, 'A Prophetic Account of a Grand National Epic Poem, to be entitled "The Wellingtoniad" and to be published in AD 2824.' Macaulay describes the author of this epic, Richard Quongti, who will study at the University of Tombuctoo under Professor Kissey Kickey. His success will allow him to travel by balloon rather than velocipede. The satire's real humour comes in the misapplication of epic tropes to contemporary history; thus, it opens with Mars, God of War, cuckolding Carlo Buonaparte to engender Napoleon, and Wellington's pistols were forged by the Cyclopes. All this is described as 'most faithful to the manners of the age to which it relates. It preserves exactly all the historical circumstances, and interweaves them most artfully with all the *speciosa miracula* of supernatural agency.' The neoclassical epic, which Macpherson had imitated for *Fingal*, is wholeheartedly debunked. When a real 'epic' of Napoleon appeared, it would be the novel *War and Peace*. That the novel would become the primary mode of literary production is Scott's most lasting legacy. Throughout *The Antiquary*, a running joke involves Monkbarns and his perpetually deferred epic, *The Caledoniad*; a topic which even recurs in the preface to *Tales of the Crusaders* as one of the unwritten projects. The punch-line to the joke occurs in our world. The true *Caledoniad* is a series of novels, and the age of epic is over.

There is a telling phrase attributed to Arthur Freed, the producer of the 1954 film *Brigadoon*. Asked why he had not filmed the musical in Scotland, he supposedly said, 'Because Scotland doesn't look like Scotland.' In that film, the local minister has cast a spell that preserves the village, allowing it to exist for only one day in every hundred years. Many would say that Scott did the same for Scotland: kept its identity, and trapped it in the past. The 'cost' of his magic is that the minister is excluded from the safeguarded Brigadoon, in much the same manner as Scott is now almost completely excluded from our literary culture. At the end of the film, 'true love' brings the village back for long enough to allow the hero to escape into it, and we should not underestimate the sincere attraction Scott-land still holds. We might call it misguided, or romantic, or even conde-scending, but we cannot doubt the genuine emotional contact and contract people can find with this vision, without ever visiting the rocks and soil place. At a greater distance in time we can appreciate Scott's singular influence while admitting its shortcomings. Benedict Anderson defined a nation, in an over-used quotation, as 'an imag-ined community', and of all its 'imagineers', to use the Disney Corporation's word, Scott is Scotland's most successful and prob-lematic. Scott-land is a hyper-real Scotland, untethered to geography, and it has allowed a sense of identity to persist through dramatic, painful and significant social, political and industrial changes. Since every identity is a form of construction, instead of pointlessly attempting to create a 'genuine' sense of Scottishness, it might be more sensible to accept that every incarnation, from the most naive patriotism to the most kitsch adoption, makes Scottishness stronger by making it more plural. Not being reductive is surely better than aiming at an impossible, unadulterated authenticity. We cannot control what others dream of us, nationally or individually.

Departure

'Lector, si monumentum requiris circumspice': Christopher Wren's epitaph in St Paul's Cathedral translates as 'Reader, if you seek his monument, look around you'. Much the same could be said of Scott, and not just if you were leaving Waverley Station. But what of the man? Dickens guessed that he did not dream of his characters – but what did he dream of? Lockhart thought that he was 'A GREAT AND GOOD MAN' – but did he think of himself as either?

Scott's constant games with masks and pseudonyms and alibis and disguises strike me, at the end of this voyage around him, as more than just games. Nor do I think that a certain dissimulation over business affairs can wholly account for a life-long and unnecessary addiction to secrecy. Any biography which claims to detect a root cause or guiding principle for something as complex as a human being is a minor form of fraud, and I do not, as I stand metaphorically at his open coffin, seek to reduce this sad, gleeful, hard-working, lazy, profound, rash, canny, superficial, loving, loveless man to a formula. But the journey through all the pages which I did not quote has left me with one overriding hunch.

Walter Scott did not want to be Walter Scott. On the most superficial level, the boy with the lame leg wanted to be a soldier. Fiction was a way to be and a way to feel like other people. The more he became famous, the more he dislocated himself into the inventions he would rather be: the strong, the glamorous, the tragic, the humorous, the wicked, the mysterious, the spear-carrier, the hero. There is something fearful, and sad, and broken about Scott. He was the understudy to his own life; the man of might-have-beens. Every success he achieved – and they were numerous, stellar and unique – must have seemed will-o'-the-wispish: they were, after all, happening to someone he didn't think he was. His was a life of second-bests. He did not marry the woman he wanted. His legal career was conducted entirely in the boondocks, not in the High Court. He lived to see his politics superseded. The King he cultivated died heirless and an embarrassment. He became famous as a poet, and then saw a wholly new form of poetry sweep his laurels away. He became even more famous as a novelist, and was acutely aware of his limitations there: nothing he wrote touches me as much as his lines in his *Journal* on Jane Austen.

> That young lady had a talent for describing the involvement and feelings and characters of ordinary life which is to me the most wonderful I ever met with. The big Bow-wow strain I can do myself like any now going, but the exquisite touch which renders ordinary commonplace things and characters interesting from the truth of the description and the sentiment is denied to me. What a pity such a gifted creature died so early!

Scott knew, I think, in his heart of hearts, that all his labours to establish a name, a title, an estate and a line were doomed.

Whenever I feel despondent about Scott, both as a man and as a cultural phenomenon, whenever I think that he was a failure and his legacy was cliché, I re-read the end of G K Chesterton's fine biographical essay, 'The Position of Sir Walter Scott'. The essay ends:

> With all his faults, and all his triumphs, he stands for the great mass of natural manliness which must be absorbed into art unless art is to be a mere luxury and freak. An appreciation of Scott might be made almost a test of decadence. If ever we lose touch with this one most reckless and defective writer, it will be a proof to us that we have erected round ourselves a false cosmos, a world of lying and horrible perfection, leaving outside of it Walter Scott and that strange old world which is as confused and as indefensible and as inspiring and as healthy as he.

Further Reading

Bibliographies, like telephone directories and encyclopaedias, are the earliest casualties of the digital age. I'm not really minded to mourn their passing: on a political level they seem braggish, and on a personal level I could never really square omitting all the books which fundamentally contributed to my writing while including the ones that were merely quoted or referenced. In that spirit, I'd commend *The Trouble With Tom*, by Paul Collins (Bloomsbury, 2006) which first planted the idea that an author's afterlife might be as curious as their mortal existence. The following list is really intended only for those who, having finished this book, would like to read more about Sir Walter Scott.

Although a great deal of Scott is out of print, his fame was such that he is almost always well represented in charity shops and second-hand booksellers. For completists, then, I used:

The Waverley Novels, 48 vols, Cadell, 1829–33

The Edinburgh Edition of the Waverley Novels, 28 vols, Edinburgh University Press, 1993–2010; and the supplementary volumes *Reliquiae Trotcosienses* (2004) and *The Seige of Malta and Bizarro* (2008)

The Miscellaneous Prose Works of Sir Walter Scott, 40 vols, Cadell, 1834–71

The Poetical Works of Sir Walter Scott, 12 vols, Cadell, 1833–4

The Life of Sir Walter Scott, Bart., John Gibson Lockhart, 7 vols, Cadell, 1837–8

The Journal of Sir Walter Scott, W E K Anderson (ed.), Canongate, 1999

The Letters of Sir Walter Scott, H J C Grierson (ed.), 12 vols, Constable, 1932–7. This is an extremely incomplete and out-of-date selection: the Millgate Union Catalogue at the National

Library of Scotland is invaluable; as is the selection of e-texts at
http://www.walterscott.lib.ed.ac.uk/etexts/index.html

The Poems of Ossian, Howard Gaskill (ed.), Edinburgh University
Press, 1996

The Complete Poetical Works of Robert Burns, James Kingsley (ed.),
3 vols, Clarendon Press, 1968

The Complete Poetical Works of Lord Byron, Jerome McGann (ed.),
7 vols, Clarendon Press, 1980

*The Stirling/South Carolina Research Edition of the Collected Works of
James Hogg*, Edinburgh University Press, 1995 (ongoing)

The Works of John Galt, D S Meldrum & William Roughead (eds),
10 vols, J Grant, 1936 – again, a new edition of Galt is sorely
needed

The Tusitala Edition of the Works of Robert Louis Stevenson, 35 vols,
Heinemann, 1924

Scott and his Influence, J H Alexander & David Hewitt (eds),
Association of Scottish Literary Studies, 1982

Michael Alexander, *Medievalism*, Yale University Press, 2007

Neal Ascherson, *Stone Voices*, Granta 2002

The Edinburgh History of the Book in Scotland, Bill Bell (ed.), 4 vols,
Edinburgh University Press, 2007

Scotland After Enlightenment, Craig Beveridge & Ronald Turnbull,
Polygon, 1997

The Eclipse of Scottish Culture, Craig Beveridge & Ronald Turnbull,
Polygon, 1989

The Scottish Enlightenment, Alexander Broadie, Birlinn, 2007

Edinburgh History of Scottish Literature, Ian Brown, Thomas Owen
Clancy, Murray Pittock & Susan Manning (eds), 3 vols, Edinburgh
University Press, 2006

Capital of the Mind, James Buchan, John Murray, 2003

Sir Walter Scott, John Buchan, Cassell, 1932

Romantics, Rebels and Reactionaries, Marilyn Butler, Oxford
University Press, 1985

Scotlands of the Mind, Angus Calder, Luath Press, 2002

'Scott', in *Literature in Perspective*, Angus & Jenni Calder, Evans
Bros, 1969

Scottish Literature, Gerard Carruthers, Edinburgh University Press, 2009

Britons, Linda Colley, Yale University Press, 1992

Edinburgh: The Golden Age, Mary Cosh, John Donald, 2003

Devolving English Literature, Robert Crawford, Edinburgh University Press, 2000

Scotland's Books, Robert Crawford, Penguin, 2007

The Bard: Roberts Burns, A Biography, Robert Crawford, Jonathan Cape, 2009

The Origins of Scottish Nationhood, Neil Davidson, Pluto Press, 2000

Kafka: Towards a Minor Literature, Gilles Deleuze & Felix Guattari, University of Minnesota Press, 1986

The Scottish Nation, T M Devine, Penguin, 2006

Scott's Shadow: The Novel in Romantic Edinburgh, Ian Duncan, Princeton University Press, 2007

Englishness, Simon Featherstone, Edinburgh University Press, 2009

The Achievement of Literary Authority: Gender, History and the Waverley Novels, Ina Ferris, Cornell University Press, 1991

Art and Enlightenment, Jonathan Friday (ed.), Imprint Academic, 2004

Edinburgh: A History, Michael Fry, Macmillan, 2009

The Scottish Empire, Michael Fry, Birlinn, 2001

Scotland, the Autobiography, Rosemary Goring (ed.), Viking, 2007

Scott the Rhymer, Nancy Goslee, University Press of Kentucky, 1988

The Great Infidel: A Life of David Hume, Roderick Graham, Birlinn, 2004

Sir Walter Scott, Bart: A New Life, Sir Herbert Grierson, Constable, 1938

Stone of Destiny, Ian Hamilton, reprinted Birlinn, 2008

Jane's Fame, Claire Harman, Canongate, 2009

Scott: The Critical Heritage, John O Hayden, Routledge & Kegan, 1970

Empires of the Imagination, Holger Hoeck, Bodley Head, 2009

James Hogg: A Life, Gillian Hughes, Edinburgh University Press, 2007

The Great Unknown, Edgar Johnson, 2 vols, Hamish Hamilton, 1970

Subverting Scotland's Past, Colin Kidd, Cambridge University Press, 1993

Highways and Byways in the Border, Andrew & John Lang, Macmillan, 1913

Enlightenment and Change, Bruce Lenman, Edinburgh University Press, 2009

Tobias Smollett, Jeremy Lewis, Jonathan Cape, 2003

Walter Scott and Modernity, Andrew Lincoln, Edinburgh University Press, 2007

Compton Mackenzie, Andro Linklater, Chatto & Windus, 1987

The Historical Novel, George Lukàcs, reprinted Peregine Books, 1969

The Ragged Lion, Allan Massie, Hutchinson, 1994

The Thistle and the Rose, Allan Massie, John Murray, 2005

Culture, Nation and the New Scottish Parliament, Caroline McCracken-Flesher (ed.), Bucknell University Press, 2007

Possible Scotlands: Walter Scott and the Story of Tomorrow, Caroline McCracken-Flesher, Oxford University Press, 2005

Contemporary Scottish Literature: A Reader's Guide to Essential Criticism, Matt McGuire, Palgrave Macmillan, 2009

Burns the Radical, Liam McIlvanney, Tuckwell Press, 2002

Walter Scott: The Making of the Novelist, Jane Millgate, Edinburgh University Press, 1984

Electric Shepherd: A Likeness of James Hogg, Karl Miller, Faber & Faber, 2003

The Borders, Alistair Moffat, Birlinn, 2007

The Reivers, Alistair Moffat, Birlinn, 2008

Scott and Scotland, Edwin Muir, reprinted Polygon Press, 1982

Anonymity, John Mullan, Faber, 2007

The Break-Up of Britain, Tom Nairn, Verso, 1981

After Britain, Tom Nairn, Granta, 2000

The Atlantic Ocean, Andrew O'Hagan, Faber & Faber, 2008

The Voyage of the Pharos, Brian Osborne (ed.), Scottish Library Association, 1998

Walter Scott: His Life and Personality, Hesketh Pearson, Methuen, 1954

The Invention of Scotland, Murray Pittock, Routledge, 1991

The King's Jaunt, John Prebble, Collins, 1998

Young Disraeli, Jane Ridley, Sinclair Stevenson, 1995

Legitimate Histories: Scott, Gothic and the Authorities of Fiction, Fiona Robertson, Clarendon Press, 1994

Reviewing Before the Edinburgh, Derek Roper, Methuen, 1978

Why Scottish Literature Matters, Carla Sassi, Saltire Society, 2005

The Edinburgh Companion to Contemporary Scottish Literature, Berthold Schoene (ed.), Edinburgh University Press, 2007

British Periodicals and Romantic Identity, Mark Schoenfield, Palgrave Macmillan, 2009

Walter Scott and Scotland, Paul Henderson Scott, William Blackwood, 1991

The Enlightenment and the Book, Richard Sher, Chicago University Press, 2007

History Meets Fiction, Beverley Southgate, Longman, 2009

The Siege of Malta Rediscovered, Donald Sultana, Scottish Academic Press, 1977

The Life of Walter Scott, John Sutherland, Blackwell, 1995

The House of Blackwood, F D Tredrey, William Blackwood, 1954

The Invention of Scotland, Hugh Trevor-Roper, Yale University Press, 2008

Sir Walter Scott: A Bibliographical History, William B Todd & Ann Bowden, Oak Knoll Press, 1998

Bardic Nationalism, Katie Trumpener, Princeton University Press, 1997

The Literary Tourist, Nicola Watson, Palgrave Macmillan, 2006

The Literature of Scotland, Roderick Watson, 2 vols, Palgrave Macmillan, 2007

The Hero of the Waverley Novels, Alexander Welsh, Yale University Press, 1963

The Laird of Abbotsford, A N Wilson, Oxford University Press, 1980

Secret Leaves, Judith Wilt, University of Chicago Press, 1985

Acknowledgements

It is a deep regret to me that this book has come out when Angus Calder (1942–2008) is no longer with us, as he was an inspirational figure with whom to discuss Scott, and I would have relished his complaints, quibbles and vast erudition. The novelists Allan Massie, Andrew Crumey and James Robertson were generous with their knowledge, as were, on vastly tangential and peculiar topics, Alison Kennedy, Walter Elliott, Kenny Farquharson, Bill Jamieson, Marc Lambert, David Stenhouse, Carolyn Becket, Peggy Hughes, Colin Fraser and David Bishop. They knew not what they did. Professors Ian Campbell, Douglas Gifford, Willy Maley and Michael Schmidt all answered my sometimes eccentric questions with accuracy and benevolence, and I wish to express particular thanks to Michael Schmidt, in his other capacity with Carcanet Press, for permission to reproduce Hugh MacDiarmid's poem. Jacqui Wright at the Abbotsford Trust and Dr Paul Barnaby at Edinburgh University provided superb access to and expertise in their respective institutions. Thanks to Hugh Andrew, Neville Moir, Jan Rutherford, Alison Rae and Kenny Redpath at Birlinn, and Peter Straus at Rogers, Coleridge & White. Finally, Brian and Carolyn Kelly started my interest in Scott, and, Dad, I can still remember the dirty version of *Lay of the Last Minstrel*. Sam, as always: just for everything.

Index